Maharshi Dayanand Saraswati Book Series-27

The Manusmṛti

The First Constitution of Humanity on the Earth

Vol. 1

Chapters 1-6

Critically Edited Sanskrit Text, Roman Transliteration, and English Translation in most modern terms

By

Prof. Ravi Prakash Arya

Chair Professor

Maharshi Dayanand Saraswati Chair (UGC)

Maharshi Dayanand University, Rohtak

Assisted by

Alois Heinrich

AMAZON BOOKS, USA

In association with

INDIAN FOUNDATION FOR VEDIC SCIENCE

1051, Sector-1, Rohtak-124001, Haryana, India

Ph. 09313033917; 9650183260

Email: vedicscience@rediffmail.com; vedicscience@gmail.com

https://vedic-sciences.com

First Edition

Christian era: 2025

Vikram era: 2082

Kali era: 5127

Kalpa Era: 1972949127

Brahma Era: 155521972949127

ISBN No. 978-93-94724-66-2

Printed by

Indian Foundation for Vedic Science, 1051, Sector-1, Rohtak-124001, Haryana

Contents

Introduction

The Manusmṛti is the first constitution of humanity on the earth. It is also considered an important source for the sociological history of ancient and medieval India. Since it forms the basis of the Varṇa system, codes of conduct, duties of various professionals.

The Manusmṛti, also known as the Mānava Dharmaśāstra, is one of humanity's most important and earliest legal texts. It is attributed to Manu, the first lawgiver. It presents a discourse in which Manu responds to a group of ṛṣis who ask him to explain the "Dharma" meaning knowledge, duties, and laws governing the state and society, focusing on the four Varṇas (professional classes formed based on Sanskāras. Manu has become the standard reference for all subsequent Dharmaśāstras.

The Manusmṛti is regarded as the last remnant of a long tradition that traces back to an original text initially instructed by Brahmā to Manu, who then passed it on to his disciples. Traditionally, the Dharmaśāstra comprised one thousand chapters detailing various rules and regulations governing society and the state. This original narrative was first conveyed by Brahmā to his son Manu, who later transmitted it to his students, including Bhṛgu. Bhṛgu then relayed this information to his own audience of pupils, continuing the tradition passed down through generations.

The text is structured as a dialogue between Manu's disciple, Bhṛgu, and his students. It begins with Manu describing the creation of the world and the societal structure based on the four professional classes known as Varṇas. Bhṛgu takes over the narrative, teaching the details of Manu's teachings for the rest of the work.

The Manusmṛiti was one of the first Sanskrit texts studied by European philologists. It was first translated into English by Sir William Jones, whose version was published in 1794. Jones regarded Manu's laws as older than those of Solon and Lycurgus, and he suggested that the latter had adopted their legal principles from Manu. William Jones writes:

"The laws of Manu very probably were considerably older than those of Solon or even of Lycurgus, although their promulgation before they were reduced to writing might have been covered by the first monarchies established in Egypt and India."

British administrative requirements sparked their interest in the Dharmaśāstras, which they believed to be legal codes. In fact, these texts encompassed not only laws but also norms related to society, polity, and economy.

In his book *Bible in India*, Louis Jacolliot writes:

> "Manusmṛti was the foundation upon which the Egyptian, the Persian, the Grecian, and the Roman codes of law were built, and the influence of Manu is still felt in Europe."

According to him, The Laws of Justinian and the Civil Death of the Code Napoleon are all formed based on *Manusmṛiti*. In this regard, his observations are given below:

> "We have seen the Indian priests, after the fall (which was their work) of Vedic civilization, institute for the security of their power, and with the design of imbuing their victims with salutary fear, this terrible penalty of rejection, partial or complete, from all caste, which placed the unhappy delinquent below the brute, since not the faintest social relation could be held with him without incurring degradation, and sinking to his level.
>
> "Even the ties of family were broken; the children of the outcast became orphans, they were relegated to a tutor; his wife became a widow, and might re-marry if of a caste in which second marriage was not prohibited; his succession failed; and, finally, if he happened to be killed, the civil law touched not his murderer, who had simply to perform the religious ceremonies of purification, because he had been defiled by contact of a paria.

"From the soil of Mediaeval India, its birth-place, this institution of theocratic despotism quickly passed to the other countries that adopted it, in their turn, as an admirable instrument of domination; and thus did *the interdiction of water and of fire* come to be considered throughout antiquity a just and salutary penalty.

"A modification it must be stated, was, however, introduced into the exercise of this severe repression.

"Thus just as India, pronounced the sentence of expulsion from caste, for faults as well as for crimes; for religious as well as for social offenses; similarly, the different nations of antiquity tainted by Indian influence, also applied this penalty to political and religious crimes, treason, and conspiracies against all authority.

"Crimes and offences against the person were subject to other laws.

"This exception, however, did not include Egypt, which retained this practice in all its rigorous and arbitrary application, and it is easy to see the reason why.

"After India, it is Egypt that exhibits to us the most painful example of stolid demoralisation and abasement of the people, who, deprived of all social and political role, deprived in some measure of the faculty of thinking, because deprived of the privilege of knowing, of acting, and of speaking; derived all initiative, their hours defined for refection, repose, and prayer, never long but docile instruments[2] producing machines to satisfy all the caprices of the small number of the elect, who elected themselves by aid of the religious idea, of terror and of lies.

"Zoroaster, while retaining this penalty, ordained that it should only be applied to great offenders in the eyes of God and of men, and made it almost exceptional. In Greece (under the name of Ostracism, it was applied to men whose political influence was feared), interdiction of fire and water was scarce ever pronounced, except as *temporary,* and it does not appear that any special laws regulated its application.

"Rome, after the example of India and of Egypt, ordained this mode of repression in its written law, under the name of *Capitis Minutio;* and, as the Oriental legislator Manu had admitted the partial or complete rejection of caste, so Roman legislation ordained degrees of this penalty: these were the great, the middle and the lesser *Minutio Capitis.*

"By the first, the citizen was deprived of all social and political rights; of all the rights of family; and placed in the same situation as the Egyptian and Indian– rejected from all caste.

"Water and fire were prohibited in the same form, and as rigorously as Indian interdicted rice, water and fire.

"He was not even allowed the resource of serving as a slave; and to kill him was not a crime.

"By the second, all the rights of father and of master were suppressed; he had no longer any control over his children, who were emancipated by the fact, and his succession divided amongst his heirs.

"By the third, or lesser *minutio capitis,* it but excluded the condemned from the magistracy, and from the service of the republic, leaving intact his paternal authority and the free disposition of his property.

"Thus adopted into the written laws of Rome, this provision became, as we see, a penalty of common law.

These modes of penalisation personal degradation by withdrawing social and political rights, were of Eastern growth; and I am not in the least astonished to see the Osiris inventing such penalties under the influence of Indian penal code. The Rome was influenced by and followed the rule of the ancient world, I do not think a sufficient reason for denouncing her, but I feel a thrill of indignation when I see that our modern legislators had inscribed in our codes this rejection of caste, this *capitis minutio,* had prescribed, in fact, this civil death.

"Civil death! Will it be believed that scarce fifteen years ago, the victim of this penalty, had no longer on earth either wife, children, or relations to articulate his name, to retain some little affection for one so unblest, and permit him, in default of hope, in the depths of his cell, to live a little upon memories?

"And 1889 had passed over without daring to touch this hideous bequest of antiquity, preserved by that sacerdotal and fanatic middle-age, that sought to re-erect in Europe all the despotism and all the degeneracies of Priestly class, by the division of castes, and domination of the priest.

"Honour and remembrance, in the name of the people, in the name of humanity; honour and recollection in the history of painfully conquered progress, honour in the name of eternal justice, to the sovereign influence that in 1853 erased from our codes this odious relic of antique immortality and corruption!

"We have said that in India, civil death, the complete exclusion from caste, was pronounced either by the judge for purely civil, or by the priest for religious offences. It was certainly necessary for Papal Rome, when in the middle ages attempting the role of Indian priests, to appropriate such customs; the instrument fitted her hand too well, and she would have invented, had she not inherited it from her illustrious ancestors.

Excommunication was nothing else than a weapon of despotism picked up in the temples, for the subjugation of people and of kings, and for triumph of the priest. We have seen it at work, in the middle ages, cursing people in their posterity [2] anathematising kings in their dynasty. We have seen Savonarola die at the stake for

> having exposed the disorders of Alexander VI., and the pious Robert, of France, abandoned by his friends and his most faithful servants, obliged to bend the knee under the hand of a religious fanatic.
>
> "We have seen human hecatombs on the burning piles of faith, and the altar reddened with blood.
>
> "Ages have passed away; we are but wakening to progress of free thought. But let us expect struggles without end, until the day when we shall have courage to arraign all sacerdotalism at the bar of liberty."[1]

The "Law of Manu" was cited favourably by Friedrich Nietzsche[2] and Aaron Ridley[3]. He deemed it "an incomparably spiritual and superior work" to the Christian Bible.

He observed that "the sun shines on the whole book" and attributed its ethical perspective to "the noble classes, the philosophers and warriors, [who] stand above the mass." He endorsed the political exclusion of Manu's system. He considered the Varṇa system to be a good idea, and stated that "Varṇa order, order of rank is just a formula for the supreme law of life itself", a "natural order, lawfulness par excellence".

He wrote that 'to prepare a book of law in the style of Manu means to give a people the right to become master one day, to become perfect, - to aspire to the highest art of life.'

A prominent Hindu revivalist and reformist Swami Dayanand Sarasvati held the text to be authentic and authoritative except few interpolations. His Magnum Opus

---

1 Quoted by present author in his book '*India: The Cradle of World Civilisations*' published by Indian Foundation for Vedic Science in association with Amazon books, USA

2 *A Philosophical Biography*, p. 515, Julian Young, Cambridge University Press

3 *The Anti-Christ, Ecce Homo, Twilight of the Idols: And Other Writings*, Cambridge University Press, P.58

'Satyarth Prakash' is based upon *Manusmṛti*. Other admirers of the text have included Annie Besant, P.D. Ouspensky, Pandurang Shastri Athavale, and Sarvepalli Radhakrishnan among many others.

Friedrich Nietzsche[1] is noted to have said "Close the Bible and open the Manusmṛti. It has an affirmation of life, a triumphing agreeable sensation in life and that to draw up a lawbook such as Manu means to permit oneself to get the upper hand, to become perfect, to be ambitious of the highest art of living." Contra Nietzsche, W.A. Borody has coined the phrase "sublimation-transmogrification logic" to describe the underlying 'state of mind' lying behind the ethical teaching of the Manu Saṁhtā 'state of mind' that would have found Nietzsche's concept of the Dionysian Übermensch abhorrent, and a 'state of mind' or 'voice' that has always been radically contested within India's various philosophical and religious traditions.

It is indisputable that the Manusmṛti is the first constitution of humanity. It presents a remarkable charter for personal, social, and political life. As the foremost text among all Dharmaśāstras, Manusmṛti encompasses the essence of the Vedas, Upaniṣads, the six systems of Indian philosophy, and the Bhagavad Gita.

This volume provides information on creation, the duties of householders, Vānaprasthis (forest dwellers), and Saṁnyāsīs (peripatetic monks). It discusses the sources of knowledge of Dharma, appropriate and legal means of livelihood, and dietary practices. Furthermore, it outlines the ways and means for the upliftment of human beings, defines the concepts of heaven and hell, and offers a comprehensive guide to life that can lead individuals towards divinity, helping them avoid degradation into lower species.

Notably, the Manusmṛti is considered to be more influential

---

1 *Will to Power*, Vol. 1

than the Bhagavad Gita or the Bible. Friedrich Nietzsche famously stated, "Close the Bible and open the Manusmṛti." I would assert, close everything else and open the Manusmṛti. This edition has been meticulously revised and updated to provide contemporary interpretations of ancient terms in English, ensuring its relevance to today's social, economic, and political contexts. I wholeheartedly believe that both readers and researchers will find this work an indispensable resource for understanding the timeless wisdom and foundational principles it offers.

Prof. Ravi Prakash Arya
Chair Professor
Maharshi Dayanand Saraswati Chair (UGC)
Maharshi Dayanand University, Rohtak, Haryana

Chapter 1: Creation of the World

This chapter discusses the brief history of time. The first chapter recounts how ten great sages approached Manu to seek guidance on the laws that sustain creation and society. In response, Manu asked the learned sage Bhṛgu, who had been meticulously trained in the metrical tenets of the law, to share his teachings.

Manu outlined the duties of all four Varṇas (professional classes based on Sanskāras). He designated the intellectuals to focus on teaching and studying the Vedas. He instructed defense personnel to protect the people and perform Yajñas while refraining from indulging in sensual pleasures. Those engaged in trade and commerce were assigned the responsibilities of domesticating animals, production, performing charitable acts, trading, and lending money. Finally, the uneducated and illiterate individuals involved in services were to engage in all activities within the service sector.

Manu also stated that a Vedic scholar whose conduct is unsatisfactory, cannot be regarded as a Vedic scholar. Conversely, one whose behaviour is virtuous is better than a so-called Vedic scholar. The sages ultimately agreed that these laws govern the core of the state and society.

Question of Sages

मनुमेकाग्रमासीनमभिगम्य महर्षयः ।
प्रतिपूज्य यथान्यायमिदं वचनमब्रुवन् ॥ 1 ॥

manumekāgramāsīnamabhigamya maharṣayaḥ /
pratipūjya yathānyāyamidaṁ vachanamabruvan // 1 //

1. The great sages approached Manu, who was seated in Samādhi, and, having paid due respect to him, spoke as follows:

भगवन् सर्ववर्णानां यथावदनुपूर्वशः ।
अन्तरप्रभवानां च धर्मान्नो वक्तुमर्हसि ॥ 2 ॥

bhagavan sarvavarṇānāṁ yathāvadanupūrvaśaḥ /
antaraprabhavānāṁ cha dharmānno vaktumarhasi //2 //

2. "Bhagvan, kindly tell us precisely and in due order the duties of all Varṇas and sub-Varṇas.

त्वमेको ह्यस्य सर्वस्य विधानस्य स्वयम्भुवः ।
अचिन्त्यस्याप्रमेयस्य कार्यतत्त्वार्थवित् प्रभो ॥ 3 ॥

tvameko hyasya sarvasya vidhānasya svayambhuvaḥ I
achintyasyāprameyasya kāryatattvārthavit prabho II 3 II

3. For you alone are the knower of truth and associated with this entire ordinance which is unknowable and unfathomable to us.

Manu's Answer

स तैः पृष्टस्तथा सम्यगमितोजा महात्मभिः ।
प्रत्युवाचार्च्य तान् सर्वान् महर्षींश्रूयतामिति ॥ 4 ॥

sa taiḥ pṛṣṭastathā samyagamitojā mahātmabhiḥ I
pratyuvāchārchya tān sarvān maharṣīṁśrūyatāmiti II 4 II

4. He, endowed with infinite energy, was asked by the great sages. He duly honoured them and replied, 'Listen!'

Origin of the World

आसीदिदं तमोभूतमप्रज्ञातमलक्षणम् ।
अप्रतर्क्यमविज्ञेयं प्रसुप्तमिव सर्वतः ॥ 5 ॥

āsīdidaṁ tamobhūtamaprajñātamalakṣaṇam I
apratarkyamavijñeyaṁ prasuptamiva sarvataḥ II 5 II

5. This (universe) existed in the shape of dark energy (inactive energy), unperceived, devoid of any kind of symptoms, incomprehensible, unknowable, wholly immersed, as it were, in deep sleep.

ततः स्वयम्भूर्भगवानव्यक्तो व्यञ्जयन्निदम् ।
महाभूतादि वृत्तोजाः प्रादुरासीत् तमोनुदः ॥ 6 ॥

tataḥ svayambhūrbhagavānavyakto vyañjayannidam I
mahābhūtādi vṛttojāḥ prādurāsīt tamonudaḥ II 6 II

6. Then the Self-existent unmanifest Brahman agitated the dark energy (vṛttaujaḥ) and created bhūtākāśa consting of five

gross evolutes (bhūtās) composed of active energy), dispelling the darkness of energy (activating energy).

योऽसावतीन्द्रियग्राह्यः सूक्ष्मोऽव्यक्तः सनातनः ।
सर्वभूतमयोऽचिन्त्यः स एव स्वयमुद्बभौ ॥ 7 ॥

yo'sāvatīndriyagrāhyaḥ sūkṣamo'vyaktaḥ sanātanaḥ /
sarvabhūtamayo'chintyaḥ sa ēva svayamudbabhau // 7 //

7. He who cannot be perceived by senses, who is subtle, unmanifest, and eternal, who contains entire bhūtākāśa in it and is incomprehensible, he desired himself to create universe.

सोऽभिध्याय शरीरात् स्वात् सिसृक्षुर्विविधाः प्रजाः ।
अप एव ससर्जादौ तासु वीर्यमवासृजत् ॥ 8 ॥

so'bhidhyāya śarīrāt svāt sisṛkṣurvividhāḥ prajāḥ /
apa ēva sasarjādau tāsu vīryamavāsṛjat // 8 //

8. He, desiring to produce beings of various kinds, [svāt śarīrāt] because of his sanskāras (information of creation in Brahman), he first [sasarja] created motion in [āpaḥ] (prakṛti or inactive energy) with the power of his saṅkalpa (sanskāras or information of creation in Brahman) [abhidhyāyāt], and so infused potency (or activated the inactive energy.

Note: Inactive material thing can only be activated by an external force of some sentient being. Before creation, when the prakṛti (energy) was in sāmyāvastha (inactive form or dark form), it was only Brahman to activate it. Dark or inactive energy cannot participate in creation. For energy to participate in creation, its activation is must.

तदण्डमभवद्धैमं सहस्रांशुसमप्रभम् ।
तस्मिञ्जज्ञे स्वयं ब्रह्मा सर्वलोकपितामहः ॥9 ॥

tadaṇḍamabhavaddhaimaṁ sahasrāṁśusamaprabham /
tasmiñjajñe svayaṁ brahmā sarvalokapitāmahaḥ //9 //

9. That active energy gave rise in due course to Bhūtākāśa, called a golden egg, which had brilliance like thousands of suns; in that egg (Bhūtākāśa) was automatically born following law of Ṛta, universe or Brahmāṇḍa (known as Svayambhā Brahmā), the prototype of the whole world.

आपो नारा इति प्रोक्ता आपो वै नरसूनवः ।
ता यदस्यायनं पूर्वं तेन नारायणः स्मृतः ॥ 10 ॥

āpo nārā iti proktā āpo vai narasūnavaḥ /
tā yadasyāyanaṁ pūrvaṁ tena nārāyaṇaḥ smṛtaḥ // 10 //

10. These āpaḥ (inactive energy particles) are called nārā. These nārās (dark energy particles) are [narasūnavaḥ] the offspring of nara [chidākāśar or Brahmākāśa); as they had their first [ayana] abode in Brahman or Brahmākāśa, so that (Brahman or Brahmākāśa) is named Nārāyaṇa.

यत् तत् कारणमव्यक्तं नित्यं सदसदात्मकम् ।
तद्विसृष्टः स पुरुषो लोके ब्रह्मैति कीर्त्यते ॥ 11 ॥

yat tat kāraṇamavyaktaṁ nityaṁ sadasadātmakam /
tadvisṛṣṭaḥ sa puruaṣo loke brahmaiti kīrtyate // 11 //

11. [yat] Because [tat] that [kāraṇam] material cause (Prakṛti or dark energy) is invisible, eternal, and both real (in the dark form real) and unreal (in the active form), (loke puruṣaḥ) the Brahmaṇḍa Puruṣa (Bhūtākāśa) is produced from that material cause (Prakṛti or dark energy) [visṛṣṭaḥ] when motion is created in it. That is known in this world (under the appellation of) Brahmā, (expanding universe).

NB: The homogeneous state of sattva, rajas and tamas is called Prakṛti or inactive energy. When the same is agiated the rise of inhomogeneity is caused by the active energy particles.

तस्मिन्नण्डे स भगवानुषित्वा परिवत्सरम् ।
स्वयमेवात्मनो ध्यानात् तदण्डमकरोद् द्विधा ॥ 12 ॥

tasminnaṇḍe sa bhagavānuṣitvā parivatsaram /
svayamevātmano dhyānāt tadaṇḍamakarod dvidhā // 12 //

12. [tasmin aṇḍe] In that Bhūtākāśa (golden egg) [bhagvān] Brahmā (Brahmāṇḍa puruṣa) [uṣitvā] resided [parivatsaram] for a period of two Brāhma years (four kalpas i.e. for 16,80,00,00,000 years). [ātmano dhyānāt] Due to the saṅkalpa (sanskāras or information of creation) in Brahman [tad aṇḍam] that Bhūtākāśa [svyam] itself following the law of Ṛta [dvidhā akarot] divided into two objects.

Note: Parivatsara is the second year. Two kalpas are equal to one year.

ताभ्यां स शकलाभ्यां च दिवं भूमिं च निर्ममे ।
मध्ये व्योम दिशश्चाष्टावपां स्थानं च शाश्वतम् ॥ 13 ॥
tābhyāṁ sa śakalābhyāṁ cha divaṁ bhūmiṁ cha nirmame
madhye vyoma diśaśchāṣṭāvapāṁ sthānaṁ cha śāśvatam ॥

13. [tābhyām] Those [śaklābhyām] two objects in the Bhūtākāśa make [divam] stars (having their own light) and [bhūmim] planets (devoid of their own light) [madhye] intervened by [vyomaḥ] space [diśaśḥ cha aṣṭau] having eight directions (four main directions and four corners) [cha] in addition to this is eternal space of [apām] dark energy.

Note: Bhūtākāśa (virāṭ) which is the abode of active energy is only 25%. This 25% energy takes part in creation. In addition to it is Chidākāśā (svrāṭ) which is the eternal space for 75% dark energy. Bhūtākāśā is not eternal, it is formed by active energy, but Chdākāśa is eternal. Whole creation is caused by the saṅkalpa of Brahman. Saṅkalpa means the sanskāras (information) of creation in Brahman.

उद्बबर्हात्मनश्चैव मनः सदसदात्मकम् ।
मनसश्चाप्यहङ्कारमभिमन्तारमीश्वरम् ॥ 14 ॥
udbabarhātmanaśchaiva manaḥ sadasadātmakam ।
manasaśchāpyahaṅkāramabhimantāramīśvaram ॥ 14 ॥

14. From [ātmanaḥ cha] Prakṛti [udbbarhaḥ] drew forth the mahat (cosmic intelligence) which is both cause and product, [manasaḥ cha] from mahat was produced [ahaṅkāram] notion of individuality (ability to maintain distinct identity) which is the [abhimantāram] ability [īśvaram] of soul to create or act.

Note: Ahaṅkāra is the ability of prakṛti to act or create. That is why in Bhagvadgitā it is said: अहंकारो कर्ता न पुरुषः । Ahaṅkāra is the actual agent and not the soul. The soul possessed of ahaṅkāra does actions.

महान्तमेव चात्मानं सर्वाणि त्रिगुणानि च ।
विषयाणां ग्रहीतृणि शनैः पञ्चेन्द्रियाणि च ॥ 15 ॥
mahāntameva chātmānaṁ sarvāṇi triguṇāni cha ।

viṣayāṇāṁ grahītṝṇi śanaiḥ pañchaindriyāṇi cha // *15* //

15. [mahāntam eva ātmānam] When the soul possesses mahat (intelligence and notion of individuality and power to act), it [śanaiḥ] is gradually influenced by (sarvāṇi triguṇāni) all three Guṇas, i.e. sattva, rajas and tamas. [cha] Additionally [pañchaindrayāṇi] it engages with the five senses, [viṣyāṇām grahītṛṇi] which are the receivers of objects made from five gross elements (bhūtas).

तेषां त्ववयवान् सूक्ष्मान् षण्णामप्यमितौजसाम् ।
संनिवेश्यात्ममात्रासु सर्वभूतानि निर्ममे ॥ 16 ॥
teṣāṁ tvavayavān sūkṣamān ṣaṇṇāmapyamitaujasām /
saṁniveśyātmamātrāsu sarvabhūtāni nirmame // *16* //

16. [sukṣmān tu avayavān] Five tanmātras or sensations like sound, touch, sight, taste, olfaction [teṣām] associated with five sensory organs [saṁniveśya] when combined with [ātmamātrāsu] their vikārās (products) like pṛthivī (solids), jala (liquids), agni (fire or light and heat), vāyu (gas) and ākāśā (space) along with ahaṅkāra [amit-aujasām ṣaṇṇām] exceedingly potent group of six [nirmame] created [sarvabhūtāni] all living and non-living objects.

Note: These six elements are called exceedingly potent because they can produce unlimited material objects in the universe.

यन् मूर्त्यवयवाः सूक्ष्मास्तानीमान्याश्रयन्ति षट् ।
तस्माच्छरीरमित्याहुस्तस्य मूर्तिं मनीषिणः ॥ 17 ॥
yan mūrtyavayavāḥ sūkṣamāstānīmānyāśrayanti ṣaṭ /
tasmāchchharīramityāhustasya mūrtiṁ manīṣiṇaḥ //*17* //

17. [yat] Because [murti] the products of prakṛti are constituted of [ṣaṭ sukṣmāḥ avayavāḥ] these six subtle elements (ahaṅkāra and five sensations). (tāni imāni) Since, all the products of prakṛti [āśrayanti] are based upon these subtle six. [tasmāt] Therefore, [maniṣīṇaḥ] the wise call [tasya mūrtim] the gross products of prakṛti [śarīram] as the body of these six subtle elements.

तदाविशन्ति भूतानि महान्ति सह कर्मभिः ।

मनश्चावयवैः सूक्ष्मैः सर्वभूतकृदव्ययम् ॥ 18 ॥
tadāviśanti bhūtāni mahānti saha karmabhiḥ /
manaśchāvayavaiḥ sūkṣamaiḥ sarvabhūtakṛdavyayam //18 //

18. The prakṛti is [sarvabhūtkṛt] creates all things and the material bodies of all beings. It is [avyayam] imperishable being the cause of all. Why prakṛti is able to create unlimited material things and objects? Because [imāni] all these material things and bodies [mahānti bhūtāni] five gross elements (ākāśa, vāyu, agni, jala and pṛthivī) [saha karmabhiḥ] together with their functions [cha], and [manaḥ] the manas [sukṣmaiḥ avayavaiḥ] along with its subtle components like buddhi, ahaṅkāra, and sense organs, [tad+āviśanti] already exist in prakṛti.

Note: The function of ākāśa (space) is voidness; the function of vāyu is vyūha (motion); the function of agni is cooking; the function of water is compactness; the function of the earth is sustaining.

तेषामिदं तु सप्तानां पुरुषाणां महौजसाम् ।
सूक्ष्माभ्यो मूर्तिमात्राभ्यः सम्भवत्यव्ययाद् व्ययम् ॥ 19 ॥
teṣāmidaṁ tu saptānāṁ puruṣāṇāṁ mahaujasām
sūkṣamābhyo mūrtimātrābhyaḥ sambhavatyavyayād vyayam

19. [sukṣmābhyaḥ mūrtimātrābhyaḥ] From the subtle products (atoms) of [teṣām] these [saptānām puruṣāṇām] seven elements (mahat, ahankāra and five tanmātrās or sensations), which proceed from [avyayāt] imperishable prakṛti and [mahaujasām] which are exceedingly potent, [sambhavati] are produced [vyayam] perishable gross objects.

आद्याद्यस्य गुणं त्वेषामवाप्नोति परः परः ।
यो यो यावतिथश्चैषां स स तावद् गुणः स्मृतः ॥ 20 ॥
ādyādyasya guṇaṁ tveṣāmavāpnoti paraḥ paraḥ /
yo yo yāvatithaśchaiṣāṁ sa sa tāvad guṇaḥ smṛtaḥ // 20 //

20. Among five gross elements [paraḥ paraḥ] each succeeding (element) [avāpnoti] acquires [guṇaḥ] the quality of [ādyā+ādyasya] the preceding one, [cha] and [yāvatithaḥ] whatever place (in the sequence) each of them occupies, [tāvad guṇaḥ] even so many qualities [smṛtaḥ] it is declared to possess.

For example, ākāśa possesses the quality of sound. Following ākāśa, vāyu has two qualities: sound, which it inherits from ākāśa, and touch, which is its own quality. Similarly, agni, which is the third element, possesses three qualities: sound and touch (inherited from the preceding two elements) and its own quality of sight. This pattern continues with subsequent elements.

सर्वेषां तु स नामानि कर्माणि च पृथक् पृथक् ।
वेदशब्देभ्य एवादौ पृथक् संस्थाश्च निर्ममे ॥ 21 ॥
sarveṣāṁ tu sa nāmāni karmāṇi cha pṛthak pṛthak /
vedaśabdebhya ēvādau pṛthak saṁsthāścha nirmame // 21 //

21. [ādau] In the beginning of creation, [vedaśabdebhyaḥ] according to the words of the Veda, [pṛthak pṛthak] different [nāmāni] the nomenclatures [sarveṣām] of all objects [cha] and [karmāṇi] actions [nirmame] were assigned, and various institutions like varṇa, āśrama and so on were made.

Note: The Veda is the information of creation in Brahman. This information was received by the seers in mokṣa in the previous creation who descended first at the beginning of human origin in the present creation.

कर्मात्मनां च देवानां सोऽसृजत् प्राणिनां प्रभुः ।
साध्यानां च गणं सूक्ष्मं यज्ञं चैव सनातनम् ॥ 22 ॥
karmātmanāṁ cha devānāṁ so'sṛjat prāṇināṁ prabhuḥ
sādhyānāṁ cha gaṇaṁ sūkṣamaṁ yajñaṁ chaiva sanātanam

22. [saḥ prabhuḥ] Almighty [asṛjat] created [sanātanam sukṣmaṁ yajñam] eternal fine-tuned process of creation [devānāṁ gaṇaṁ cha], so that [prāṇinām] human beings, divine beings and seekers may attain the objective of life (mokṣa) [karmātmanām] by performing actions.

Creation of the Veda

अग्निवायुरविभ्यस्तु त्रयं ब्रह्म सनातनम् ।
दुदोह यज्ञसिद्ध्यर्थं ऋग्यजुस्सामलक्षणम् ॥ 23 ॥
agnivāyuravibhyastu trayaṁ brahma sanātanam /
dudoha yajñasiddhyarthaṁ ṛgyajussāmalakṣaṇam // 23 //

23. From out of three seers Agni, Vāyu and Sūrya, [trayam] three [sanātana] eternal [brahma] Vedas called Ṛk, Yajus, and Sāman [dudoha] were milked (extracted) [siddhyartham] to understand [yajña] the process of creation.

Creation of Time

कालं कालविभक्तीश्च नक्षत्राणि ग्रहांस्तथा ।
सरितः सागरान् शैलान् समानि विषमानि च ॥ 24 ॥
kālaṁ kālavibhaktīścha nakṣatrāṇi grahāṁstathā /
saritaḥ sāgarān śailān samāni viṣamāni cha // 24 //

24. Time and its divisions, such as kalpas, manvantara, yugas, years, months, fortnights, days, hours, palas, violas, etc.; the constellations and planets; the rivers, the oceans; the mountains, plains, and uneven ground.

Creation of Emotions

तपो वाचं रतिं चैव कामं च क्रोधमेव च ।
सृष्टिं ससर्ज चैवैमां स्रष्टुमिच्छन्निमाः प्रजाः ॥ 25 ॥
tapo vāchaṁ ratiṁ chaiva kāmaṁ cha krodhameva cha /
sṛṣṭiṁ sasarja chaivaimāṁ sraṣṭumichchhannimāḥ prajāḥ //

25. Austerity, speech, pleasure, desire, anger, this whole creation was produced by Brahman, when He desired to create these living beings.

Differentiation of Dharma and Adharma

कर्मणां च विवेकार्थं धर्माधर्मौ व्यवेचयत् ।
द्वन्द्वैरयोजयच्चैमाः सुखदुःखादिभिः प्रजाः ॥ 26 ॥
karmaṇāṁ cha vivekārthaṁ dharmādharmau vyavechayat /
dvandvairayojayachchaimāḥ sukhaduḥkhādibhiḥ prajāḥ //

26. [vivekārtham] For the due discrimination of actions, Brahman [vyavechayat] separated [dharmādharmau] dharma (permissible actions) from adharma (non-permissible actions), and [imāḥ prajāḥ] these creatures [ayojayet] were connected [dvandvaiḥ] with the dvandvas of [sukh-duḥkhādibhiḥ] pleasure and pain.

Order of Origin of things

अण्व्यो मात्रा विनाशिन्यो दशार्धानां तु याः स्मृताः ।
ताभिः सार्धमिदं सर्वं सम्भवत्यनुपूर्वशः ॥ 27 ॥
aṇvyo mātrā vināśinyo daśārdhānāṁ tu yāḥ smṛtāḥ /
tābhiḥ sārdhamidaṁ sarvaṁ sambhavatyanupūrvaśaḥ //

27. [sarvam] The entire creation [sambhavati] came into being [anupūrvaśaḥ] in due order from micro to macro to gross [tābhiḥ] alongwith [vināśinyaḥ] the perishable [aṇvyaḥ mātrāḥ] tanmātras (sensations) [yāḥ smṛtāḥ] as they are called, [daśārdhānām] of five gross of elements.

Karma-based

यस्तु कर्मणि यस्मिन् स न्ययुङ्क्त प्रथमं प्रभुः ।
स तदेव स्वयं भेजे सृज्यमानः पुनः पुनः ॥ 28 ॥
yastu karmaṇi yasmin sa nyayuṅkta prathamaṁ prabhuḥ /
sa tadeva svayaṁ bheje sṛjyamānaḥ punaḥ punaḥ // 28 //

28. At the beginning of creation, Paramātmā (God) associated different actions with the bodies of living beings of various species. Every living being occupies a body in subsequent lives that aligns with their karmas.

हिंस्राहिंस्रे मृदुक्रूरे धर्माधर्मावृतानृते ।
यद् यस्य सोऽदधात् सर्गे तत् तस्य स्वयमाविशत् ॥ 29 ॥
hiṁsrāhiṁsre mṛdukrūre dharmādharmāvṛtānṛte /
yad yasya so'dadhāt sarge tat tasya svayamāviśat // 29 //

29. Whatever traits God assigned to each species at the beginning of creation—harmfulness or harmlessness, gentleness or cruelty, dharma (righteousness) or adharma (non-righteousness), truth or falsehood—became their natural traits.

यथर्तुलिङ्गान्यर्तवः स्वयमेवर्तुपर्यये ।
स्वानि स्वान्यभिपद्यन्ते तथा कर्माणि देहिनः ॥ 30 ॥
yathartuliṅgānyartavaḥ svayamevartuparyaye /
svāni svānyabhipadyante tathā karmāṇi dehinaḥ //30 //

30. Just as with the change of the seasons, each season adopts its unique characteristics. In a similar way, souls reborn

into various species according to their karmas automatically resume the actions assigned to the body of the concerned species.

Creation of four Varṇās (Sanskāras)

लोकानां तु विवृद्ध्यर्थं मुखबाहूरुपादतः ।
ब्राह्मणं क्षत्रियं वैश्यं शूद्रं च निरवर्तयत् ॥ 31 ॥

lokānāṁ tu vivṛddhyarthaṁ mukhabāhūrupādataḥ /
brāhmaṇaṁ kṣatriyaṁ vaiśyaṁ śūdraṁ cha niravartayat //

31. [vvṛddhyartham lokānām] For the sake of human progress, every individual is endowed with the sanskāras (qualities) of Brahmaṇa, Kṣatriya, Vaiśya, and Śudra which are compatible with their mouth, arms, thighs, and feet respectively.

Note: Every human being has the freedom to achieve progress and prosperity by carefully accumulating any or all of the four sanskāras (qualities) through food habits, actions, and thoughts. These four sanskāras are reflected in the four types of Varṇas in society.

Actions of Various Species

येषां तु यादृशं कर्म भूतानामिह कीर्तितम् ।
तत् तथा वोऽभिधास्यामि क्रमयोगं च जन्मनि ॥ 32 ॥

yeṣāṁ tu yādṛśaṁ karma bhūtānāmiha kīrtitam /
tat tathā vo'bhidhāsyāmi kramayogaṁ cha janmani // 32 //

32. [tat karma vaḥ abhidhāsyāmi] I will narrate the actions associated with [bhūtānām] each of the living being [yādṛśam iha kīrtitam] in this world [kramayogaṁ cha janmani] in respect of their birth order.

पशवश्च मृगाश्चैव व्यालाश्चोभयतोदतः ।
रक्षांसि च पिशाचाश्च मनुष्याश्च जरायुजाः ॥ 33 ॥

paśavaścha mṛgāśchaiva vyālāśchobhayatodataḥ /
rakṣāṁsi cha piśāchāścha manuṣyāścha jarāyujāḥ // 33 //

33. [paśavaḥ] Domestic animals, [mṛgāścha] wild animals, [vyālāḥ] carnivorous animals and [ubhayodataḥ] omnivores

with two rows of teeth, [rākṣāṁsi] people residing in southern regions [piśāchas] non-vegetarian humans and vegetarian humans are [jarāyujāḥ] viviparous.

अण्डजाः पक्षिणः सर्पा नक्रा मत्स्याश्च कच्छपाः ।
यानि चैवं प्रकाराणि स्थलजान्यौदकानि च ॥ 34 ॥

aṇḍajāḥ pakṣiṇaḥ sarpā nakrā matsyāścha kachchhapāḥ /
yāni chaivaṁ prakārāṇi sthalajānyaudakāni cha // 34 //

34. Birds, snakes, crocodiles, fishes, tortoises, as well as similar terrestrial and aquatic (animals) are called aṇḍjas (oviparous).

स्वेदजं दंशमशकं यूकामक्षिकमत्कुणम् ।
ऊष्मणश्चोपजायन्ते यच्चान्यत् किं चिदीदृशम् ॥ 35 ॥

svedajaṁ daṁśamaśakaṁ yūkāmakṣikamatkuṇam /
ūṣmaṇaśchopajāyante yachchānyat kiṁ chidīdṛśam // 35 //

35. Biting, stinging insects, mosquitoes, lice, flies, bugs, and all other (creatures) of that kind like aquatic animals and those which are produced by heat are called Svedaja.

उद्भिज्जाः स्थावराः सर्वे बीजकाण्डप्ररोहिणः ।
ओषध्यः फलपाकान्ता बहुपुष्पफलोपगाः ॥ 36 ॥
udbhijjāḥ sthāvarāḥ sarve bījakāṇḍaprarohiṇaḥ /
ōṣadhyaḥ phalapākāntā bahupuṣpaphalopagāḥ // 36 //

36. In the category of Udbhijas are included all trees, plants, and shrubs growing from seeds or from shoots; herbs, and plants bearing fruits and flowers;

Categories of Plants and Trees

अपुष्पाः फलवन्तो ये ते वनस्पतयः स्मृताः ।
पुष्पिणः फलिनश्चैव वृक्षास्तूभयतः स्मृताः ॥ 37 ॥

apuṣpāḥ phalavanto ye te vanaspatayaḥ smṛtāḥ /
puṣpiṇaḥ phalinaśchaiva vṛkṣāstūbhayataḥ smṛtāḥ // 37 //

37. (Those trees) which bear fruit without flowers are called Vanaspati; also those which bear both flowers and fruit are called Vṛkṣa.

गुच्छगुल्मं तु विविधं तथैव तृणजातयः ।

बीजकाण्डरुहाण्येव प्रताना वल्लय एव च ॥ 38 ॥

guchchhagulmaṁ tu vividhaṁ tathaiva tṛṇajātayaḥ /
bījakāṇḍaruhāṇyeva pratānā vallaya ēva cha // *38* //

38. Also various [guccha] shrubs, [gulma] bushes and different kinds of grasses, [pratāna] plants with tendrils, and [vallaya] creepers those spring forth from seed or [kāṇḍa] stem.

Plants have life. Their Cause of the Origin

तमसा बहुरूपेण वेष्टिताः कर्महेतुना ।
अन्तस्सञ्ज्ञा भवन्त्येते सुखदुःखसमन्विताः ॥ 39 ॥

tamasā bahurūpeṇa veṣṭitāḥ karmahetunā /
antassañjñā bhavantyete sukhaduḥkhasamanvitāḥ // *39* //

39. This plant world is [veṣṭitāḥ] wrept [bahurupeṇa tamasā] in darkness and tamoguṇa [karmahetunā] as a result of past karmas (when in human species). [ete] This immovable plant world (categorized as Udbhija) also [antaḥ sañjā] has life and [sukhaduḥkha-samanvitāḥ] experiences pleasure and pain.

Karma is the Cause of Birth of Soul in various species

एतदन्तास्तु गतयो ब्रह्माद्याः समुदाहृताः ।
घोरेऽस्मिन् भूतसंसारे नित्यं सततयायिनि ॥ 40 ॥

ētadantāstu gatayo brahmādyāḥ samudāhṛtāḥ /
ghore'smin bhūtasaṁsāre nityaṁ satatayāyini // *40* //

40. This is the status of birth (birth is caused by karma) of creatures starting from Brahmā to immovable plants in this scary mundane world which goes on perpetually

Cause of Motion of the World and its Dissolution

यदा स देवो जागर्ति तदेवं चेष्टते जगत् ।
यदा स्वपिति शान्तात्मा तदा सर्वं निमीलति ॥ 41 ॥

yadā sa devo jāgarti tadevaṁ cheṣṭate jagat /
yadā svapiti śāntātmā tadā sarvaṁ nimīlati // *41* //

41. When the Almighty Brahman awakens from sleep (expresses a desire to create the universe), the world becomes active. Conversely, when He sleeps—withdraws His desire—

with a tranquil mind, the entire universe dissolves.

Note: In this context, the period of creation is linked to Brahman's awakening, while dissolution corresponds to His state of rest.

तस्मिन् स्वपिति तु स्वस्थे कर्मात्मानः शरीरिणः ।
स्वकर्मभ्यो निवर्तन्ते मनश्च ग्लानिमृच्छति ॥ 42 ॥

tasmin svapiti tu svasthe karmātmānaḥ śarīriṇaḥ /
svakarmabhyo nivartante manaścha glānimṛchchhati // 42 //

42. But when he sleeps, the action-oriented corporeal beings, cease to act and their minds weaken.

Condition during Dissolution

युगपत् तु प्रलीयन्ते यदा तस्मिन् महात्मनि ।
तदाऽयं सर्वभूतात्मा सुखं स्वपिति निर्वृतः ॥ 43 ॥

yugapat tu pralīyante yadā tasmin mahātmani /
tadā'yaṁ sarvabhūtātmā sukhaṁ svapiti nirvṛtaḥ // 43 //

43. When all creatures are absorbed simultaneously into that great soul (Brahman) during the period of dissolution, the Brahman, who is the shelter of the entire universe, sleeps comfortably, free from all care and occupation.

Rise of Individual Souls in New Creation Cycle

तमोऽयं तु समाश्रित्य चिरं तिष्ठति सैन्द्रियः ।
न च स्वं कुरुते कर्म यत उत्क्रामति मूर्तितः ॥ 44 ॥

tamo'yaṁ tu samāśritya chiraṁ tiṣṭhati saindriyaḥ /
na cha svaṁ kurute karma yata utkrāmati mūrtitaḥ // 44 //

44. [ayaṁ tu] The individual souls also [tamaḥ smāśritya] enter into deep sleep and [chiraṁ tiṣṭhati] rests for a long time [sendriyaḥ] in the company of its subtle body consisting of manas, buddhi and ahaṅkāra, [na cha svaṁ kurute karma] and performs no action by itself, [yat utkrāmati mūrtitaḥ] as it is without corporeal frame, which is the only means of doing action.

यदाऽणुमात्रिको भूत्वा बीजं स्थाणु चरिष्णु च ।

समाविशति संसृष्टस्तदा मूर्तिं विमुञ्चति ॥ 45 ॥

yadā'ṇumātriko bhūtvā bījaṁ sthāṇu chariṣṇu cha /
samāviśati saṁsṛṣṭastadā mūrtiṁ vimuñchati // 45 //

45. [yadā] When the next creation cycle begins, the individuated soul, [aṇumātriko bhūtvā] in its atomic form, [sansṛṣṭaḥ] becoming united with its subtle body [bījam] according to the seed of its kārmika sanskāras, [smāviśati] attains the life of immovable creatures like plants and moveable creatures like humans and animals etc., [tadā] then it [vimuñchati] assumes [mūrtim] a (new) corporeal frame (body).

एवं स जाग्रत्स्वप्नाभ्यामिदं सर्वं चराचरम् ।
सञ्जीवयति चाजस्रं प्रमापयति चाव्ययः ॥ 46 ॥

ēvaṁ sa jāgratsvapnābhyāmidaṁ sarvaṁ charācharam /
sañjīvayati chājasraṁ pramāpayati chāvyayaḥ // 46 //

46. [evam] Thus [saḥ] He (Brahman), [avyayam] the imperishable one, [jāgṛt-svapnābhyām] by (alternately) waking and sleeping, [ajasram] incessantly [sañjīvayati] revivifies [cha] and [pramāpayati] destroys [sarvam] this whole [charācharam] animate and inanimate world.

Origin of Dharmaśāstra (Code of Natural Law)

इदं शास्त्रं तु कृत्वाऽसौ मामेव स्वयमादितः ।
विधिवद् ग्राहयामास मरीच्यादींस्त्वहं मुनीन् ॥ 47 ॥

idaṁ śāstraṁ tu kṛtvā'sau māmeva svayamāditaḥ /
vidhivad grāhayāmāsa marīchyādīṁstvahaṁ munīn // 47 //

47. This Dharmaśāstra, or code of natural law, was created by Brahman Himself during the formation of the universe. (Manu's Dharmaśāstra is grounded in these natural laws). He (Brahman) personally imparted this knowledge to me while I was in deep meditation (Samādhi). I then passed it on to Marīci and the other sages.

एतद् वोऽयं भृगुः शास्त्रं श्रावयिष्यत्यशेषतः ।
एतद् हि मत्तोऽधिजगे सर्वमेषोऽखिलं मुनिः ॥ 48 ॥

ētad vo'yaṁ bhṛguḥ śāstraṁ śrāvayiṣyatyaśeṣataḥ /

ētad hi matto'dhijage sarvameṣo'khilaṁ muniḥ // 48 //

48. Bhṛgu, here, will pass on this Śāstra to you; as that sage [adhijage] learned the entire Śāstra [mattaḥ] from me.

ततस्तथा स तेनोक्तो महर्षिमनुना भृगुः ।
तानब्रवीद् ऋषीन् सर्वान् प्रीतात्मा श्रूयतामिति ॥ 49 ॥

tatastathā sa tenokto maharṣimanunā bhṛguḥ /
tānabravīd ṛṣīn sarvān prītātmā śrūyatāmiti // 49 //

49. Then that great sage Bhṛgu, thus addressed by Manu, spoke, pleased in his heart, to all the sages, "Listen!

Manvantaras

स्वायम्भुवस्यास्य मनोः षड्वंश्या मनवोऽपरे ।
सृष्टवन्तः प्रजाः स्वाः स्वा महात्मानो महौजसः ॥ 50 ॥

svāyambhuvasyāsya manoḥ ṣaḍvaṁśyā manavo'pare /
sṛṣṭavantaḥ prajāḥ svāḥ svā mahātmāno mahaujasaḥ // 50 //

50. "There are six other great, very energetic Manus (manvantara periods] in the chain of Svayambhu Manu who witnessed the creation of living beings during their tenures.

NB: Presently we are living in Vaivasvata Manvantara which is the seventh in a series of the present Śveta vārāha kalpa. The present Manvantara commenced 120,533,116 years ago. The names of Manvantaras that have passed since the beginning of the present Kalpa are: Svāyambhūva Manvantara (the first one), Svārociṣa (second Manvantara), Uttama (third Manvantara), Tāmasa (fourth Manvantara), Raivata (fifth Manvantara), Cākṣuṣa (sixth Manvantara) and Vaivasvata (current seventh Manvantara)

स्वारोचिषश्चोत्तमश्च तामसो रैवतस्तथा ।
चाक्षुषश्च महातेजा विवस्वत्सुत एव च ॥ 51 ॥

svārochiṣaśchottamaścha tāmaso raivatastathā /
chākṣuṣaścha mahātejā vivasvatsuta ēva cha // 51 //

51. The six [suta] descending Manus (manvantaras) are Svārociṣa Manu, Uttama Manu, Tāmasa Manu, Raivata Manu, Cākṣuṣa Manu, and Vaivasvata Manu, the current one.

स्वायम्भुवाद्याः सप्तैते मनवो भूरितेजसः ।
स्वे स्वेऽन्तरे सर्वमिदमुत्पाद्यापुश्चराचरम् ॥ 52 ॥

svāyambhuvādyāḥ saptaite manavo bhūritejasaḥ /
sve sve'ntare sarvamidamutpādyāpuścharācharam // 52 //

52. These seven distinguished Manus, beginning with Svāyambhuva, [utpādya] created and [āpuḥ] safeguarded [charācharam] this entire movable and immovable creation, each during their respective periods.

NB: Their periods are:

Svāyambhūva Manu= 1972949116-1662773115

Svārociṣa Manu = 1662773116-1354325115

Uttama Manu =1354325116-1045877115

Tāmasa Manu = 1045877116-737429115

Raivata Manu =737429116-428981115

Cākṣuṣa Manu = 428981116-120533115

Vaivasvata Manu= 120533116-5115 Kali

Measure of Time From Micro Units to Macro Units

निमेषा दश चाष्टौ च काष्ठा त्रिंशत् तु ताः कला ।
त्रिंशत् कला मुहूर्तः स्यादहोरात्रं तु तावतः ॥ 53 ॥

nimeṣā daśa chāṣṭau cha kāṣṭhā triṁśat tu tāḥ kalā /
triṁśat kalā muhūrtaḥ syādahorātraṁ tu tāvataḥ // 53 //

53. (The time has been divided into micro units as well as macro units). To explain the measurement Manvantara period, micro units of time have been explained first).

(1 Nimeṣa=0.088 seconds)

18 Nimeṣas (twinklings of the eye) =1 Kāṣṭhā (1.6 seconds)

30 Kāṣṭhās = 1 Kalā (48 seconds)

30 Kalās = 1 Muhurta (24 minutes) (According to Bhāskara 1 Muhurta = 48 Minutes)

60 Muhurtas= One day and night (24 hours) (According to

Bhāskara 30 Muhurtas = One day and night)

अहोरात्रे विभजते सूर्यो मानुषदैविके ।
रात्रिः स्वप्नाय भूतानां चेष्टायै कर्मणामहः ॥ 54 ॥

ahorātre vibhajate sūryo mānuṣadaivike /
rātriḥ svapnāya bhūtānāṁ cheṣṭāyai karmaṇāmahaḥ // 54 //

54. The sun splits the days and nights for humans (residing in equatorial regions) and devas (residing in polar regions); the night is meant for the rest of created beings, while the day is for action.

Day and Night of Pitaras and Pitṛloka

पित्र्ये रात्र्यहनी मासः प्रविभागस्तु पक्षयोः ।
कर्मचेष्टास्वहः कृष्णः शुक्लः स्वप्नाय शर्वरी ॥ 55 ॥

pitraye rātrayahanī māsaḥ pravibhāgastu pakṣayoḥ /
karmacheṣṭāsvahaḥ kṛṣṇaḥ śuklaḥ svapnāya śarvarī // 55 //

55. [māsaḥ] A lunar month of humans is equivalent [rātryahanī] to a day and a night [pitrye] for the Pitaras [moon], as the far side of the moon experiences a night for a dark fortnight (15 days) and day for a bright fortnight and vice versa. The bright fortnight is the day on the moon for performing actions, and the dark (fortnight) is the night for sleep.

Note: Lunar dark and bright fortnights are equal to a month of humans on the earth.

The lunar surface is called Pitṛloka.

Day and Nights of Devas

दैवे रात्र्यहनी वर्षं प्रविभागस्तयोः पुनः ।
अहस्तत्रोदगयनं रात्रिः स्याद् दक्षिणायनम् ॥ 56 ॥

daive rātrayahanī varṣaṁ pravibhāgastayoḥ punaḥ /
ahastatrodagayanaṁ rātriḥ syād dakṣiṇāyanam // 56 //

56. [varṣam] A year of Manuṣya loka (equatorial region) is equivalent to [rātryahanī] a day and a night [daive] for the Devaloka (polar regions); [tayoḥ pravibhāgaḥ] their division is (as follows): the [udagayanam] the Udgayana period or

Devayāna (six months from 21st March to 23rd Sept. when the sun tenants northern hemisphere of the earth) [ahaḥ tatra] is the day for polar regions, as there is day for continuous six months), and [dakṣiṇāyanam syāt rātriḥ] that Dakṣiṇāyana period or Pitṛyāna period from 23rd Sept to 21st March when the Sun remains in southern hemisphere of the earth) is the night for Devas (polar regions).

Note: The Equatorial region is called Manuṣyaloka and the Polar region is called Devaloka. A year on the equator is equivalent to a day and night of six months each in polar regions.

Days and Nights of Brahmā and Yuga-Cycle

ब्राह्मस्य तु क्षपाहस्य यत् प्रमाणं समासतः ।
एकैकशो युगानां तु क्रमशस्तन्निबोधत ॥ 57 ॥

brāhmasya tu kṣapāhasya yat pramāṇaṁ samāsataḥ /
ēkaikaśo yugānāṁ tu kramaśastannibodhata // 57 //

57. [tat nibodhat] Now be informed [samāsataḥ] briefly [yat pramāṇam] about the duration [brāhmasya kṣpā] of a Brāhma night and [ahasya] a Brāhma day and [ekaikaśaḥ yugānām] of each Yuga [kramaśah] according to their order.

चत्वार्याहुः सहस्राणि वर्षाणां तत् कृतं युगम् ।
तस्य तावत्शती सन्ध्या सन्ध्यांशश्च तथाविधः ॥ 58 ॥

chatvāryāhuḥ sahasrāṇi varṣāṇāṁ tat kṛtaṁ yugam /
tasya tāvatśatī sandhyā sandhyāṁśaścha tathāvidhaḥ // 58 //

58. Four thousand Deva years (or 4000X360=1440000 human years) make one Kṛta yuga; as many hundred years (i.e. 400 Deva years or 400X360= 14400 human years) constitute the sandhi and sandhyāñśa period to be prefixed and suffixed to the same. This means one Kṛta yuga is equivalent to 400+4000+400=4800 Deva years or 1728000 human years.

इतरेषु ससन्ध्येषु ससन्ध्यांशेषु च त्रिषु ।
एकापायेन वर्तन्ते सहस्राणि शतानि च ॥ 59 ॥

itareṣu sasandhyeṣu sasandhyāṁśeṣu cha triṣu /
ēkāpāyena vartante sahasrāṇi śatāni cha // 59 //

59. The other three Yugas along with their sandhis and sandhyāñśas prefixed and suffixed to them are constituted of thousands and hundreds diminished successively by one each. For example

Tretāyuga consists of 300+3000+300= 3600 Deva years or 1296000 human years

Dvāparayuga consists of 200+2000+200=2400 Deva years or 864000 human years

Kaliyuga consists of 100+1000+100=1200 Deva years or 432000 human years.

यदेतत् परिसङ्ख्यातमादावेव चतुर्युगम् ।
एतद् द्वादशसाहस्रं देवानां युगमुच्यते ॥ 60 ॥

yadetat parisaṅkhyātamādāveva chaturyugam /
ētad dvādaśasāhasraṁ devānāṁ yugamuchyate // 60 //

60. The Chaturyuga mentioned above consists a total of 12000 (Deva) years. These Chaturyugas of twelve thousand years are also known as Devayuga which are equal to 43,20,000 human years. (If Devayears are multiplied by 360, they convert into human years).

दैविकानां युगानां तु सहस्रं परिसङ्ख्यया ।
ब्राह्ममेकमहर्ज्ञेयं तावतीं रात्रिमेव च ॥ 61 ॥

daivikānāṁ yugānāṁ tu sahasraṁ parisaṅkhyayā /
brāhmamekamaharjñeyaṁ tāvatīṁ rātrimeva cha // 61 //

61. 1000 Devayugas or Chaturyugas (4,320,000,000 human years) make one day of Brahman and his night has also the same length (4320000000 years). Thus a day and night of Brahmā is equivalent to 86,40,00,00,00 years

तद् वै युगसहस्रान्तं ब्राह्मं पुण्यमहर्विदुः ।
रात्रिं च तावतीमेव तेऽहोरात्रविदो जनाः ॥ 62 ॥

tad vai yugasahasrāntaṁ brāhmaṁ puṇyamaharviduḥ /
rātriṁ cha tāvatīmeva te'horātravido janāḥ // 62 //

62. Thus the astronomers know that a Brāhma day (day of Brahman) lasts for 1000 Devayugas (4,320,000,000 human

years) and that his night lasts as long (1000 Devayugas or 4,320,000,000 human years).

Brahman Activates Cosmic Mind (Prakṛti) for Creation

तस्य सोऽहर्निशस्यान्ते प्रसुप्तः प्रतिबुध्यते ।
प्रतिबुद्धश्च सृजति मनः सदसदात्मकम् ॥ 63 ॥

tasya so'harniśasyānte prasuptaḥ pratibudhyate /
pratibuddhaścha sṛjati manaḥ sadasadātmakam // 63 //

63. When only one day and night (equivalent to 8,640,000,000 years) of his sleep remains, Brahman awakens. Upon awakening, he activates his cosmic mind (prakṛti), which is eternal in its causal form but perishable in its effectual form.

Note: It is important to note that prakṛti represents the cosmic mind of Brahman, containing the information necessary for creation. Additionally, there is a gap of 800 million (8 Arab) and 640 million (64 Crore) years between each cycle of creation.

Sequence of Creation

मनः सृष्टिं विकुरुते चोद्यमानं सिसृक्षया ।
आकाशं जायते तस्मात् तस्य शब्दं गुणं विदुः ॥ 64 ॥

manaḥ sṛṣṭiṁ vikurute chodyamānaṁ sisṛkṣayā /
ākāśaṁ jāyate tasmāt tasya śabdaṁ guṇaṁ viduḥ // 64 //

64. Cosmic mind (prakṛti or inactive energy), [chodyamānaḥ] agitated or impelled [sisṛkṣayā] by Brahman's desire to create, [sṛṣṭiṁ vikurute] performs the work of creation, [tasmāt] thence [ākāśam jāyate] Bhūtākāśa (elemental space that which illuminates all around) or Virāṭ is formed.

Śabda (vibration/wave) is said to be the indicative of this Ākāśa (Bhūtākāśa or elemental space), as vibration/wave can only travel in Ākāśā (Bhūtākāśa).

आकाशात् तु विकुर्वाणात् सर्वगन्धवहः शुचिः ।
बलवाञ्जायते वायुः स वै स्पर्शगुणो मतः ॥ 65 ॥

ākāśāt tu vikurvāṇāt sarvagandhavahaḥ śuchiḥ /
balavāñjāyate vāyuḥ sa vai sparśaguṇo mataḥ // 65 //

65. From Bhūtākāśa (elemental space) [vikurvāṇāt], buzzing with active energy, pure and strong vāyu (vāyu here is the technical term used for gases) is formed. Vāyu can carry all types of scents. It is associated with the sensory property of sparśa (touch).

Note: In Ākāśa, active energy resulted in the formation of neutrinos, quarks, and electrons, which eventually led to the creation of protons and neutrons. These protons and neutrons combined to form hydrogen nuclei, which subsequently merged to create helium, hydrogen, oxygen, and other gases. In gases, the intermolecular distance is significant, and the molecules float with high frequency. When these frequently moving molecules collide with a surface, the impact is strong and noticeable, whereas slower collisions are less perceptible. This phenomenon is referred to as sparśa (touch) in Vedic terminology.

वायोरपि विकुर्वाणाद् विरोचिष्णु तमोनुदम् ।
ज्योतिरुत्पद्यते भास्वत् तद् रूपगुणमुच्यते ॥ 66 ॥

vāyorapi vikurvāṇād virochiṣṇu tamonudam /
jyotirutpadyate bhāsvat tad rūpaguṇamuchyate // 66 //

66. From vāyu (hydrogen, oxygen etc. gases) originated fire which dispelled darkness. Fire is luminous and possesses the property of rūpa (luminosity).

Note: Hydrogen has the characteristic of burning, and oxygen aids in this process. As a result, fire (or heat) is produced when hydrogen and oxygen combine. The fire has a visible luminosity, which is why the origin of the fire is considered the herald of the beginning of the visible world.

ज्योतिषश्च विकुर्वाणादापो रसगुणाः स्मृताः ।
अद्भ्यो गन्धगुणा भूमिरित्येषा सृष्टिरादितः ॥ 67 ॥

jyotiṣaścha vikurvāṇādāpo rasaguṇāḥ smṛtāḥ /
adbhyo gandhaguṇā bhūmirityeṣā sṛṣṭirāditaḥ // 67 //

67. Water originated from fire, specifically from its gaseous components. Water possesses the sensory property of taste. Earth, in turn, originated from water, which has the unique

property of smell.

To elaborate, water comes into existence after the element of fire (or heat). In fact, when the two constituents of fire—hydrogen (which facilitates combustion) and oxygen (the oxidizing agent)—combine in a specific ratio, they form water.

As the temperature rises above zero degrees Celsius, the molecules of water move closer together, resulting in reduced intermolecular distance. At this point, matter occupies the liquid state, which in Vedic terminology is referred to as Jala or Āpaḥ. In this state, the matter can be tasted, highlighting its sensory property of taste.

In contrast, the solid form of matter is referred to as Pṛthivī in Vedic terminology. When the temperature drops, the molecules fuse and the intermolecular distance becomes negligible. This leads to the formation of solid matter, known as Pṛthivī. Solid matter is characterized by its exclusive property of olfaction, or smell. It is important to note that the sense of smell is unique to Earth and can only be found in its evolutes; for instance, flowers are also evolutions of Earth.

In the Vedas, the elements of water (Āpaḥ), fire (Agni), and air (Vāyu) are collectively referred to as 'pavitra,' meaning purifying agents. Therefore, smell cannot exist independently in water, heat, or air/gas; rather, it is a property that emerges from the combination of these elements with earthly matter.

Measure of a Manvantara

यद् प्राग् द्वादशसाहस्रमुदितं दैविकं युगम् ।
तदेकसप्ततिगुणं मन्वन्तरमिहोच्यते ॥ 68 ॥

yad prāg dvādaśasāhasramuditaṁ daivikaṁ yugam /
tadekasaptatiguṇaṁ manvantaramihochyate // 68 //

68. The before-mentioned Devayuga (Chaturyuga) of twelve thousand deva years (43,20,000 human years), being multiplied by seventy-one, (constitutes what) is here named the period of a Manvantara.

मन्वन्तराण्यसङ्ख्यानि सर्गः संहार एव च ।

क्रीडन्निवैतत् कुरुते परमेष्ठी पुनः पुनः ॥ 69 ॥

manvantarāṇyasaṅkhyāni sargaḥ saṁhāra ēva cha /
krīḍannivaitat kurute parameṣṭhī punaḥ punaḥ // 69 //

69. There are an infinite number of the manvantaras, the creation and decreation cycles; sporting, as it were, Brahman repeats this again and again.

Representation of Chaturyga by Dharma

चतुष्पात् सकलो धर्मः सत्यं चैव कृते युगे ।
इतरेष्वागमाद् धर्मः पादशस्त्ववरोपितः ॥ 70 ॥

chatuṣpāt sakalo dharmaḥ satyaṁ chaiva kṛte yuge /
itareṣvāgamād dharmaḥ pādaśastvavaropitaḥ // 70 //

70. Chaturyuga which spans 43,20,000 years, is referred to as equal to Dharma. Dharma refers to the number 10. The entire period [chatuṣpāt] is divided into four portions 1:2:3:4. The Kritayuga consists of four portions (4320000/10*4 =17,68,000 years). The other three yugas are progressively diminished by a portion of dharma (4 portions). For example, Tretāyuga consists of three portions, making it have a duration of (4320000/10 * 3 = 1296000 years); Dvāparayuga is made up of two portions, resulting in (4320000/10 * 2 = 864000 years); and Kaliyuga consists of one portion, leading to (4320000/10 * 1 = 432000 years).

Span of Human life in each Yuga

अरोगाः सर्वसिद्धार्थाश्चतुर्वर्षशतायुषः ।
कृते त्रेतादिषु ह्येषामायुर्ह्रसति पादशः ॥ 71 ॥

arogāḥ sarvasiddhārthāśchaturvarṣaśatāyuṣaḥ /
kṛte tretādiṣu hyeṣāmāyurhrasati pādaśaḥ // 71 //

71. In Kṛtayuga, people may live upto 400 years, enjoying successful healthy lives. However, in Tretā yuga, their lifespan decreased to 300 years. This decline continued in each subsequent yuga: in Dvāpara yuga, people lived for 200 years, and in Kaliyuga, their lifespan was reduced to just 100 years.

वेदोक्तमायुर्मर्त्यानामाशिषश्चैव कर्मणाम् ।

फलन्त्यनुयुगं लोके प्रभावश्च शरीरिणाम् ॥ 72 ॥

vedoktamāyurmartyānāmāśiṣaśchaiva karmaṇām /
phalantyanuyugaṁ loke prabhāvaścha śarīriṇām // 72 //

72. [āyuḥ] The age, [āśiṣaḥ cha eva karmaṇām] fruits of karmas and [prabhāvaḥ cha] power of [śarīriṇām] physical bodies of the people, [vedoktam] mentioned in the Vedas, [loke phalanti] have different bearings [anuyugam] in different yugas.

For instance, Veda talks about human beings' age of 100 years. जीवेम शरदः शतम्. This age is for a single yuga or Kaliyuga. For dvāpara, it will be twice, i.e. 200 years; for tretā, 300 years, and Satyayuga, 400 years.

Change of Values according to Yugas

अन्ये कृतयुगे धर्मास्त्रेतायां द्वापरेऽपरे ।
अन्ये कलियुगे नृणां युगह्रासानुरूपतः ॥ 73 ॥

anye kṛtayuge dharmāstretāyāṁ dvāpare'pare /
anye kaliyuge nṝṇāṁ yugahrāsānurūpataḥ // 73 //

73. The set of values and duties change according to yugas. For example, values and duties prescribed in the Kritayuga, differ from the ones prescribed in the Tretā, the Dvāpara, and the Kali.

तपः परं कृतयुगे त्रेतायां ज्ञानमुच्यते ।
द्वापरे यज्ञमेवाहुर्दानमेकं कलौ युगे ॥ 74 ॥

tapaḥ paraṁ kṛtayuge tretāyāṁ jñānamuchyate /
dvāpare yajñamevāhurdānamekaṁ kalau yuge // 74 //

74. Yoga and austerity [param] find the highest place in the Kṛtayuga; Jñāna (knowledge) is given prominence in the Tretā; Yajña in the Dvāpara and charity in the Kaliyuga.

In other words, we can say that tapa (yoga and austerity) find the highest place equivalent to the Kṛtayuga; Jñāna (knowledge) is given prominence equivalent to the Tretā; Yajña to the Dvāpara and charity to in the Kaliyuga.

Distribution of Duties of the Four Main Professions

सर्वस्यास्य तु सर्गस्य गुप्त्यर्थं स महाद्युतिः ।
मुखबाहूरुपज्जानां पृथक्कर्माण्यकल्पयत् ॥ 75 ॥

sarvasyāsya tu sargasya guptyarthaṁ sa mahādyutiḥ ।
mukhabāhūrupajjānāṁ pṛthakkarmāṇyakalpayat ॥ *75* ॥

75. [sargasya guptyartham] To ensure the safety and proper functioning [sarvasya asya] of all living beings, [saḥ] Brahman, [mahādyuti] the most resplendent one, [akalpayat] designated [pṛthak] distinct [karmāṇi] functions to different professionals applying different organs of the body like mouth, arms, and others to execute their professional duties.

The human body has four principal organs: the mouth, arms, thighs, and belly. So, all professions concerning human beings have also been divided into three main categories. The first one is the Teaching profession; the second one is Administration, which includes legislative, executive, judiciary, defense, and other related professions; the third one is production and business, including trading, marketing, etc.; and the fourth one is jobs of skilled and unskilled workers in the above three main professions.

For instance, a teacher is supposed to execute his/her duty by applying the organ of the mouth, an administrator or kṣatriya arms, vaiśya thighs or belly (traveling), and skilled and non-skilled applying feet.

अध्यापनमध्ययनं यजनं याजनं तथा ।
दानं प्रतिग्रहं चैव ब्राह्मणानामकल्पयत् ॥ 76 ॥

adhyāpanamadhyayanaṁ yajanaṁ yājanaṁ tathā ।
dānaṁ pratigrahaṁ chaiva brāhmaṇānāmakalpayat ॥ *76* ॥

76. To those pursuing the professional duty of a teacher, he designated the function of teaching and studying, performing yajña for one's own benefit and others, work of charity, and making approvals.

Note: Manu is known as the originator of the Varṇa system, not the caste system. According to Manu, a person of the Brāhmaṇa Varṇa is comparable to a modern-day teacher. While there is also a Brāhmaṇa caste in India, it is important to note that the caste system developed much later, during the Muslim period. People often confuse the term 'Brāhmaṇa varṇa' with the 'Brāhmaṇa caste.' It is not necessary that a person from Brāhmaṇa caste may also belong to Brāhmaṇa varṇa. Therefore, from now on, we will translate the term 'Brāhmaṇa' as used by Manu in the context of varṇa to mean 'teacher' to avoid confusion between Brāhmaṇa caste and Brāhmaṇa Varṇa.

Similarly, Manu originally employed the term "Śudra" to denote two key meanings: first, as a reference to individuals lacking education, and second, to refer to skilled and unskilled workers. However, in today's society, the term "Śudra" is predominantly linked to the notion of low caste. To better resonate with contemporary understandings and to foster clarity, I have chosen to use more precise terms such as "uneducated" and "skilled or unskilled worker," depending on the context. This approach not only respects the original intent of the Manu but also provides a more accurate representation of individuals' roles in society.

प्रजानां रक्षणं दानमिज्याऽध्ययनमेव च ।
विषयेष्वप्रसक्तिश्च क्षत्रियस्य समासतः ॥ 77 ॥

prajānāṁ rakṣaṇaṁ dānamijyā'dhyayanameva cha /
viṣayeṣvaprasaktiścha kṣatriyasya samāsataḥ // 77 //

77. To those pursuing the professional duty of Kṣatriyas (legislature, executive, judiciary, defence, and other administrative and civil services), he assigned the function of protection of the interests of the people and nationa, work of charity, performance of yajña, study, and abstaining from sensual pleasures;

पशूनां रक्षणं दानमिज्याऽध्ययनमेव च ।
वणिक्पथं कुसीदं च वैश्यस्य कृषिमेव च ॥ 78 ॥

paśūnāṁ rakṣaṇaṁ dānamijyā'dhyayanameva cha /
vaṇikpathaṁ kusīdaṁ cha vaiśyasya kṛṣimeva cha // 78 //

78. To those pursuing the professional duty of a Vaiśya (farmers, manufacturers, businessman and traders) He assigned the function of domestication of animals, charity, the

performance of Yajña, study, trading and manufacturing, money lending/banking, and agriculture.

एकमेव तु शूद्रस्य प्रभुः कर्म समादिशत् ।
एतेषामेव वर्णानां शुश्रूषामनसूयया ॥ 79 ॥

ēkameva tu śūdrasya prabhuḥ karma samādiśat ।
ēteṣāmeva varṇānāṁ śuśrūṣāmanasūyayā ॥ 79 ॥

79. To those providing services as skilled and non-skilled workers in other professions, he assigned only one function and that is to provide skilled or unskilled services in other professions.

Progressive Excellence in Body-parts

ऊर्ध्वं नाभेर्मेध्यतरः पुरुषः परिकीर्तितः ।
तस्मान् मेध्यतमं त्वस्य मुखमुक्तं स्वयम्भुवा ॥ 80 ॥

ūrdhvaṁ nābhermedhyataraḥ puruṣaḥ parikīrtitaḥ ।
tasmān medhyatamaṁ tvasya mukhamuktaṁ svayambhuvā

80. A human is considered purer above the navel than below; thus, the Self-existent (Svayambhū) Brahman has stated that the purest part of a human is his head /mouth.

Progressive Excellence in Species and Human Professions

भूतानां प्राणिनः श्रेष्ठाः प्राणिनां बुद्धिजीविनः ।
बुद्धिमत्सु नराः श्रेष्ठा नरेषु ब्राह्मणाः स्मृताः ॥ 81 ॥

bhūtānāṁ prāṇinaḥ śreṣṭhāḥ prāṇināṁ buddhijīvinaḥ ।
buddhimatsu narāḥ śreṣṭhā nareṣu brāhmaṇāḥ smṛtāḥ ॥

81. Among unanimated and animated beings, the most excellent are the animated ones; of the animated beings, those that subsist by using mind (animals and humans); of those using mind, humans; and among humans, teachers;

ब्राह्मणेषु च विद्वांसो विद्वत्सु कृतबुद्धयः ।
कृतबुद्धिषु कर्तारः कर्तृषु ब्रह्मवेदिनः ॥ 82 ॥

brāhmaṇeṣu cha vidvāṁso vidvatsu kṛtabuddhayaḥ ।
kṛtabuddhiṣu kartāraḥ kartṛṣu brahmavedinaḥ ॥ 82 ॥

82. Among teachers, the most excellent are scholars; of the

scholars, those who understand their duties; among those who understand their duties, those who actually perform; among the performers, those who have realised Brahman.

उत्पत्तिरेव विप्रस्य मूर्तिर्धर्मस्य शाश्वती ।
स हि धर्मार्थमुत्पन्नो ब्रह्मभूयाय कल्पते ॥ 83 ॥

utpattireva viprasya mūrtirdharmasya śāśvatī /
sa hi dharmārthamutpanno brahmabhūyāya kalpate // 83 //

83. The very birth of a teacher is considered to be an eternal incarnation of dharma (knowledge); for he is born for the proliferation of this knowledge, and can qualify for mokṣa.

तस्य कर्मविवेकार्थं शेषाणामनुपूर्वशः ।
स्वायम्भुवो मनुर्धीमानिदं शास्त्रमकल्पयत् ॥ 84 ॥

tasya karmavivekārthaṁ śeṣāṇāmanupūrvaśaḥ /
svāyambhuvo manurdhīmānidaṁ śāstramakalpayat // 84 //

84. In order to clearly settle the duties of teachers and those of the others (legislature, executive, judiciary, and defence; farmers, manufacturers and traders; and skilled and unskilled workers) according to their profession, wise Manu born in the family of Svyambhū Brahmā, composed this Śāstra.

Note: The progressive excellence emphasizes the importance of advancing based on one's abilities, skills, and achievements. This principle not only rewards hard work and talent but also fosters a culture of excellence and fairness, driving individuals to reach their full potential. These professional classes were made so that every human being can judge his excellence on this scale and strive hard to make advances to as redeem the spiritual objective of human life (mokṣa)

Role of a good Teacher

विदुषा ब्राह्मणेनैदमध्येतव्यं प्रयत्नतः ।
शिश्येभ्यश्च प्रवक्तव्यं सम्यग् नान्येन केन चित् ॥ 85 ॥

viduṣā brāhmaṇenaidamadhyetavyaṁ prayatnataḥ /
śiśyebhyaścha pravaktavyaṁ samyaga nānyena kena chit //

85. A learned teacher must carefully read it, and he must

duly instruct his pupils in it, as nobody else can do it.

Note: It is essential to guide students toward the most effective paths for both material and spiritual growth, empowering them to make informed choices that resonate with their individual aspirations. This freedom of choice not only nurtures their development but also fosters a deeper sense of responsibility and commitment to their journey.

इदं शास्त्रमधीयानो ब्राह्मणः शंसितव्रतः ।
मनोवाक्देहजैर्नित्यं कर्मदोषैर्न लिप्यते ॥ 86 ॥

idaṁ śāstramadhīyāno brāhmaṇaḥ śaṁsitavrataḥ /
manovākdehajairnityaṁ karmadoṣairna lipyate // 86 //

104. A teacher who studies these Sāstras and faithfully fulfils the duties (of teaching this Śāstra), will never be tainted by actions inviting blemishness done through mind, speech, and body. That is, he will never do wrong actions.

पुनाति पङ्क्तिं वंश्यांश्च सप्तसप्त परावरान् ।
पृथिवीमपि चैवेमां कृत्स्नामेकोऽपि सोऽर्हति ॥ 87 ॥

punāti paṅktiṁ vaṁśyāṁścha saptasapta parāvarān /
pṛthivīmapi chaivemāṁ kṛtsnāmeko'pi so'rhati // 87 //

87. A person who excels in this Dharmaśāstra, he sanctifies any company (which he may enter), seven lines of his seniors and seven lines of juniors, and he alone deserves (to possess) this whole earth.

इदं स्वस्त्ययनं श्रेष्ठमिदं बुद्धिविवर्धनम् ।
इदं यशस्यमायुष्यं इदं निःश्रेयसं परम् ॥ 88 ॥

idaṁ svastyayanaṁ śreṣṭhamidaṁ buddhivivardhanam /
idaṁ yaśasyamāyuṣyaṁ idaṁ niḥśreyasaṁ param // 88 //

88. The study of this Śastra bestows success, knowledge/understanding, name, fame and long life. It (leads to) supreme bliss.

अस्मिन् धर्मेऽखिलेनोक्तौ गुणदोषौ च कर्मणाम् ।
चतुर्णामपि वर्णानामाचारश्चैव शाश्वतः ॥ 89 ॥

asmin dharme'khilenoktau guṇadoṣau cha karmaṇām /

chaturṇāmapi varṇānāmāchāraśchaiva śāśvataḥ // 89 //

89. In this Dharmaśāstra, both the good and bad qualities of human actions are fully stated alongside the duties and conduct of all four Varṇas (the professional classes based on sanskāras).

Significance of Good Conduct

आचारः परमो धर्मः श्रुत्योक्तः स्मार्त एव च ।
तस्मादस्मिन् सदा युक्तो नित्यं स्यादात्मवान् द्विजः ॥ 90 ॥

āchāraḥ paramo dharmaḥ śrutyoktaḥ smārta ēva cha /
tasmādasmin sadā yukto nityaṁ syādātmavān dvijaḥ // 90 //

90. The value of good conduct is paramount, whether taught in the Śrutis (Vedas) or in the Smṛtis (Dharmaśāstras). Therefore, an educated person desiring self-elevation should always follow it.

आचाराद् विच्युतो विप्रो न वेदफलमश्नुते ।
आचारेण तु संयुक्तः सम्पूर्णफलभाग् भवेत् ॥ 91 ॥

āchārād vichyuto vipro na vedaphalamaśnute /
āchāreṇa tu saṁyuktaḥ sampūrṇaphalabhāg bhavet // 91 //

91. An educated person who displays improper conduct fails to reap the benefits of good actions performed in accordance with the Vedas and Śāstras. In contrast, a person who upholds good conduct will receive the rewards of all their good deeds carried out according to the Vedas.

एवमाचारतो दृष्ट्वा धर्मस्य मुनयो गतिम् ।
सर्वस्य तपसो मूलमाचारं जगृहुः परम् ॥ 92 ॥

ēvamāchārato dṛṣṭvā dharmasya munayo gatim /
sarvasya tapaso mūlamāchāraṁ jagṛhuḥ param // 92 //

92. The sages who discovered that Dharma can be attained through good conduct, have established good conduct as the foundation of all austerities.

Contexts of This Dharmaśāstra

जगतश्च समुत्पत्तिं संस्कारविधिमेव च ।
व्रतचर्योपचारं च स्नानस्य च परं विधिम् ॥ 93 ॥

jagataścha samutpattiṁ saṁskāravidhimeva cha |
vratacharyaupachāraṁ cha snānasya cha paraṁ vidhim || 93

93. The following subjects have been covered in this text: the creation of the universe, the procedures of the sanskāras, the observance of various vratas (saṅkalpas), [upachāra] conducts and attitudes, and the excellent procedure of graduation.

दाराधिगमनं चैव विवाहानां च लक्षणम् ।
महायज्ञविधानं च श्राद्धकल्पं च शाश्वतम् ॥ 94 ॥

dārādhigamanaṁ chaiva vivāhānāṁ cha lakṣaṇam |
mahāyajñavidhānaṁ cha śrāddhakalpaṁ cha śāśvatam ||94

94. (The law of) marriage and the definition of the (various) forms of marriages, the procedure of Pañcha-Mahāyajñas (five main Yajñas) and the eternal rules of care for elderly persons of family and society.

वृत्तीनां लक्षणं चैव स्नातकस्य व्रतानि च ।
भक्ष्याभक्ष्यं च शौचं च द्रव्याणां शुद्धिमेव च ॥ 95 ॥

vṛttīnāṁ lakṣaṇaṁ chaiva snātakasya vratāni cha |
bhakṣayābhakṣayaṁ cha śauchaṁ cha dravyāṇāṁ
śuddhimeva cha || 95 ||

95. The explanation of various means of livelihood and the practices of a Gṛhastha (householder) who has graduated in the Vedas and other Śāstras, including which foods are beneficial to eat and which to avoid, as well as methods for self-purification and cleaning things.

स्त्रीधर्मयोगं तापस्यं मोक्षं संन्यासमेव च ।
राज्ञश्च धर्ममखिलं कार्याणां च विनिर्णयम् ॥ 96 ॥

strīdharmayogaṁ tāpasyaṁ mokṣaṁ saṁnyāsameva cha |
rājñaścha dharmamakhilaṁ kāryāṇāṁ cha vinirṇayam || 96

96. Duties of women, duties of Vānaprasthis, Saṁnyāsīs and procedure of mokṣa, the duties of a king and the manner of deciding lawsuits,

साक्षिप्रश्नविधानं च धर्मं स्त्रीपुंसयोरपि ।
विभागधर्मं द्यूतं च कण्टकानां च शोधनम् ॥ 97 ॥

sākṣipraśnavidhānaṁ cha dharmaṁ strīpuṁsayorapi /
vibhāgadharmaṁ dyūtaṁ cha kaṇṭakānāṁ cha śodhanam //

97. The rules for the examination of witnesses, the duties of husband and wife, the law of (inheritance and) division of property, the laws to deal with gambling and unsocial elements,

वैश्यशूद्रोपचारं च सङ्कीर्णानां च सम्भवम् ।
आपद्धर्मं च वर्णानां प्रायश्चित्तविधिं तथा ॥ 98 ॥

vaiśyaśūdropachāraṁ cha saṅkīrṇānāṁ cha sambhavam /
āpaddharmaṁ cha varṇānāṁ prāyaśchittavidhiṁ tathā // *98*

98. The law governing the conduct and treatment of Vaiśyas (manufacturers and trader) and Śūdras (service providers), adulteration, emergency duties of various professionals, and the methods of expiation (in case of commission of mistakes and crimes),

संसारगमनं चैव त्रिविधं कर्मसम्भवम् ।
निःश्रेयसं कर्मणां च गुणदोषपरीक्षणम् ॥ 99 ॥

saṁsāragamanaṁ chaiva trividhaṁ karmasambhavam /
niḥśreyasaṁ karmaṇāṁ cha guṇadoṣaparīkṣaṇam // *99* //

99. Threefold of transmigration of soul on the basis of karmas (actions): uttama (first class), madhyam (second class) and adhama (third class); rules of emancipation and the examination of the good and bad qualities of actions.

देशधर्मान्जातिधर्मान् कुलधर्मांश्च शाश्वतान् ।
पाषण्डगणधर्मांश्च शास्त्रेऽस्मिन्नुक्तवान् मनुः ॥ 100 ॥

deśadharmānjātidharmān kuladharmāṁścha śāśvatān /
pāṣaṇḍagaṇadharmāṁścha śāstre'sminnuktavān manuḥ //

100. The eternal laws for governing a nation, managing various species of living beings, overseeing dynasties, and regulating heretics are outlined in this Śāstra.

यथैदमुक्तवांशास्त्रं पुरा पृष्टो मनुर्मया ।
तथैदं यूयमप्यद्य मत्सकाशान्निबोधत ॥ 101 ॥

yathaidamuktavāṁśāstraṁ purā pṛṣṭo manurmayā /
tathaidaṁ yūyamapyadya matsakāśānnibodhata // *101* //

101. As Manu, in reply to my questions, formerly promulgated this Śāstra, even so learn you the (whole work) from me.

Chapter 2: Sources of Dharma

The present chapter addresses the proper conduct expected of students, their initiation into student life through the sacred thread ceremony, and the period of disciplined study dedicated to learning the Vedas under the guidance of a teacher. Manu specifies that a student aspiring to become a teacher should wear a sacred thread made of cotton, while those engaged in legislative, executive, judiciary, and defense roles should use a hemp thread. In contrast, individuals involved in manufacturing, farming, and trading should wear a woolen thread.

Manu also emphasizes the behavior a student should exhibit while learning the Vedas. A student should begin by respectfully touching the feet of their teacher and making a gesture of reverence called Brahmāñjali by joining their hands. Additionally, the student should always recite the syllable "OM" at both the beginning and the end of their studies of the Vedas.

How to Know Dharma

विद्वद्भिः सेवितः सद्भिर्नित्यमद्वेषरागिभिः ।
हृदयेनाभ्यनुज्ञातो यो धर्मस्तं निबोधत ॥ 1 ॥

vidvadbhiḥ sevitaḥ sadbhirnityamadveṣarāgibhiḥ /
hṛdayenābhyanujñāto yo dharmastaṁ nibodhata // 1 //

1. Know that Dharma which is followed by learned men and assented from the core of their hearts by the virtuous ever free from attachment and hatred.

Excessive Desires Deprecated

कामात्मता न प्रशस्ता न चैवैहास्त्यकामता ।
काम्यो हि वेदाधिगमः कर्मयोगश्च वैदिकः ॥ 2 ॥

kāmātmatā na praśastā na chaivaihāstyakāmatā /
kāmyo hi vedādhigamaḥ karmayogaścha vaidikaḥ // 2 //

2. It is not laudable to act solely from a desire for rewards,

nor is the desirelessness appreciable. Because it is the desire that makes one study the Veda and perform actions prescribed by the Veda.

सङ्कल्पमूलः कामो वै यज्ञाः सङ्कल्पसम्भवाः ।
व्रतानि यमधर्माश्च सर्वे सङ्कल्पजाः स्मृताः ॥ 3 ॥

saṅkalpamūlaḥ kāmo vai yajñāḥ saṅkalpasambhavāḥ /
vratāni yamadharmāścha sarve saṅkalpajāḥ smṛtāḥ // 3 //

3. The desires are rooted in our saṅkalpa (resolutions), and the performance of yajñas is also based upon our resolutions. Observance of vows, as well as yamas (non-violence, truthfulness, non-stealing, celibacy, non-hoarding) and niyamas (purification of body, speech and mind, contentment, austerity, study of Vedas, meditation) arise from our resolutions.

अकामस्य क्रिया का चिद् दृश्यते नैह कर्हि चित् ।
यद् यद् हि कुरुते किं चित् तत् तत् कामस्य चेष्टितम् ॥ 4 ॥

akāmasya kriyā kā chid dṛśyate naiha karhi chit /
yad yad hi kurute kiṁ chit tat tat kāmasya cheṣṭitam // 4 //

4. Every action here seems to be driven by desire. Everything that is done occurs because of the impulse of that desire.

तेषु सम्यग् वर्तमानो गच्छत्यमरलोकताम् ।
यथा सङ्कल्पितांश्चेह सर्वान् कामान् समश्नुते ॥ 5 ॥

teṣu samyag vartamāno gachchhatyamaralokatām /
yathā saṅkalpitāṁśchaiha sarvān kāmān samaśnute // 5 //

5. He who conducts himself properly while performing actions prescribed in the Vedas, reaches the state of emancipation as well as fulfills all desires as per his resolution.

Sources of Dharma

वेदोऽखिलो धर्ममूलं स्मृतिशीले च तद्विदाम् ।
आचारश्चैव साधूनामात्मनस्तुष्टिरेव च ॥ 6 ॥

vedo'khilo dharmamūlaṁ smṛtiśīle cha tadvidām /
āchāraśchaiva sādhūnāmātmanastuṣṭireva cha // 6 //

6. The Veda is the primary source of dharma (moral and

ethical values, knowledge, duties, laws, and code of conduct) followed in order by Smṛtis, the virtuous scholars well versed in the Veda and Smṛtis, also the conduct of saints, and finally self-satisfaction.

As such a person should perform those actions either sanctioned in Vedas and Smṛtis or followed by Vedic scholars or reflected in the conduct of saints or which provide him/her self-satisfaction.

यः कश्चित् कस्य चिद् धर्मो मनुना परिकीर्तितः ।
स सर्वोऽभिहितो वेदे सर्वज्ञानमयो हि सः ॥ 7 ॥

yaḥ kaśchit kasya chid dharmo manunā parikīrtitaḥ /
sa sarvo'bhihito vede sarvajñānamayo hi saḥ // 7 //

7. All duties and conduct prescribed by Manu are fully ordained in the Veda, as the Veda is the source of all knowledge.

सर्वं तु समवेक्ष्यैदं निखिलं ज्ञानचक्षुषा ।
श्रुतिप्रामाण्यतो विद्वान् स्वधर्मे निविशेत वै ॥ 8 ॥

sarvaṁ tu samavekṣayaidaṁ nikhilaṁ jñānachakṣuṣā /
śrutiprāmāṇyato vidvān svadharme niviśeta vai // 8 //

8. However, a knowledgeable person, having gained insight into all this through wisdom, should perform his duties in alignment with the Vedas.

श्रुतिस्मृत्योदितं धर्ममनुतिष्ठन् हि मानवः ।
इह कीर्तिमवाप्नोति प्रेत्य चानुत्तमं सुखम् ॥ 9 ॥

śrutismṛtyoditaṁ dharmamanutiṣṭhan hi mānavaḥ /
iha kīrtimavāpnoti pretya chānuttamaṁ sukham // 9 //

9. For a man who adheres to the code of conduct as outlined in the Śruti (Veda) and Smṛti (Dharmaśāstras based on the Vedas), he gains fame in this world and achieves supreme bliss (emancipation) after death.

श्रुतिस्तु वेदो विज्ञेयो धर्मशास्त्रं तु वै स्मृतिः ।
ते सर्वार्थेष्वमीमांस्ये ताभ्यां धर्मो हि निर्बभौ ॥ 10 ॥
śrutistu vedo vijñeyo dharmaśāstraṁ tu vai smṛtiḥ /
te sarvārtheṣvamīmāṁsye tābhyāṁ dharmo hi nirbabhau //

10. Śruti refers to the Veda, while Smṛti signifies the Dharmaśāstra (based on Vedas). Both of these texts are considered undisputed authorities, as dharma emerges from them.

Note: There are dharmaśāstras or smṛtis that do not follow Veda, so they cannot be considered undisputed sources of Dharma.

योऽवमन्येत ते मूले हेतुशास्त्राश्रयाद् द्विजः ।
स साधुभिर्बहिष्कार्यो नास्तिको वेदनिन्दकः ॥ 11 ॥

yo'vamanyeta te mūle hetuśāstrāśrayād dvijaḥ ।
sa sādhubhirbahiṣkāryo nāstiko vedanindakaḥ ॥ 11 ॥

11. A scholar who disregards these two sources of dharma (Veda and Smṛtis based upon Vedas) relying on [hetuśāstrāśrayāt] science of logic, must be ousted by the gentlemen, as someone who denounces the Veda is essentially an atheist.

वेदः स्मृतिः सदाचारः स्वस्य च प्रियमात्मनः ।
एतच्चतुर्विधं प्राहुः साक्षाद् धर्मस्य लक्षणम् ॥ 12 ॥

vedaḥ smṛtiḥ sadāchāraḥ svasya cha priyamātmanaḥ ।
ētachchaturvidhaṁ prāhuḥ sākṣād dharmasya lakṣaṇam ॥

12. The Veda, the Smṛti, good conduct, and well-being of oneself are declared to be the fourfold means of dharma.

अर्थकामेष्वसक्तानां धर्मज्ञानं विधीयते ।
धर्मं जिज्ञासमानानां प्रमाणं परमं श्रुतिः ॥ 13 ॥

arthakāmeṣvasaktānāṁ dharmajñānaṁ vidhīyate ।
dharmaṁ jijñāsamānānāṁ pramāṇaṁ paramaṁ śrutiḥ ॥

13. The individuals who don't crave material possessions and the fulfillment of worldly desires can attain a deeper understanding of Dharma. For those who seek Dharma, the Śruti (Veda) is the highest authority.

How to Solve the Conflicting views of the Vedic Texts

श्रुतिद्वैधं तु यत्र स्यात् तत्र धर्मावुभौ स्मृतौ ।
उभावपि हि तौ धर्मौ सम्यगुक्तौ मनीषिभिः ॥ 14 ॥

śrutidvaidhaṁ tu yatra syāt tatra dharmāvubhau smṛtau /
ubhāvapi hi tau dharmau samyaguktau manīṣibhiḥ // 14 //

14. If there are two prescriptions in the Śruti (Vedas), both prescriptions should be taken as Dharma, since both prescriptions are pronounced by the wise (to be) valid.

उदितेऽनुदिते चैव समयाध्युषिते तथा ।
सर्वथा वर्तते यज्ञ इतीयं वैदिकी श्रुतिः ॥ 15 ॥

udite'nudite chaiva samayādhyuṣite tathā /
sarvathā vartate yajña itīyaṁ vaidikī śrutiḥ // 15 //

15. For example, the Vedas provide two prescriptions for performing Agnihotra: (1) it should be done at sunrise or sunset, or [*samayādhyuṣite*] (2) if the time for sunrise or sunset has passed [*samayādhyuṣita*], Agnihotra must still be performed. This indicates that the yajña should be conducted regularly, regardless of the times of sunrise and sunset—such is the instruction given in the Veda.

Who is the Subject of this Śāstra?

निषेकादिश्मशानान्तो मन्त्रैर्यस्योदितो विधिः ।
तस्य शास्त्रेऽधिकारोऽस्मिन् ज्ञेयो नान्यस्य कस्य चित् ॥ 16 ॥

niṣekādiśmaśānānto mantrairyasyodito vidhiḥ /
tasya śāstre'dhikāro'smin jñeyo nānyasya kasya chit // 16 //

16. Know that this Śāstra is meant for no others (animal etc.) but human beings in general for whom the 16 Sanskāras (process for transformation of human beings) beginning with [niṣeka] the conception (Garbhādhana) and ending with [śmaśānāntaḥ] the last rite/funeral rite (Antyeṣṭi) are prescribed.

Countries qualified to enacting the rules of this Śāstra

सरस्वतीदृशद्वत्योर्देवनद्योर्यदन्तरम् ।
तं देवनिर्मितं देशं ब्रह्मावर्तं प्रचक्षते ॥ 17 ॥

sarasvatīdṛśadvatyordevanadyoryadantaram /
taṁ devanirmitaṁ deśaṁ brahmāvartaṁ prachakṣate // 17 //

17. The region [devanirmitam] with natural landscape, situated between the two rivers Sarasvatī and Dṛṣadvati

(Chautanga), is referred to as Brahmāvarta (Āryāvarta) and at least in this regions, the rules of this Śāstra should be implemented.

तस्मिन् देशे य आचारः पारम्पर्यक्रमागतः ।
वर्णानां सान्तरालानां स सदाचार उच्यते ॥ 18 ॥

tasmin deśe ya āchāraḥ pāramparyakramāgataḥ ।
varṇānāṁ sāntarālānāṁ sa sadāchāra uchyate ॥ 18 ॥

18. Those countries are also qualified for the implementation of the rules of this Dharmaśātra where the code of conduct followed traditionally since time immemorial by the people of four varṇas [sāntarālānām] along with āśramas is called Sadāchāra (moral and ethical code of conduct). They are:

कुरुक्षेत्रं च मत्स्याश्च पञ्चालाः शूरसेनकाः ।
एष ब्रह्मर्षिदेशो वै ब्रह्मावर्तादनन्तरः ॥ 19 ॥

kurukṣetraṁ cha matsyāścha pañchālāḥ śūrasenakāḥ ।
ēṣa brahmarṣideśo vai brahmāvartādanantaraḥ ॥ 19 ॥

19. Kurukshetra, the kingdom of the Matsyas, Panchālas, and Śūrasenakas, together called Brahmarṣi country located immediately after Brahmāvarta.

Matsyas ruled a kingdom located south of the Kurus, and west of the Yamuna river which separated it from the kingdom of the Pañchālas. It roughly corresponded to the former state of Jaipur in Rajasthan and included the whole of Hindaun, Alwar with portions of Bharatpur. The capital of Matsya was at Virāṭ Nagari (present-day Bairat) which is said to have been named after its founder king, Virāṭa. In Pali literature, the Matsya tribe is usually associated with the Śūrasena. The western Matsya was the hill tract on the north bank of the Chambal River.

The Pañchāla kingdom extends from the Himalayas in the north; to the Charmaṇvati river; with the Kuru, Śūrasena and Matsya kingdoms to the west; and the Naimiṣa Forest to the east. Later, Pañchāla was divided into Southern Pañchāla (Pañchāla proper, centered at Kāmpilya, ruled by

King Drupada, the father-in-law of Pāṇḍavas); and Northern Pañchāla (centered at Ahichatrā, ruled by Aśvathāma, the son of Droṇa. Droṇa was Drupada's friend who later became his enemy). The Ganges River separated the two Pañchālas.

Śūrsena was an ancient Indian region corresponding to the present-day Braj region in Uttar Pradesh.

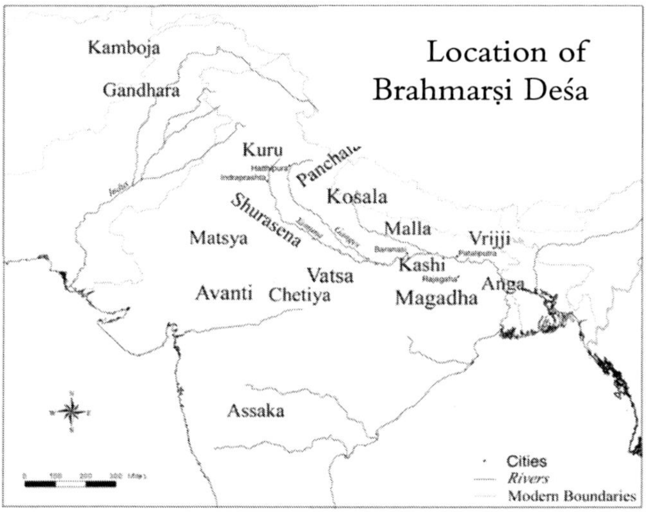

एतद् देशप्रसूतस्य सकाशादग्रजन्मनः ।
स्वं स्वं चरित्रं शिक्षेरन् पृथिव्यां सर्वमानवाः ॥ 20 ॥

ētad deśaprasūtasya sakāśādagrajanmanaḥ /
svaṁ svaṁ charitraṁ śikṣeran pṛthivyāṁ
sarvamānavāḥ //20 //

20. From the inhabitants of this country who were first born human beings on the globe, people from all parts of the globe learn the education of code of conduct.

हिमवद्विन्ध्ययोर्मध्यं यत् प्राग् विनशनादपि ।
प्रत्यगेव प्रयागाच्च मध्यदेशः प्रकीर्तितः ॥ 21 ॥

ā samudrāt tu vai pūrvādā samudrāchcha paśchimāt /
tayorevāntaraṁ giryorāryāvartaṁ vidurbudhāḥ // 22 //

21. That (country) which is located between the Himalayas and the Vindhya (mountains) to the west of Prayāga (modern Allahabad) and to the east of Vinaśana (modern Bisan near Beri

in Rohtak District of Haryana) is called Madhyadeśa (the central region).

आ समुद्रात् तु वै पूर्वादा समुद्राच्च पश्चिमात् ।
तयोरेवान्तरं गिर्योरार्यावर्तं विदुर्बुधाः ॥ 22 ॥

ā samudrāt tu vai pūrvādā samudrāchcha paśchimāt /
tayorevāntaraṁ giryorāryāvartaṁ vidurbudhāḥ // 22 //

22. But (the area) between those two mountains (just mentioned), which extends between the eastern ocean (Bay of Bengal) and the western ocean (Arabian sea) is called Āryāvarta by scholars.

कृष्णसारस्तु चरति मृगो यत्र स्वभावतः ।
स ज्ञेयो यज्ञियो देशो म्लेच्छदेशस्त्वतः परः ॥ 23 ॥

kṛṣṇasārastu charati mṛgo yatra svabhāvataḥ /
sa jñeyo yajñiyo deśo mlechchhadeśastvataḥ paraḥ // 23 //

23. The land where the black antelope naturally roams is known to be suitable for performing Yajñas; a region distinct from this is the country of the Mlechchhas (those who do not follow the Vedic code of conduct).

एतान्द्विजातयो देशान् संश्रयेरन् प्रयत्नतः ।
शूद्रस्तु यस्मिन् कस्मिन् वा निवसेद् वृत्तिकर्शितः ॥ 24 ॥

ētāndvijātayo deśān saṁśrayeran prayatnataḥ /
śūdrastu yasmin kasmin vā nivased vṛttikarśitaḥ // 24 //

24. Vedic scholars may choose to reside in Mlechchha countries to educate the locals about moral and ethical values. However, a Śudra (an uneducated person) is free to choose any place to live in order to make a living.

Summing up

एषा धर्मस्य वो योनिः समासेन प्रकीर्तिता ।
सम्भवश्चास्य सर्वस्य वर्णधर्मान्निबोधत ॥ 25 ॥

ēṣā dharmasya vo yoniḥ samāsena prakīrtitā /
sambhavaśchāsya sarvasya varṇadharmānnibodhata // 25 //

25. Thus [yoniḥ] the source of Dharma is briefly described to you as also the origin of this universe; learn (now) the

dharmas (moral and ethical codes of conduct and duties) of the different Varṇas.

Duties and Sixteen Sanskāras

वैदिकैः कर्मभिः पुण्यैर्निषेकादिर्द्विजन्मनाम् ।
कार्यः शरीरसंस्कारः पावनः प्रेत्य चैह च ॥ 26 ॥

vaidikaiḥ karmabhiḥ puṇyairniṣekādirdvijanmanām ।
kāryaḥ śarīrasaṁskāraḥ pāvanaḥ pretya chaiha cha ॥ 26 ॥

26. Sixteen Vedic auspicious Sanskāras starting from [niṣeka] conception to the last ceremony should be performed by educated individuals for their children. This practice helps the child develop into a transformed being (in this life) and hereafter (after death).

Note: This verse emphasizes that at least educated individuals (dvijas) are required to perform Sanskāras for their children. However, it should be noted that even uneducated individuals (Śudras) are not prohibited from conducting these ceremonies.

गार्भैर्होमैर्जातकर्मचौडमौञ्जीनिबन्धनैः ।
बैजिकं गार्भिकं चैनं द्विजानामपमृज्यते ॥ 27 ॥

gārbhairhomairjātakarmachauḍamauñjīnibandhanaiḥ ।
baijikaṁ gārbhikaṁ chainaṁ dvijānāmapamṛjyate ॥ 27 ॥

27. The Sanskāras of Garbhādāna (conception), Jātakarma (birth ceremony), Cūḍākarma (baby's first haircut ceremony), Mauñjibandhan (Girdle ceremony) are meant for treating genetic disorders or disorders related to pregnancy, sperm and ovum.

स्वाध्यायेन व्रतैर्होमैस्त्रैविद्येनेज्यया सुतैः ।
महायज्ञैश्च यज्ञैश्च ब्राह्मीयं क्रियते तनुः ॥ 28 ॥

svādhyāyena vratairhomaistraividyenejyayā sutaiḥ ।
mahāyajñaiścha yajñaiścha brāhmīyaṁ kriyate tanuḥ ॥ 28 ॥

28. Svādhyāya (the study of the Vedas), Vrata (vow for practice of austerity), Yajñas, Traividyā (threefold sciences: Ādhyātmika, Ādhidaivika, and Ādhibhautika), Ijyā (Iṣṭis), Suta (procreation), Mahāyajñas [5 great yajñas: Brahmayajña

(aquisition of knowledge), Devayajña (agnihotra for purification of environment), Pitṛyajña (care for elders), Atithiyajña (hosting peripatetic monks and scholars) Balivaiśvadevayajña (feeding of animals and birds] and other Śrauta yajñas (allegorical Vedic yajñas explaining the process of creation at different levels) are meant to transform the human body into a Brāhmī (divine) body or to make human body eligible for uniting with Brahman (liberation).

Jātakarma Sanskāra

प्राङ् नाभिवर्धनात् पुंसो जातकर्म विधीयते ।
मन्त्रवत् प्राशनं चास्य हिरण्यमधुसर्पिषाम् ॥ 29 ॥

prāṅ nābhivardhanāt puṁso jātakarma vidhīyate /
mantravat prāśanaṁ chāsya hiraṇyamadhusarpiṣām // 29 //

29. Before the navel-string is cut, the Jātakarma (birth-ceremony) must be performed [punsaḥ] in case of child; and he must be fed honey and cow ghee/butter in a golden spoon.

Nāmakaraṇa Sanskāra

नामधेयं दशम्यां तु द्वादश्यां वाऽस्य कारयेत् ।
पुण्ये तिथौ मुहूर्ते वा नक्षत्रे वा गुणान्विते ॥ 30 ॥

nāmadheyaṁ daśamyāṁ tu dvādaśyāṁ vā'sya kārayet /
puṇye tithau muhūrte vā nakṣatre vā guṇānvite // 30 //

30. Naming ceremony should be performed on tenth or twelfth day after birth, on an auspicious lunar day or muhurta or constellation.

मङ्गल्यं ब्राह्मणस्य स्यात् क्षत्रियस्य बलान्वितम् ।
वैश्यस्य धनसंयुक्तं शूद्रस्य तु जुगुप्सितम् ॥ 31 ॥

maṅgalyaṁ brāhmaṇasya syāt kṣatriyasya balānvitam /
vaiśyasya dhanasaṁyuktaṁ śūdrasya tu jugupsitam // 31 //

31. In this verse, the author emphasizes the significant influence that a name can have on shaping an individual's personality. The idea is that a person's name can mirror their character.

If you want your child to grow into a high-profile Teacher

or scientist, you should choose a name that is associated with auspiciousness. To nurture qualities suitable for a member of the defense forces, legislative, executive, or judiciary, consider a name linked to power. If your aim is for your child to excel as a businessman, trader, farmer, or manufacturer, select a name connected with wealth. Finally, if you want your child to thrive in the service sector, choose a name that is suitable for a service provider.

शर्मवद् ब्राह्मणस्य स्याद् राज्ञो रक्षासमन्वितम् ।
वैश्यस्य पुष्टिसंयुक्तं शूद्रस्य प्रेष्यसंयुतम् ॥ 32 ॥

śarmavad brāhmaṇasya syād rājño rakṣāsamanvitaṁ /
vaiśyasya puṣṭisaṁyuktaṁ śūdrasya preṣyasaṁyutam // 32 //

32. For example, if you want to make your child a professor or scientist, choose a name that signifies happiness, prosperity, spirituality, bliss, or comfort. If you hope for your child to develop the qualities necessary for a role in the legislative, defense forces, executive, or judiciary, select a name that embodies shelter, protection, safety, security, guardianship, and defense. For a child intending to pursue farming, business, trading, or manufacturing, choose a name that represents richness, wealth, prosperity, nourishment, growth, and development. Lastly, if you wish for your child to excel in providing services, consider a name that conveys notions of service, messenger, bearer, or command.

स्त्रीणां सुखौद्यमक्रूरं विस्पष्टार्थं मनोहरम् ।
मङ्गल्यं दीर्घवर्णान्तमाशीर्वादाभिधानवत् ॥ 33 ॥

strīṇāṁ sukhaudyamakrūraṁ vispaṣṭārthaṁ manoharam /
maṅgalyaṁ dīrghavarṇāntamāśīrvādābhidhānavat // 33 //

33. The names of female children [sukhodyam] should be easy to pronounce, not imply anything dreadful, possess a plain meaning, be pleasing to the heart and auspicious, end in long vowels, and contain a word of benediction.

Niṣkramaṇa and Annaprāśana Sanskāra

चतुर्थे मासि कर्तव्यं शिशोर्निष्क्रमणं गृहात् ।
षष्ठेऽन्नप्राशनं मासि यद् वैष्टं मङ्गलं कुले ॥ 34 ॥

chaturthe māsi kartavyaṁ śiśorniṣkramaṇaṁ gṛhāt ।
ṣaṣṭhe'nnaprāśanaṁ māsi yad vaiṣṭaṁ maṅgalaṁ kule ॥

34. In the fourth month, the Niṣkramaṇa Sanskāra (first outing ceremony) of the child should be performed, in the sixth month the Annaprāśana Sanskāra (feeding first solid food) or as required by (the custom of) the family should be performed.

Chūḍākarma Sanskāra

चूडाकर्म द्विजातीनां सर्वेषामेव धर्मतः ।
प्रथमेऽब्दे तृतीये वा कर्तव्यं श्रुतिचोदनात् ॥ 35 ॥

chūḍākarma dvijātīnāṁ sarveṣāmeva dharmataḥ ।
prathame'bde tṛtīye vā kartavyaṁ śrutichodanāt ॥ *35* ॥

35. As per the Śrutis' ordinance, the Cūdākarma Sanskāra (first haircut ceremony) must be performed by all educated individuals in either the first or third year as a mandatory duty. Uneducated individuals are exempt from these requirements.

Upanayana Sanskāra

गर्भाष्टमेऽब्दे कुर्वीत ब्राह्मणस्यौपनायनम् ।
गर्भादेकादशे राज्ञो गर्भात् तु द्वादशे विशः ॥ 36 ॥

garbhāṣṭame'bde kurvīta brāhmaṇasyaupanāyanam ।
garbhādekādaśe rājño garbhāt tu dvādaśe viśaḥ ॥ *36* ॥

36. In the eighth year after conception, the upanayana (sacred thread) sanskāra should be performed for a child who possesses the qualities of a teacher or guru. In the eleventh year after conception, this ceremony should be performed for a child who embodies the attributes of someone in the legislative, executive, judicial, or defense sectors. Finally, in the twelfth year after conception, the ceremony should be conducted for a child who reflects the qualities of a businessman, farmer, or trader.

ब्रह्मवर्चसकामस्य कार्यो विप्रस्य पञ्चमे ।
राज्ञो बलार्थिनः षष्ठे वैश्यस्यैहार्थिनोऽष्टमे ॥ 37 ॥

brahmavarchasakāmasya kāryo viprasya pañchame ।
rājño balārthinaḥ ṣaṣṭhe vaiśyasyaihārthino'ṣṭame ॥ *37* ॥

37. A student who aspires to attain Brahmavarchasva, which is the aura of bioelectric current surrounding the face gained through the study of the Vedas, should be initiated into studies in the fifth year after their conception. A student seeking prowess should begin their studies in the sixth year, while a student desiring success in business should be initiated in the eighth year after conception.

आ षोडशाद् ब्राह्मणस्य सावित्री नातिवर्तते ।
आ द्वाविंशात् क्षत्रबन्धोराचतुर्विंशतेर्विशः ॥ 38 ॥

ā ṣoḍaśād brāhmaṇasya sāvitrī nātivartate /
ā dvāviṁśāt kṣatrabandhorāchaturviṁśatervisaḥ // *38* //

38. The upanayana sanskāra for a child who is endowed with the sanskāras (qualities) associated with the teaching profession cannot be performed after the age of sixteen years from conception. For a child endowed with qualities related to legislative, executive, judiciary, or defence roles, the initiation cannot extend beyond twenty-two years. Additionally, for a child with qualities related to business, the initiation must occur before the age of twenty-four years from conception.

अत ऊर्ध्वं त्रयोऽप्येते यथाकालमसंस्कृताः ।
सावित्रीपतिता व्रात्या भवन्त्यार्यविगर्हिताः ॥ 39 ॥

ata ūrdhvaṁ trayo'pyete yathākālamasaṁskṛtāḥ /
sāvitrīpatitā vrātyā bhavantyāryavigarhitāḥ // *39* //

39. If they do not complete their initiation by the maximum time limit prescribed for them, they will remain uneducated (asanskrit), and so attain (vrātya) the status of śudra. [sāvitrī patitā] They will lack the Upanayana Sanskāra and will be viewed unfavourably (vigarhitā) by their peers.

नैतैरपूतैर्विधिवदापद्यपि हि कर्हि चित् ।
ब्राह्मान् यौनांश्च सम्बन्धान्नाचरेद् ब्राह्मणः सह ॥ 40 ॥

naitairapūtairvidhivadāpadyapi hi karhi chit /
brāhmān yaunāṁścha sambandhānnāchared brāhmaṇaḥ saha // *40* //

40. With such people of low profile who remain uneducated, no (Brāhmaṇa) educated person should ever, even

in times of distress, form a relationship through [yaunān] marriage [brāhmān] because he is born to educated parents.

The author highlights that Brāhmaṇa status is achieved through education rather than being determined by birth. Therefore, a person is considered educated (Brāhmaṇa) only if they have successfully graduated from the educational system; lineage or birth alone does not confer education or Brāhmaṇa status.

कार्ष्णरौरवबास्तानि चर्माणि ब्रह्मचारिणः ।
वसीरन्नानुपूर्व्येण शाणक्षौमाविकानि च ॥ 41 ॥

kārṣṇarauravabāstāni charmāṇi brahmachāriṇaḥ /
vasīrannānupūrvyeṇa śāṇakṣaumāvikāni cha // 41 //

41. A specific dress code has been established to differentiate students pursuing various professions.

Students in the teaching program are required to use seats made of black wool and wear clothing made from jute. Those studying administration should use seats crafted from wool sourced from the Tibetan antelope, known as 'Chiru' and their clothing should be made of linen. Finally, students in the business profession should use seats made from cashmere goats and wear clothing made from wool.

मौञ्जी त्रिवृत् समा श्लक्ष्णा कार्या विप्रस्य मेखला ।
क्षत्रियस्य तु मौर्वी ज्या वैश्यस्य शणतान्तवी ॥ 42 ॥

mauñjī trivṛt samā ślakṣaṇā kāryā viprasya mekhalā /
kṣatriyasya tu maurvī jyā vaiśyasya śaṇatāntavī // 42 //

42. A student pursuing a teaching profession should wear a girdle made of a smooth and soft triple cord of Muñja grass. For those studying administration or defence studies, the girdle should consist of a bowstring made from Murvā (hemp) strings. Meanwhile, a student preparing for a business profession should wear a girdle made of jute threads.

मुञ्जालाभे तु कर्तव्याः कुशाश्मन्तकबल्वजैः ।
त्रिवृता ग्रन्थिनैकेन त्रिभिः पञ्चभिरेव वा ॥ 43 ॥

muñjālābhe tu kartavyāḥ kuśāśmantakabalvajaiḥ /

trivṛtā granthinaikena tribhiḥ pañchabhireva vā // 43 //

43. In case of non-availability of Muñja grass, etc. (the girdles) may be made of Kuśa grass, Aśmantaka, and Balvaja (a kind of coarse grass) fibres. A girdle should have three strings folded into one with three or five knots.

कार्पासमुपवीतं स्याद् विप्रस्यौर्ध्ववृतं त्रिवृत् ।
शणसूत्रमयं राज्ञो वैश्यस्याविकसौत्रिकम् ॥ 44 ॥

kārpāsamupavītaṁ syād viprasyaurdhvavṛtaṁ trivṛt /
śaṇasūtramayaṁ rājño vaiśyasyāvikasautrikam // 44 //

44. The Yajñopavīta (initiation thread) of a student initiating into the teaching profession shall be made of cotton, that of the student getting education of administration of jute, (and) that of a student learning commerce and business of woollen. It shall be twisted upward with the right hand, (and consist) of three threads.

ब्राह्मणो बैल्वपालाशौ क्षत्रियो वाटखादिरौ ।
पैलवौदुम्बरौ वैश्यो दण्डानर्हन्ति धर्मतः ॥ 45 ॥

brāhmaṇo bailvapālāśau kṣatriyo vāṭakhādirau /
pailavaudumbarau vaiśyo daṇḍānarhanti dharmataḥ // 45 //

45. As per rule, a student pursuing teaching profession shall (carry) a stick made of wood apple (Bilva) or Palāśa (Butea Frondosa) tree; a student getting education of Kṣatriya profession will carry a stick made of Vaṭa (Banyan) or Khadira (Acacia) tree; and a student initiating into Vaiśya profession will carry a stick made of Pīlu (Palm) or Udumbara (fig) tree.

केशान्तिको ब्राह्मणस्य दण्डः कार्यः प्रमाणतः ।
ललाटसम्मितो राज्ञः स्यात् तु नासान्तिको विशः ॥ 46 ॥

keśāntiko brāhmaṇasya daṇḍaḥ kāryaḥ pramāṇataḥ /
lalāṭasammito rājñaḥ syāt tu nāsāntiko viśaḥ // 46 //

46. The height of a stick for a student pursuing a teaching profession should be long enough to reach his hair. For a student studying for the Kṣatriya profession, the stick should reach his forehead. In the case of a student training for the Vaiśya profession, it should reach the tip of his nose.

ऋजवस्ते तु सर्वे स्युरव्रणाः सौम्यदर्शनाः ।
अनुद्वेगकरा नृणां सत्वचोऽनग्निदूषिताः ॥ 47 ॥

ṛjavaste tu sarve syuravraṇāḥ saumyadarśanāḥ ।
anudvegakarā nṛṇāṁ satvacho'nagnidūṣitāḥ ॥ *47* ॥

47. Let all the sticks be straight, unblemished, and good looking, with their bark untouched by fire.

प्रतिगृह्येप्सितं दण्डमुपस्थाय च भास्करम् ।
प्रदक्षिणं परीत्याग्निं चरेद् भैक्षं यथाविधि ॥ 48 ॥

pratigṛhyepsitaṁ daṇḍamupasthāya cha bhāskaram ।
pradakṣiṇaṁ parītyāgniṁ chared bhaikṣaṁ yathāvidhi 48 ॥

48. After selecting a stick of his choice, the student should stand facing the sun, walk around the fire of Yajña, and then beg for alms according to the prescribed rules.

भवत्पूर्वं चरेद् भैक्षमुपनीतो द्विजोत्तमः ।
भवन्मध्यं तु राजन्यो वैश्यस्तु भवदुत्तरम् ॥ 49 ॥

bhavatpūrvaṁ chared bhaikṣamupanīto dvijottamaḥ ।
bhavanmadhyaṁ tu rājanyo vaiśyastu bhavaduttaram ॥*49* ॥

49. A student pursuing the profession of teacher should beg, beginning his request with the word '*bhavati*' (e.g. *bhavati bhikṣāṁ dehi*); a student initiating into profession of Kṣatriya, placing the word 'bhavati' in the middle (e.g. *bhikṣāṁ bhavati dehi*), and of Vaiśya profession, placing it at the end (e.g. *bhikṣāṁ dehi bhavati*).

मातरं वा स्वसारं वा मातुर्वा भगिनीं निजाम् ।
भिक्षेत भिक्षां प्रथमं या चैनं नावमानयेत् ॥ 50 ॥

mātaraṁ vā svasāraṁ vā māturvā bhaginīṁ nijām ।
bhikṣeta bhikṣāṁ prathamaṁ yā chainaṁ nāvamānayet ॥

50. Let him first beg of his mother, or of his sister, or of his own maternal aunt, or another such women who will not insult him (with a refusal).

समाहृत्य तु तद् भैक्षं यावदन्नममायया ।
निवेद्य गुरवेऽश्नीयादाचम्य प्राङ्मुखः शुचिः ॥ 51 ॥

samāhṛtya tu tad bhaikṣaṁ yāvadannamamāyayā ।

nivedya gurave'śnīyādāchamya prāṅmukhaḥ śuchiḥ // 51 //

51. Having obtained as much food as is required by begging without fraud or cheating, let him eat it turning his face towards the east beginning with a sip of water.

आयुष्यं प्राङ्मुखो भुङ्क्ते यशस्यं दक्षिणामुखः ।
श्रियं प्रत्यङ्मुखो भुङ्क्ते ऋतं भुङ्क्ते ह्युदङ्मुखः ॥ 52 ॥

āyuṣyaṁ prāṅmukho bhuṅkte yaśasyaṁ dakṣiṇāmukhaḥ /
śriyaṁ pratyaṅmukho bhuṅkte ṛtaṁ bhuṅkte hyudaṅmukhaḥ // 52 //

52. He will attain long life, if he eats facing the east; fame, if he eats facing the south; prosperity, if he eats turning his face to the west; truthfulness, if he faces the east.

उपस्पृश्य द्विजो नित्यमन्नमद्यात् समाहितः ।
भुक्त्वा चौपस्पृशेत् सम्यगद्भिः खानि च संस्पृशेत् ॥ 53 ॥

upaspṛśya dvijo nityamannamadyāt samāhitaḥ /
bhuktvā chaupaspṛśet samyagadbhiḥ khāni cha saṁspṛśet //

53. Let a student always take his food having taken a sip of water; and after he has taken food, let him duly wash his mouth and hands and touch/sprinkle the cavities (of his head) with water.

पूजयेदशनं नित्यमद्याच्चैतदकुत्सयन् ।
दृष्ट्वा हृष्येत् प्रसीदेच्च प्रतिनन्देच्च सर्वशः ॥ 54 ॥

pūjayedaśanaṁ nityamadyāchchaitadakutsayan /
dṛṣṭvā hṛṣyet prasīdechcha pratinandechcha sarvaśaḥ // 54 //

54. Let him give due regard to the food, and eat it without condemnation; when he has a glance of it, let him rejoice, pleased, and pray that he may always obtain it.

पूजितं ह्यशनं नित्यं बलमूर्जं च यच्छति ।
अपूजितं तु तद् भुक्तमुभयं नाशयेदिदम् ॥ 55 ॥

pūjitaṁ hyaśanaṁ nityaṁ balamūrjaṁ cha yachchhati /
apūjitaṁ tu tad bhuktamubhayaṁ nāśayedidam // 55 //

55. Food when taken with due regard, always provides power and energy; but when taken contrarily, it destroys both

power and energy.

नौच्छिष्टं कस्य चिद् दद्यान्नाद्यादेतत् तथाऽन्तरा ।
न चैवात्यशनं कुर्यान्न चौच्छिष्टः क्व चिद् व्रजेत् ॥ 56 ॥

nauchchhiṣṭaṁ kasya chid dadyānnādyādetat tathā'ntarā /
na chaivātyaśanaṁ kuryānna chauchchhiṣṭaḥ kva chid vrajet // 56 //

56. Never give leavings or stale food to anyone; never take food between the two meals (i.e. take food only two times in the morning after sunrise and evening before sunset and never take lunch). Never over-eat yourself, nor go anywhere without washing his mouth after food.

अनारोग्यमनायुष्यमस्वर्ग्यं चातिभोजनम् ।
अपुण्यं लोकविद्विष्टं तस्मात् तत् परिवर्जयेत् ॥ 57 ॥

anārogyamanāyuṣyamasvargyaṁ chātibhojanam /
apuṇyaṁ lokavidviṣṭaṁ tasmāt tat parivarjayet // 57 //

57. Excessive eating is prejudicial to health, long life, and emancipation. It is criticised by people, so it should be avoided.

ब्राह्मेण विप्रस्तीर्थेन नित्यकालमुपस्पृशेत् ।
कायत्रैदशिकाभ्यां वा न पित्र्येण कदा चन ॥ 58 ॥

brāhmeṇa viprastīrthena nityakālamupaspṛśet /
kāyatraidaśikābhyāṁ vā na pitrayeṇa kadā chana // 58 //

58. Let a student always sip water with Brāhma tīrtha (with palm of hand at the base of thumb), or with (ka) prajāpati tīrtha (root of fingers) or (tridaśa) deva tīrtha (tips of fingers), and never with pitṛ tīrtha (portion between thumb and fore-finger).

अङ्गुष्ठमूलस्य तले ब्राह्मं तीर्थं प्रचक्षते ।
कायमङ्गुलिमूलेऽग्रे देवं पित्र्यं तयोरधः ॥ 59 ॥

aṅguṣṭhamūlasya tale brāhmaṁ tīrthaṁ prachakṣate /
kāyamaṅgulimūle'gre devaṁ pitrayaṁ tayoradhaḥ // 59 //

59. The palm of the hand at the base of the thumb is known as Brāhma tīrtha, while the base of the fingers is referred to as Ka/Prajāpati tīrtha. The tips of the fingers are called Deva tīrtha, and the area between the forefinger and

the thumb is known as Pitṛ tīrtha.

त्रिराचामेदपः पूर्वं द्विः प्रमृज्यात् ततो मुखम् ।
खानि चैव स्पृशेदद्भिरात्मानं शिर एव च ॥ 60 ॥

trirāchāmedapaḥ pūrvaṁ dviḥ pramṛjyāt tato mukham ।
khāni chaiva spṛśedadbhirātmānaṁ śira ēva cha ॥ *60* ॥

60. [triḥ+āchamet apaḥ] Let him first take three sips of water followed by face wash; and lastly he should touch with water his head and all cavities therein.

अनुष्णाभिरफेनाभिरद्भिस्तीर्थेन धर्मवित् ।
शौचेप्सुः सर्वदाऽचामेदेकान्ते प्रागुदङ्मुखः ॥ 61 ॥

anuṣṇābhiraphenābhiradbhistīrthena dharmavit ।
śauchepsuḥ sarvadā'chāmedekānte prāgudaṅmukhaḥ ॥ *61* ॥

61. He who is familiar with the code of dharma and seeks purity shall always take a sip of water which is neither hot nor frothy, with the (prescribed) tīrtha (mentioned above), in a secluded place facing the east or the north.

हृद्गाभिः पूयते विप्रः कण्ठगाभिस्तु भूमिपः ।
वैश्योऽद्भिः प्राशिताभिस्तु शूद्रः स्पृष्टाभिरन्ततः ॥ 62 ॥

hṛdgābhiḥ pūyate vipraḥ kaṇṭhagābhistu bhūmipaḥ ।
vaiśyo'dbhiḥ prāśitābhistu śūdraḥ spṛṣṭābhirantataḥ ॥ *62* ॥

62. The water that is sipped purifies a student who aspires to be educated in the teaching profession if it reaches their heart. This same sip can also purify a student pursuing an education in the Kṣatriya profession (which encompasses the legislative, executive, judiciary, management and defense roles) if it reaches their throat. A student studying for a Vaiṣya profession (involving manufacturing, trading, and farming) is purified by the sip of water taken into their mouth, while a student getting training for the Śudra profession (skilled worker) or not is purified if the water merely touches their lips.

In this context, the complexity of a job correlates with its responsibility: the more complex the job, the greater the responsibility and the higher the risk of mistakes, which in turn requires greater means of purification. Conversely, less complex jobs come with less responsibility, fewer chances of mistakes, and therefore, lesser means of purification.

उद्धृते दक्षिणे पाणावुपवीत्यौच्यते द्विजः ।
सव्ये प्राचीनावीती निवीती कण्ठसज्जने ॥ 63 ॥

uddhṛte dakṣiṇe pāṇāvupavītyauchyate dvijaḥ /
savye prāchīnāvītī nivītī kaṇṭhasajjane // 63 //

63. There are three styles of wearing sacred thread by a student, which are as under:

A student is called upavītī when the sacred thread rests on his left shoulder and passed underneath his right arm; he is called prāchīnāvītī when the sacred thread rests on his right shoulder and passed underneath his left arm; and nivītī when it hangs down from the neck in the manner of a rosary.

मेखलामजिनं दण्डमुपवीतं कमण्डलुम् ।
अप्सु प्रास्य विनष्टानि गृह्णीतान्यानि मन्त्रवत् ॥ 64 ॥

mekhalāmajinaṁ daṇḍamupavītaṁ kamaṇḍalum /
apsu prāsya vinaṣṭāni gṛhṇītānyāni mantravat // 64 //

64. The girdle, the fur, the stick, the initiation thread, and the Kamaṇḍalu (vessel made of wood), must be discarded into waters, when they have become useless, and new ones must be taken reciting mantras.

Keśānta Sanskāra

केशान्तः षोडशे वर्षे ब्राह्मणस्य विधीयते ।
राजन्यबन्धोर्द्वाविंशे वैश्यस्य द्व्यधिके मतः ॥ 65 ॥

keśāntaḥ ṣoḍaśe varṣe brāhmaṇasya vidhīyate /
rājanyabandhordvāviṁśe vaiśyasya dvyadhike mataḥ // 65 //

65. Keśānta (hair clipping ceremony) is performed in the sixteenth year (from conception) for a student initiating into the teaching profession; for a student initiating into the profession of Kṣatriya, in the twenty-second year; and for a student getting an education in Vaiśya profession, 24th year from conception.

Necessity of All Sanskāras for Female Child

समन्त्रिका तु कार्यैयं स्त्रीणामावृदशेषतः ।
संस्कारार्थं शरीरस्य यथाकालं यथाक्रमम् ॥ 66 ॥

samantrikā tu kāryaiyaṁ strīṇāmāvṛdaśeṣataḥ /
saṁskārārthaṁ śarīrasya yathākālaṁ yathākramam // 66 //

66. This whole series of Sanskāras must be performed in respect of females for their consecration, at the proper time and in the proper order with mantras.

Note: In some manuscripts, amantrikā word has been used, it also means without mantraṇā (consultation and thought). Meaning to say that the sanskāras of ladies should also be done with mantras without any second thought.

वैवाहिको विधिः स्त्रीणां संस्कारो वैदिकः स्मृतः ।
पतिसेवा गुरौ वासो गृहार्थोऽग्निपरिक्रिया ॥ 67 ॥

vaivāhiko vidhiḥ strīṇāṁ saṁskāro vaidikaḥ smṛtaḥ /
patisevā gurau vāso gṛhārtho'gniparikriyā // 67 //

67. After marriage, the following household duties are to be performed by ladies as Vedic Sanskāras: assisting and helping their husbands, living along with elderly persons of the house, taking care of Gṛhyāgni (family sanskāras) for the smooth and successful conduct of Gṛhastha Āśrama.

एष प्रोक्तो द्विजातीनामौपनायनिको विधिः ।
उत्पत्तिव्यञ्जकः पुण्यः कर्मयोगं निबोधत ॥ 68 ॥

ēṣa prokto dvijātīnāmaupanāyaniko vidhiḥ /
utpattivyañjakaḥ puṇyaḥ karmayogaṁ nibodhata // 68 //

68. This has been described as the guideline for initiating students into various professions, serving as an indicator of a new birth in terms of their education. This process is beneficial for their future lives. It is important to learn about their responsibilities (duties) now.

Duties of a Student

उपनीयं गुरुः शिष्यं शिक्षयेत्शौचमादितः ।
आचारमग्निकार्यं च सन्ध्यौपासनमेव च ॥ 69 ॥

upanīyaṁ guruḥ śiṣyaṁ śikṣayetśauchamāditaḥ /

āchāramagnikāryaṁ cha sandhyaupāsanameva cha // 69 //

69. The Guru must first instruct the admitted student on personal purification, conduct, agnihotra, the other 16 sanskāras, and sandhyā, which involves performing agnihotra twice daily during twilight hours, as well as upāsanā (meditation).

Rules of Study

अध्येष्यमाणस्त्वाचान्तो यथाशास्त्रमुदङ्मुखः ।
ब्रह्माञ्जलिकृतोऽध्याप्यो लघुवासा जितेन्द्रियः ॥70॥

adhyeṣyamāṇastvāchānto yathāśāstramudaṅmukhaḥ /
brahmāñjalikṛto'dhyāpyo laghuvāsā jitaindriyaḥ //70 //

70. A student who is about to begin his studies or training should first sip water, as per the rules, while facing north. He should then offer a Brahmāñjali, which involves praying for knowledge with folded hands. Additionally, he should wear a simple and modest outfit, and fully restrain his mind and senses.

ब्रह्मारम्भेऽवसाने च पादौ ग्राह्यौ गुरोः सदा ।
संहत्य हस्तावध्येयं स हि ब्रह्माञ्जलिः स्मृतः ॥ 71 ॥

brahmārambhe'vasāne cha pādau grāhyau guroḥ sadā /
saṁhatya hastāvadhyeyaṁ sa hi brahmāñjaliḥ smṛtaḥ // 71 //

71. At the beginning and the end of his class, he must always touch both feet of his teacher and put his hands together in prayer; this is called Brahmāñjali, a prayer for the sake of education.

व्यत्यस्तपाणिना कार्यमुपसङ्ग्रहणं गुरोः ।
सव्येन सव्यः स्प्रष्टव्यो दक्षिणेन च दक्षिणः ॥ 72 ॥

vyatyastapāṇinā kāryamupasaṅgrahaṇaṁ guroḥ /
savyena savyaḥ spraṣṭavyo dakṣiṇena cha dakṣiṇaḥ // 72 //

72. A student must touch his teacher's feet with his hands crossed, meaning he should touch the left foot with his left hand and the right foot with his right hand.

अध्येष्यमाणं तु गुरुर्नित्यकालमतन्द्रितः ।
अधीष्व भो इति ब्रूयाद् विरामोऽस्त्विति चारमेत् ॥ 73 ॥

adhyeṣyamāṇaṁ tu gururnityakālamatandritaḥ /
adhīṣva bho iti brūyād virāmo'stviti chāramet // 73 //

73. While delivering a lecture to students, Guru should speak '*adhiṣva bho*' (let us start with our lesson) and while (cha āramet) terminating his lecture, he should pronounce '*virāmo astu*' (you may leave now) without any sluggishness.

ब्रह्मणः प्रणवं कुर्यादादावन्ते च सर्वदा ।
स्रवत्यनोङ्कृतं पूर्वं परस्ताच्च विशीर्यति ॥ 74 ॥

brahmaṇaḥ praṇavaṁ kuryādādāvante cha sarvadā /
sravatyanoṅkṛtaṁ pūrvaṁ parastāchcha viśīryati // 74 //

74. Let him always pronounce the name of Brahman i.e. 'Om' in the beginning and at the end of a lesson; (for) want of the pronunciation of Om in the beginning and at the end, the whole lesson becomes waste.

प्राक्कूलान् पर्युपासीनः पवित्रैश्चैव पावितः ।
प्राणायामैस्त्रिभिः पूतस्तत ओंकारमर्हति ॥ 75 ॥

prākkūlān paryupāsīnaḥ pavitraiśchaiva pāvitaḥ /
prāṇāyāmaistribhiḥ pūtastata ōṁkāramarhati // 75 //

75. Seated on blades of Kuśa grass with their points facing east, purified by all means of purification, and further cleansed by three Prāṇāyāmas, one can pronounce 'Om'.

अकारं चाप्युकारं च मकारं च प्रजापतिः ।
वेदत्रयान्निरदुहद् भूर्भुवः स्वरितीति च ॥ 76 ॥

akāraṁ chāpyukāraṁ cha makāraṁ cha prajāpatiḥ /
vedatrayānniraduhad bhūrbhuvaḥ svaritīti cha // 76 //

76. [Prajāpatiḥ] In our galaxy, three Vyāhṛtis- Bhūḥ, Bhuvaḥ, Svaḥ and three sounds - A, U, and M, represents three Vedas-Ṛgveda (contains information of bhūloka or planets), Yajurveda (contains information of antarikṣaloka or space between planets and stars) and Sāmaveda (contains information about Dyauloka or stars).

त्रिभ्य एव तु वेदेभ्यः पादं पादमदूदुहत् ।
तदित्यर्चोऽस्याः सावित्र्याः परमेष्ठी प्रजापतिः ॥ 77 ॥

tribhya ēva tu vedebhyaḥ pādaṁ pādamadūduhat ।
tadityarcho'syāḥ sāvitrayāḥ parameṣṭhī prajāpatiḥ ॥ 77 ॥

77. Moreover [Parameṣṭhī Prajāpatiḥ] in our galaxy, [pādaṁ pādam] every quarter of [sāvitryāḥ] Gāyatrī mantra (*tadityarchaḥ*) which begins with the word '*tad savatur*' represent the three Vedas- the Ṛgveda, the Yajurveda and the Sāmaveda, inversely three lokas (worlds): Bhū, Bhuvaḥ and Svaḥ.

tatsavitur vareṇyam -----Ṛgveda or Bhūloka

bhargo devasya dhimahi---Yajurveda or Bhuvaḥ loka

dhiyo yo naḥ prachodayāt-----Sāmaveda or Svaḥloka

Note: Here the verb '√duh' is used in the sense of representation.

एतदक्षरमेतां च जपन् व्याहृतिपूर्विकाम् ।
सन्ध्ययोर्वेदविद् विप्रो वेदपुण्येन युज्यते ॥ 78 ॥

ētadakṣarametāṁ cha japan vyāhṛtipūrvikām ।
sandhyayorvedavid vipro vedapuṇyena yujyate ॥ 78 ॥

78. A student well versed in the Vedas, who chants during both twilights that syllable 'Om' followed by Gāyatrī mantra preceded by the three Vyāhṛtis, is enriched by the fruit of the Vedic knoweldge.

सहस्रकृत्वस्त्वभ्यस्य बहिरेतत् त्रिकं द्विजः ।
महतोऽप्येनसो मासात् त्वचैवाहिर्विमुच्यते ॥ 79 ॥

sahasrakṛtvastvabhyasya bahiretat trikaṁ dvijaḥ ।
mahato'pyenaso māsāt tvachaivāhirvimuchyate ॥ 79 ॥

79. A student who (daily) repeats the set of three, i.e.

1. Om

2. Three vyāhṛtis

3. Gāyatrī mantra) like

Oṁ bhūrbhuvaḥ svaḥ tat savtur vareṇyaṁ bhargo devasya dhīmahi dhiyo yo naḥ pracodayat –

One thousand times outside (the village or city), will

abandon even significant pāpa actions (leading to his downfall) after a month, just as a snake sheds its skin.

एतयात्र्ऋचा विसंयुक्तः काले च क्रियया स्वया ।
ब्रह्मक्षत्रियविड्योनिर्गर्हणां याति साधुषु ॥ 80 ॥

ētayāṛchā visaṁyuktaḥ kāle cha kriyayā svayā /
brahmakṣatriyaviḍyonirgarhaṇāṁ yāti sādhuṣu // *80* //

80. A student receiving an education as a teacher, kṣatriya, or Vaiśya, who neglects the timely chanting of the Gāyatrī mantra and fails to perform other necessary sanskāras prescribed for him/her will find no respect among saintly persons.

ओङ्कारपूर्विकास्तिस्रो महाव्याहृतयोऽव्ययाः ।
त्रिपदा चैव सावित्री विज्ञेयं ब्रह्मणो मुखम् ॥ 81 ॥

ōṅkārapūrvikāstisro mahāvyāhṛtayo'vyayāḥ /
tripadā chaiva sāvitrī vijñeyaṁ brahmaṇo mukham // *81* //

81. The three imperishable Mahāvyāhṛtis, preceded by the syllable 'Om', and (followed) by the Gāyatrī mantras consisting of three pādas should be known as [mukham] the gateway [brahmaṇaḥ] to Brahman (mokṣa).

योऽधीतेऽहन्यहन्येतां त्रीणि वर्षाण्यतन्द्रितः ।
स ब्रह्म परमभ्येति वायुभूतः खमूर्तिमान् ॥ 82 ॥

yo'dhīte'hanyahanyetāṁ trīṇi varṣāṇyatandritaḥ /
sa brahma paramabhyeti vāyubhūtaḥ khamūrtimān // *82* //

82. Anyone who recites the Gāyatrī mantra daily, preceded by three vyāhṛtis and 'Om', without fatigue, for three years will realize the supreme Brahman, who has an atomic form and is without a physical body.

एकाक्षरं परं ब्रह्म प्राणायामः परं तपः ।
सावित्र्यास्तु परं नास्ति मौनात् सत्यं विशिष्यते ॥ 83 ॥

ēkākṣaraṁ paraṁ brahma prāṇāyāmaḥ paraṁ tapaḥ /
sāvitrayāstu paraṁ nāsti maunāt satyaṁ viśiṣyate // *83* //

83. The monosyllabic 'Om' is the designation of supreme Brahman, prāṇāyāma is the highest form of austerity, there is no mantra that can surpass the Gāyatrī mantra and speaking truth is better than observing silence.

क्षरन्ति सर्वा वैदिक्यो जुहोतियजतिक्रियाः ।
अक्षरं दुष्करं ज्ञेयं ब्रह्म चैव प्रजापतिः ॥ 84 ॥

kṣaranti sarvā vaidikyo juhotiyajatikriyāḥ ।
akṣaraṁ duṣkaraṁ jñeyaṁ brahma chaiva prajāpatiḥ ॥ *84* ॥

84. All rites ordained in the Veda, action of offering oblations and performing yajñas are perishable, but 'Om' and (prajāpati brahma eva) Prajāpati Brahman only is [duṣkaram] imperishable.

विधियज्ञाज् जपयज्ञो विशिष्टो दशभिर्गुणैः ।
उपांशुः स्यात्शतगुणः साहस्रो मानसः स्मृतः ॥ 85 ॥

vidhiyajñāj japayajño viśiṣṭo daśabhirguṇaiḥ ।
upāṁśuḥ syātśataguṇaḥ sāhasro mānasaḥ smṛtaḥ ॥ *85* ॥

85. Japayajña (chanting of Om and svādhyāya/study of Vedas) is ten times more efficacious than a Vidhiyajña (ritual exercises described in Śrauta or Smārta Yajñas); [upāñśuḥ] a prayer uttered in low voice surpasses it a hundred times, and [mānasaḥ] meditation a thousand times.

ये पाकयज्ञाः चत्वारो विधियज्ञसमन्विताः ।
सर्वे ते जपयज्ञस्य कलां नार्हन्ति षोडशीम् ॥ 86 ॥

ye pākayajñāḥ chatvāro vidhiyajñasamanvitāḥ ।
sarve te japayajñasya kalāṁ nārhanti ṣoḍaśīm ॥ *86* ॥

86. The four Pākayajñas (ritual prescribed in Gṛhyasūtras where cooked food is offered to eat as a part of yajña like pitṛyajña, balivaiśvadevayajña, Agnihotra, atithiyajña) together with Vidhiyajñas are not worth the sixteenth part of the Japayajña (chanting Om and study of Vedas).

Pitṛyajña means taking care of the elderly person in the family.

Balivaiśvadeva-yajña means feeding animals in our surroundings.

Atithiyajña means hosting visiting Vedic scholars and Saṁnyāsīs.

जप्येनैव तु संसिध्येद् ब्राह्मणो नात्र संशयः ।

कुर्यादन्यन्न वा कुर्यान् मैत्रो ब्राह्मण उच्यते ॥ 87 ॥

japyenaiva tu saṁsidhyed brāhmaṇo nātra saṁśayaḥ /
kuryādanyanna vā kuryān maitro brāhmaṇa uchyate // 87 //

87. Undoubtedly, a student pursuing the teaching profession succeeds [japyena] through repeated study, whether he engages in any other activities or not. A person is considered a teacher if he possesses a friendly nature.

Restraining Sensory Desires

इन्द्रियाणां विचरतां विषयेष्वपहारिषु ।
संयमे यत्नमातिष्ठेद् विद्वान् यन्तैव वाजिनाम् ॥ 88 ॥

indriyāṇāṁ vicharatāṁ viṣayeṣvapahāriṣu /
saṁyame yatnamātiṣṭhed vidvān yantaiva vājinām // 88 //

88. [vidvān] A wise man [yatnam ātiṣṭhet] should strive to [indriyāṇāṁ sañyame] restrain his sense organs [viṣyeṣu apahāriṣu] running after their stimuli, [iva] like a [yantā] charioteer his [vājinām] horses.

एकादशेन्द्रियाण्याहुर्यानि पूर्वे मनीषिणः ।
तानि सम्यक् प्रवक्ष्यामि यथावदनुपूर्वशः ॥ 89 ॥

ēkādaśendriyāṇyāhuryāni pūrve manīṣiṇaḥ /
tāni samyak pravakṣayāmi yathāvadanupūrvaśaḥ // 89 //

89. I will accurately list the eleven sense organs in order mentioned by previous scholars.

श्रोत्रं त्वक् चक्षुषी जिह्वा नासिका चैव पञ्चमी ।
पायूपस्थं हस्तपादं वाक् चैव दशमी स्मृता ॥ 90 ॥

śrotraṁ tvak chakṣuṣī jihvā nāsikā chaiva pañchamī /
pāyūpasthaṁ hastapādaṁ vāk chaiva daśamī smṛtā // 90 //

90. The ear, the skin, the eyes, the tongue, and the nose as the fifth, the anus, the reproductive organ, hands, feet, and the (organ of) speech, named as the tenth.

बुद्धीन्द्रियाणि पञ्चैषां श्रोत्रादीन्यनुपूर्वशः ।
कर्मेन्द्रियाणि पञ्चैषां पाय्वादीनि प्रचक्षते ॥ 91 ॥

buddhīndriyāṇi pañchaiṣāṁ śrotrādīnyanupūrvaśaḥ /
karmendriyāṇi pañchaiṣāṁ pāyvādīni prachakṣate // 91 //

91. First five of them, starting from the ear to the nose are called organs of sense, and the rest five starting from the anus to the organ of speech are called motor organs.

एकादशं मनो ज्ञेयं स्वगुणेनौभयात्मकम् ।
यस्मिन् जिते जितावेतौ भवतः पञ्चकौ गणौ ॥ 92 ॥

ēkādaśaṁ mano jñeyaṁ svaguṇenaubhayātmakam /
yasmin jite jitāvetau bhavataḥ pañchakau gaṇau // *92* //

92. Manas (mind), the internal sense organ, is the eleventh. It has the ability to perform the functions of both sets of five organs. When the mind is subdued, both sets of five organs are also subdued.

इन्द्रियाणां प्रसङ्गेन दोषं ऋच्छत्यसंशयम् ।
संनियम्य तु तान्येव ततः सिद्धिं निगच्छति ॥ 93 ॥

indriyāṇāṁ prasaṅgena doṣaṁ ṛchchhatyasaṁśayam /
saṁniyamya tu tānyeva tataḥ siddhiṁ nigachchhati // *93* //

93. By attaching his sense organs to various stimuli, a man will inevitably accumulate painful experiences; however, if he maintains complete control over them, he will achieve success in his life.

न जातु कामः कामानामुपभोगेन शाम्यति ।
हविषा कृष्णवर्त्मैव भूय एवाभिवर्धते ॥ 94 ॥

na jātu kāmaḥ kāmānāmupabhogena śāmyati /
haviṣā kṛṣṇavartmaiva bhūya ēvābhivardhate // *94* //

94. Desire to respond to stimuli will never be satiated, but will evoke further excitement, much [iva] like [haviṣā] oblation of clarified butter never extinguishes [kṛṣṇavartmā] fire, but [bhūya eva vardhate] stimulates it further.

यश्चैतान् प्राप्नुयात् सर्वान् यश्चैतान् केवलांस्त्यजेत् ।
प्रापणात् सर्वकामानां परित्यागो विशिष्यते ॥ 95 ॥

yaśchaitān prāpnuyāt sarvān yaśchaitān kevalāṁstyajet /
prāpaṇāt sarvakāmānāṁ parityāgo viśiṣyate // *95* //

95. Between the one who attains all worldly desire and another who renounce them, renouncing all worldly desires is far better than attaining them.

न तथैतानि शक्यन्ते संनियन्तुमसेवया ।
विषयेषु प्रजुष्टानि यथा ज्ञानेन नित्यशः ॥ 96 ॥

na tathaitāni śakyante saṁniyantumasevayā ।
viṣayeṣu prajuṣṭāni yathā jñānena nityaśaḥ ॥ *96* ॥

96. [viṣayeṣu prajuṣṭāni etāni] Sense organs that are strongly attached to stimuli [sṁniyantuṁ na śakyante] cannot be effectively restrained [asevayā] by abstaining from them, as with the support of knowledge.

वेदास्त्यागश्च यज्ञाश्च नियमाश्च तपांसि च ।
न विप्रदुष्टभावस्य सिद्धिं गच्छति कर्हि चित् ॥ 97 ॥

vedāstyāgaścha yajñāścha niyamāścha tapāṁsi cha ।
na vipraduṣṭabhāvasya siddhiṁ gachchhati karhi chit ॥ *97*

97. Neither (the study of) the Vedas, nor renunciation, nor Yajñas, nor any niyama (self-discipline like contentment, penance, studies, and mediation), nor austerities, ever procure success to a man [vipraduṣṭabhāvaḥ] whose mind is responding to stimuli.

श्रुत्वा स्पृष्ट्वा च दृष्ट्वा च भुक्त्वा घ्रात्वा च यो नरः ।
न हृष्यति ग्लायति वा स विज्ञेयो जितेन्द्रियः ॥ 98 ॥

śrutvā spṛṣṭvā cha dṛṣṭvā cha bhuktvā ghrātvā cha yo naraḥ
na hṛṣyati glāyati vā sa vijñeyo jitendriyaḥ ॥ *98* ॥

98. That man may be considered to have (really) subdued his mind, who on hearing, touching, seeing, tasting and smelling (favourable things) neither rejoices nor repents.

इन्द्रियाणां तु सर्वेषां यद्येकं क्षरतीन्द्रियम् ।
तेनास्य क्षरति प्रज्ञा दृतेः पादादिवोदकम् ॥ 99 ॥

indriyāṇāṁ tu sarveṣāṁ yadyekaṁ kṣaratīndriyam ।
tenāsya kṣarati prajñā dṛteḥ pādādivodakam ॥ *99* ॥

99. Even if a single sense organ slips away (from control), it causes disturbance to the whole system of wisdom, like a single whole in the leather water beg allows the whole water slip away from it.

वशे कृत्वेन्द्रियग्रामं संयम्य च मनस्तथा ।
सर्वान् संसाधयेदर्थानक्षिण्वन् योगतस्तनुम् ॥ 100 ॥

vaśe kṛtvendriyagrāmaṁ saṁyamya cha manastathā /
sarvān saṁsādhayedarthānakṣiṇvan yogatastanum // *100* //

100. One should perform all his works keeping all the senses as well as the mind in control with efforts without torturing his body.

पूर्वां सन्ध्यां जपंस्तिष्ठेत् सावित्रीमाऽर्कदर्शनात् ।
पश्चिमां तु समासीनः सम्यग् ऋक्षविभावनात् ॥ 101 ॥

pūrvāṁ sandhyāṁ japaṁstiṣṭhet sāvitrīmā'rkadarśanāt /
paśchimāṁ tu samāsīnaḥ samyag ṛkṣavibhāvanāt // *101* //

101. The time for morning Sandhyā and chanting the Gāyatrī mantra is from 48 minutes before sunrise until sunrise. Similarly, the time for evening Sandhyā is from sunset until the constellations rise on the horizon.

Importance of Sandhyā

पूर्वां सन्ध्यां जपंस्तिष्ठन्नैशमेनो व्यपोहति ।
पश्चिमां तु समासीनो मलं हन्ति दिवाकृतम् ॥ 102 ॥

pūrvāṁ sandhyāṁ japaṁstiṣṭhannaiśameno vyapohati /
paśchimāṁ tu samāsīno malaṁ hanti divākṛtam // *102* //

102. Morning Sandhyā absolves the (enaḥ) bad ideas accumulated during night (naiśam) and evening Sandhyā removes dirt gathered on mind during the day.

अपां समीपे नियतो नैत्यकं विधिमास्थितः ।
सावित्रीमप्यधीयीत गत्वाऽरण्यं समाहितः ॥ 104 ॥

apāṁ samīpe niyato naityakaṁ vidhimāsthitaḥ /
sāvitrīmapyadhīyīta gatvā'raṇyaṁ samāhitaḥ // *104* //

104. One should perform his daily Sandhyā and chant the Gāyatrī mantra near water in the forest with concentrated mind.

वेदौपकरणे चैव स्वाध्याये चैव नैत्यके ।
नानुरोधोऽस्त्यनध्याये होममन्त्रेषु चैव हि ॥ 105 ॥

vedaupakaraṇe chaiva svādhyāye chaiva naityake /
nānurodho'styanadhyāye homamantreṣu chaiva hi // *105* //

105. There can be no break/holiday so far as the study of

Vedas and six Vedāṅgas (Sikṣā, Kalpa, Jyotiṣa, Vyākaraṇa, Chhanda and Nirukta), daily sandhyā and chanting of Havana/Homa Mantras is concerned,

नैत्यके नास्त्यनध्यायो ब्रह्मसत्रं हि तत् स्मृतम् ।
ब्रह्माहुतिहुतं पुण्यमनध्यायवषट् कृतम् ॥ 106 ॥

naityake nāstyanadhyāyo brahmasatraṁ hi tat smṛtam /
brahmāhutihutaṁ puṇyamanadhyāyavaṣaṭ kṛtam // 106 //

106. There are no breaks for the [naityake] daily karmas like yajñā or sandhyā, dāna, and tapa, as these are collectively known as Brahmayajña. Even during breaks [vaṣaṭkṛtam], actions performed with the exclamation "vaṣaṭ," such as Balivaiśvadevayajña (feeding animals) and offerings made to Brahman (God) during the yajña, [puṇya] spiritually elevate a person.

यः स्वाध्यायमधीतेऽब्दं विधिना नियतः शुचिः ।
तस्य नित्यं क्षरत्येष पयो दधि घृतं मधु ॥ 107 ॥

yaḥ svādhyāyamadhīte'bdaṁ vidhinā niyataḥ śuchiḥ /
tasya nityaṁ kṣaratyeṣa payo dadhi ghṛtaṁ madhu // 107 //

107. A student who regularly and honestly undertakes his studies [abdam] for a year, is pouring milk, curd, clarified butter and honey.

Continuation of the Duties of a Student

अग्नीन्धनं भैक्षचर्यामधःशय्यां गुरोर्हितम् ।
आ समावर्तनात् कुर्यात् कृतोपनयनो द्विजः ॥ 108 ॥

agnīndhanaṁ bhaikṣacharyāmadhaḥśayyāṁ gurorhitam /
ā samāvartanāt kuryāt kṛtopanayano dvijaḥ // 108 //

108. Let a student (daily) collect samidhās (firewood) for Agnihotra, observe mendicancy, sleep on the ground and serve his teacher, from the time of initiation into studies until graduation ceremony [Samāvartana].

Eligibilities for Studies

आचार्यपुत्रः शुश्रूषुर्ज्ञानदो धार्मिकः शुचिः ।
आप्तः शक्तोऽर्थदः साधुः स्वोऽध्याप्या दश धर्मतः ॥ 109 ॥

āchāryaputraḥ śuśrūṣurjñānado dhārmikaḥ śuchiḥ ।
āptaḥ śakto'rthadaḥ sādhuḥ svo'dhyāpyā daśa dharmataḥ ॥

109. Following ten persons are eligible for studies:

1. A person who shows respect to their teacher.

2. A person eager to study and learn.

3. A person who imparts knowledge.

4. A person who possesses moral and ethical values.

5. An honest person.

6. A person who seeks truth.

7. A person who is competent.

8. A person who gives to charity.

9. A person who is obedient.

10. A person who is our own.

नापृष्टः कस्य चिद् ब्रूयान्न चान्यायेन पृच्छतः ।
जानन्नपि हि मेधावी जडवल्लोक आचरेत् ॥ 110 ॥

nāpṛṣṭaḥ kasya chid brūyānna chānyāyena pṛchchhataḥ ।
jānannapi hi medhāvī jaḍavalloka ācharet ॥ *110* ॥

110. One should refrain from explaining matters to others unless asked, nor should one respond to unjust inquiries. During such instances, a wise individual, even if knowledgeable, should behave as if they are unaware.

अधर्मेण च यः प्राह यश्चाधर्मेण पृच्छति ।
तयोरन्यतरः प्रैति विद्वेषं वाऽधिगच्छति ॥ 111 ॥

adharmeṇa cha yaḥ prāha yaśchādharmeṇa pṛchchhati ।
tayoranyataraḥ praiti vidveṣaṁ vā'dhigachchhati ॥ *111* ॥

111. Of the two individuals, the one who maliciously explains anything and the one who maliciously asks a question will incur blame or the other's enmity.

धर्मार्थौ यत्र न स्यातां शुश्रूषा वाऽपि तद्विधा ।
तत्र विद्या न वप्तव्या शुभं बीजमिवौषरे ॥ 112 ॥

dharmārthau yatra na syātāṁ śuśrūṣā vā'pi tadvidhā /
tatra vidyā na vaptavyā śubhaṁ bījamivauṣare // 112 //

112. Knowledge should not be nurtured where there is no merit, purpose, or proper obedience; just as seeds sown in barren land are wasted.

विद्ययैव समं कामं मर्तव्यं ब्रह्मवादिना ।
आपद्यपि हि घोरायां न त्वेनामिरिणे वपेत् ॥ 113 ॥

vidyayaiva samaṁ kāmaṁ martavyaṁ brahmavādinā /
āpadyapi hi ghorāyāṁ na tvenāmiriṇe vapet // 113 //

113. [api ghorāyām āpadi] Even in times of dire distress [brahmāvādinā] a teacher [kāmaṁ martavyaṁ vidyayā samaṁ] should rather die with his knowledge [enām iriṇe tu na vapet] than sow it in barren soil.

In short, we can say that even in times of dire distress, a teacher should choose to retain their knowledge rather than share it with those who cannot appreciate it.

विद्या ब्राह्मणमेत्याह शेवधिस्तेऽस्मि रक्ष माम् ।
असूयकाय मां मा दास्तथा स्यां वीर्यवत्तमा ॥ 114 ॥

vidyā brāhmaṇametyāha śevadhiste'smi rakṣa mām /
asūyakāya māṁ mā dāstathā syāṁ vīryavattamā // 114 //

114. Knowledge approached a scholar and said to him: 'I am [te śevadhi] thy treasure, preserve me, deliver me not to a [asukāya] ridiculer of knowledge; so (preserved) I shall become supremely strong.'

यमेव तु शुचिं विद्यान्नियतब्रह्मचारिणम् ।
तस्मै मां ब्रूहि विप्राय निधिपायाप्रमादिने ॥ 115 ॥

yameva tu śuchiṁ vidyānniyatabrahmachāriṇam /
tasmai māṁ brūhi viprāya nidhipāyāpramādine // 115 //

115. But deliver me to a student who is honest, chaste, attentive and [nidhipāya] guard me like a treasure,

ब्रह्म यस्त्वननुज्ञातमधीयानादवाप्नुयात् ।
स ब्रह्मस्तेयसंयुक्तो नरकं प्रतिपद्यते ॥ 116 ॥

brahma yastvananujñātamadhīyānādavāpnuyāt /

sa brahmasteyasaṁyukto narakaṁ pratipadyate || 116 ||

116. Obtaining knowledge [ananujñānāt] without recognizing [adhiyānāt] its source [brahmasteya sañyuktaḥ] constitutes piracy and plagiarism, which may result in the Naraka (lower species) in the next life.

Copy Right Law or Plagiarism Deprecated

लौकिकं वैदिकं वाऽपि तथाऽध्यात्मिकमेव वा ।
आददीत यतो ज्ञानं तं पूर्वमभिवादयेत् ॥ 117 ॥

laukikaṁ vaidikaṁ vā'pi tathā'dhyātmikameva vā |
ādadīta yato jñānaṁ taṁ pūrvamabhivādayet || 117 ||

117. The law of copyright is described in this śloka.

A scholar or student should first reverentially acknowledge the teacher or source from whom or where he receives material of Vedic or Spiritual knowledge.

Importance of Self-Discipline

सावित्रीमात्रसारोऽपि वरं विप्रः सुयन्त्रितः ।
नायन्त्रितस्त्रिवेदोऽपि सर्वाशी सर्वविक्रयी ॥ 118 ॥

sāvitrīmātrasāro'pi varaṁ vipraḥ suyantritaḥ |
nāyantritastrivedo'pi sarvāśī sarvavikrayī || 118 ||

118. A scholar who understands the essence of the Gāyatri Mantra alone and has mastery over his mind and senses is superior to someone who knows the three Vedas but lacks self-control and is ready to eat all kinds of food, (whether vegetarian or non-vegetarian) and engages in trading all sorts of items, (even those that are prohibited).

Protocol of Senior and Junior

शय्याऽऽसनेऽध्याचरिते श्रेयसा न समाविशेत् ।
शय्याऽऽसनस्थश्चैवेनं प्रत्युत्थायाभिवादयेत् ॥ 119 ॥

śayyā''sane'dhyācharite śreyasā na samāviśet |
śayyā''sanasthaśchaivenaṁ pratyutthāyābhivādayet || 119 ||

119. One should not take a seat reserved for a senior, and if

one has taken it, one should rise to greet the senior.

ऊर्ध्वं प्राणा ह्युत्क्रमन्ति यूनः स्थविर आयति ।
प्रत्युत्थानाभिवादाभ्यां पुनस्तान् प्रतिपद्यते ॥ 120 ॥

ūrdhvaṁ prāṇā hyutkramanti yūnaḥ sthavira āyati /
pratyutthānābhivādābhyāṁ punastān pratipadyate // 120 //

120. The life energy of a young man tends to diminish in excitement when a senior, who is more knowledgeable, approaches him; however, by rising and offering a greeting, he stabilizes his energy.

अभिवादनशीलस्य नित्यं वृद्धोपसेविनः ।
चत्वारि तस्य वर्धन्ते आयुर्धर्मो यशो बलम् ॥ 121 ॥

abhivādanaśīlasya nityaṁ vṛddhopasevinaḥ /
chatvāri tasya vardhante āyurdharmo yaśo balam // 121 //

121. A student who is humble, well-behaved, and respectful to teachers and elders, and who is always willing to offer sincere assistance, gains four important benefits: a longer life, increased knowledge, a good reputation, and good health.

On the other hand, those who lack these qualities miss out on these advantages.

अभिवादात् परं विप्रो ज्यायांसमभिवादयन् ।
असौ नामाहमस्मीति स्वं नाम परिकीर्तयेत् ॥ 122 ॥
abhivādāt paraṁ vipro jyāyāṁsamabhivādayan /
asau nāmāhamasmīti svaṁ nāma parikīrtayet // 122 //

122. After the salutation, a scholar greeting a senior in knowledge must introduce themselves by saying, 'I am so and so.'

नामधेयस्य ये के चिदभिवादं न जानते ।
तान् प्राज्ञोऽहमिति ब्रूयात् स्त्रियः सर्वास्तथैव च ॥ 123 ॥

nāmadheyasya ye ke chidabhivādaṁ na jānate /
tān prājño'hamiti brūyāt striyaḥ sarvāstathaiva cha // 123 //

123. For those who do not recognize someone who greets them, a wise person should immediately introduce themselves by saying, 'It is me,' and do the same when encountering any unfamiliar woman.

भोः शब्दं कीर्तयेदन्ते स्वस्य नाम्नोऽभिवादने ।
नाम्नां स्वरूपभावो हि भोभाव ऋषिभिः स्मृतः ॥ 124 ॥

bhoḥ śabdaṁ kīrtayedante svasya nāmno'bhivādane /
nāmnāṁ svarūpabhāvo hi bhobhāva ṛṣibhiḥ smṛtaḥ // 124

124. When saluting, an individual should say the word 'bhoḥ' after their name; the term 'bhoḥ' has the same significance as proper names.

आयुष्मान् भव सौम्यैति वाच्यो विप्रोऽभिवादने ।
अकारश्चास्य नाम्नोऽन्ते वाच्यः पूर्वाक्षरः प्लुतः ॥ 125 ॥

āyuṣmān bhava saumyaiti vāchyo vipro'bhivādane /
akāraśchāsya nāmno'nte vāchyaḥ pūrvākṣaraḥ plutaḥ // 125

125. When a scholar receives a greeting, they should reply, "May you live long, O gentle one!" The vowels, such as 'a' at the end of the person's name, along with the preceding consonant, should be pronounced in an elongated manner.

For example, if the person giving the greeting is named Rāma, the scholar should respond by pronouncing the name as 'Rām३'.

यो न वेत्त्यभिवादस्य विप्रः प्रत्यभिवादनम् ।
नाभिवाद्यः स विदुषा यथा शूद्रस्तथैव सः ॥ 126 ॥

yo na vettyabhivādasya vipraḥ pratyabhivādanam /
nābhivādyaḥ sa viduṣā yathā śūdrastathaiva saḥ // 126 //

126. A scholar who ignores a greeting deserves no respect from a learned person, as he is no better than an individual devoid of sanskāras.

ब्राह्मणं कुशलं पृच्छेत् क्षत्रबन्धुमनामयम् ।
वैश्यं क्षेमं समागम्य शूद्रमारोग्यमेव च ॥ 127 ॥

brāhmaṇaṁ kuśalaṁ pṛchchhet kṣatrabandhumanāmayam
vaiśyaṁ kṣemaṁ samāgamya śūdramārogyameva cha // 127

127. When meeting individuals, one should inquire about the following: a teacher about his ability to impart knowledge (either spiritual knowledge, known as vidyā, or material

knowledge, known as avidyā); a kṣatriya about his health and freedom from illness (referred to as anāmaya); a vaiśya about his prosperity (known as kṣema); and a skilled or non-skilled worker about his overall health (referred to as ārogya).

अवाच्यो दीक्षितो नाम्ना यवीयानपि यो भवेत् ।
भोभवत्पूर्वकं त्वेनमभिभाषेत धर्मवित् ॥ 128 ॥

avāchyo dīkṣito nāmnā yavīyānapi yo bhavet /
bhobhavatpūrvakaṁ tvenamabhibhāṣeta dharmavit // 128 //

128. He [dikṣitaḥ] who has realized the truth [avāchya] must not be addressed [nāmnā] by his name, [yaviyān api yaḥ bhavet] even though he be a younger man; he should be addressed by the respectable title of 'Bho' or 'Bhavān' by the one who is well versed with [dharmavit] the code of conduct.

परपत्नी तु या स्त्री स्यादसम्बन्धा च योनितः ।
तां ब्रूयाद् भवतीत्येवं सुभगे भगिनीति च ॥ 129 ॥

parapatnī tu yā strī syādasambandhā cha yonitaḥ /
tāṁ brūyād bhavatītyevaṁ subhage bhaginīti cha // 129 //

129. A lady who is the wife of another man, and not a blood-relation, must be addressed by the title 'Bhavati', 'Subhage' or 'Sister!'

मातुलांश्च पितृव्यांश्च श्वशुरान् ऋत्विजो गुरून् ।
असावहमिति ब्रूयात् प्रत्युत्थाय यवीयसः ॥ 130 ॥

mātulāṁścha pitṛvyāṁścha śvaśurān ṛtvijo gurūn /
asāvahamiti brūyāt pratyutthāya yavīyasaḥ // 130 //

130. One should rise to meet his maternal and paternal uncles, fathers-in-law, officiating priests, (and other) elderly persons stating one's name, even though they be younger.

मातृश्वसा मातुलानी श्वश्रूरथ पितृश्वसा ।
सम्पूज्या गुरुपत्नीवत् समास्ता गुरुभार्यया ॥ 131 ॥

mātṛśvasā mātulānī śvaśrūratha pitṛśvasā /
sampūjyā gurupatnīvat samāstā gurubhāryayā // 131 //

131. A maternal aunt, the wife of a maternal uncle, a mother-in-law, and a paternal aunt must be honoured like the wife of

one's teacher; they are equal to the wife of one's teacher.

भ्रातुर्भार्यौपसङ्ग्राह्या सवर्णाऽहन्यहन्यपि ।
विप्रोष्य तूपसङ्ग्राह्या ज्ञातिसम्बन्धियोषितः ॥ 132 ॥

bhrāturbhāryaupasaṅgrāhyā savarṇā'hanyahanyapi /
viproṣya tūpasaṅgrāhyā jñātisambandhiyoṣitaḥ // 132 //

132. One should [upasaṅgrāhyāḥ] greet daily the wife of one's own elderly brother, [jñātisaṁbandhi-yoṣitaḥ] the wives of other elderly relatives may be greeted [viproṣyasaṅgrāhyāḥ] upon their return from a journey.

पितुर्भगिन्यां मातुश्च ज्यायस्यां च स्वसर्यपि ।
मातृवद् वृत्तिमातिष्ठेन् माता ताभ्यो गरीयसी ॥ 133 ॥

piturbhaginyāṁ mātuścha jyāyasyāṁ cha svasaryapi /
mātṛvad vṛttimātiṣṭhen mātā tābhyo garīyasī // 133 //

133. One should show a motherly gesture towards a father's sister, a mother's sister, and one's own elder sister; however, the mother is superior to all.

Norms of Seniority and Juniority

दशाब्दाख्यं पौरसख्यं पञ्चाब्दाख्यं कलाभृताम् ।
त्र्यब्दपूर्वं श्रोत्रियाणां स्वल्पेनापि स्वयोनिषु ॥ 134 ॥

daśābdākhyaṁ paurasakhyaṁ pañchābdākhyaṁ kalābhṛtām
trayabdapūrvaṁ śrotriyāṇāṁ svalpenāpi svayoniṣu // 134 //

134. Fellow citizens are regarded as equals, even if one person is ten years older than another. Similarly, individuals practicing the same fine art are considered equals, regardless of a five-year age difference. Śrotriyas, who are reciters of the four Vedas, are also treated as equals, even if there is a three-year age gap between them. However, [sva-yoniṣu] blood relations are only seen as equals if the age difference is very small.

ब्राह्मणं दशवर्षं तु शतवर्षं तु भूमिपम् ।
पितापुत्रौ विजानीयाद् ब्राह्मणस्तु तयोः पिता ॥ 135 ॥

brāhmaṇaṁ daśavarṣaṁ tu śatavarṣaṁ tu bhūmipam /

pitāputrau vijānīyād brāhmaṇastu tayoḥ pitā // 135 //

135. A teacher (spiritual or material) with ten years of experience and a kṣatriya (a person engaged in legislative, executive, judiciary, management, or defence roles) with a hundred years of experience have a relationship similar to that of a father and son. In this dynamic, the person with intellectual authority can be considered the father.

Note: Here the protocol is defined. teachers, Researchers, and scientists are prioritized over individuals serving legislative, executive, judiciary, management, and the armed forces.

वित्तं बन्धुर्वयः कर्म विद्या भवति पञ्चमी ।
एतानि मान्यस्थानानि गरीयो यद् यदुत्तरम् ॥ 136 ॥

vittaṁ bandhurvayaḥ karma vidyā bhavati pañchamī /
ētāni mānyasthānāni garīyo yad yaduttaram // 136 //

136. Wealth, relationships, age, profession, and education are, in that order, titles to respect; however, each subsequent category is superior to the previous ones.

पञ्चानां त्रिषु वर्णेषु भूयांसि गुणवन्ति च ।
यत्र स्युः सोऽत्र मानार्हः शूद्रोऽपि दशमीं गतः ॥ 137 ॥

pañchānāṁ triṣu varṇeṣu bhūyāṁsi guṇavanti cha /
yatra syuḥ so'tra mānārhaḥ śūdro'pi daśamīṁ gataḥ // 137 //

137. A person from any of the three educated professions—Teaching, Kṣatriya, or Vaiśya—who possesses the maximum qualities among five specific attributes (wealth, relationships, age, profession, and education), both in terms of quantity and degree, deserves to be honored. Additionally, an uneducated individual who has reached their nineties (the tenth decade of life) also deserves of respect.

चक्रिणो दशमीस्थस्य रोगिणो भारिणः स्त्रियाः ।
स्नातकस्य च राज्ञश्च पन्था देयो वरस्य च ॥ 138 ॥

chakriṇo daśamīsthasya rogiṇo bhāriṇaḥ striyāḥ /
snātakasya cha rājñaścha panthā deyo varasya cha // 138 //

138. We must prioritize allowing the following [panthā

deyaḥ] to pass first on the road: [rogiṇaḥ] an ambulance carrying a patient, [chakriṇaḥ daśamīśthaḥ] a vehicle transporting a senior citizen in his nineties, [bhāriṇaḥ] a person carrying a load, [striyāḥ] a woman, a student, a king, and [varasya] a marriage procession featuring a bridegroom.

तेषां तु समवेतानां मान्यौ स्नातकपार्थिवौ ।
राजस्नातकयोश्चैव स्नातको नृपमानभाक् ॥ 139 ॥

teṣāṁ tu samavetānāṁ mānyau snātakapārthivau /
rājasnātakayośchaiva snātako nṛpamānabhāk // 139 //

139. Among all those gathered, a Snātaka (graduate) and the king must be the most honored; and between the king and a Snātaka (a graduate), respect is given to the Snātaka, [nṛpamānabhāk] as if he were a king.

Definition of Āchārya

उपनीय तु यः शिष्यं वेदमध्यापयेद् द्विजः ।
सकल्पं सरहस्यं च तमाचार्यं प्रचक्षते ॥ 140 ॥

upanīya tu yaḥ śiṣyaṁ vedamadhyāpayed dvijaḥ /
sakalpaṁ sarahasyaṁ cha tamāchāryaṁ prachakṣate // 140 //

140. A teacher who initiates a student and instructs him in the Veda along with all kalpa-sūtras and [sarahasyam] Vedānta Darśana is called Āchārya.

Definition of Upādhyāya

एकदेशं तु वेदस्य वेदाङ्गान्यपि वा पुनः ।
योऽध्यापयति वृत्त्यर्थमुपाध्यायः स उच्यते ॥ 141 ॥

ēkadeśaṁ tu vedasya vedāṅgānyapi vā punaḥ /
yo'dhyāpayati vṛttyarthamupādhyāyaḥ sa uchyate // 141 //

141. He who teaches any part of the Veda or a Vedāṅga for his livelihood is called Upādhyāya.

Definition of a Guru

निषेकादीनि कर्माणि यः करोति यथाविधि ।
सम्भावयति चान्नेन स विप्रो गुरुरुच्यते ॥ 142 ॥

niṣekādīni karmāṇi yaḥ karoti yathāvidhi /
sambhāvayati chānnena sa vipro gururuchyate // 142 //

142. A scholar who performs Sanskāras starting from Garbhādāna as prescribed in Gṛhyasūtras, and [annena sambhāvayati] acts as a foster father, is referred to as the Guru.

Definition of a Ṛtvik

अग्न्याधेयं पाकयज्ञानग्निष्टोमादिकान् मखान् ।
यः करोति वृतो यस्य स तस्यर्त्विगिहोच्यते ॥ 143 ॥

agnyādheyaṁ pākayajñānagniṣṭomādikān makhān /
yaḥ karoti vṛto yasya sa tasyartvigihochyate // 143 //

143. [yaḥ] He who, is [vṛtaḥ] duly officially chosen to perform [agnyādheyam] Agnihotra, as well as [pākayajñan] the Pākayajñas like balivaiśvadeva yajña, and the Somayajñas such as Agniṣṭoma for his or her client, is called Ṛtvija (officiating priest).

Degrees of Respect

य आवृणोत्यवितथं ब्रह्मणा श्रवणावुभौ ।
स माता स पिता ज्ञेयस्तं न द्रुह्येत् कदा चन ॥ 144 ॥

ya āvṛṇotyavitathaṁ brahmaṇā śravaṇāvubhau /
sa mātā sa pitā jñeyastaṁ na druhyet kadā chana // 144 //

144. The teacher who [āvṛṇoti ubhau śravaṇau brahmaṇā] imparts true Vedic knowledge to his pupil should be revered like parents; he should never be offended.

उपाध्यायान् दशाचार्य आचार्याणां शतं पिता ।
सहस्रं तु पितॄन् माता गौरवेणातिरिच्यते ॥ 145 ॥

upādhyāyān daśāchārya āchāryāṇāṁ śataṁ pitā /
sahasraṁ tu pitṝn mātā gauraveṇātirichyate // 145 //

145. An Āchārya is ten times more venerable than an Upādhyāya; the father is a hundred times more venerable than the Āchārya, but the mother is a thousand times more

venerable than the father.

उत्पादकब्रह्मदात्रोर्गरीयान् ब्रह्मदः पिता ।
ब्रह्मजन्म हि विप्रस्य प्रेत्य चैह च शाश्वतम् ॥ 146 ॥

utpādakabrahmadātrorgarīyān brahmadaḥ pitā /
brahmajanma hi viprasya pretya chaiha cha śāśvatam // 146

146. The teacher who imparts Vedic knowledge is more venerable than the biological father; for [brahma-janma] the sanskāras of knowledge accompany the scholar in this life and the next, while the physical body deteriorates in this life itself.

कामान् माता पिता चैनं यदुत्पादयतो मिथः ।
सम्भूतिं तस्य तां विद्याद् यद् योनावभिजायते ॥ 147 ॥

kāmān mātā pitā chainaṁ yadutpādayato mithaḥ /
sambhūtiṁ tasya tāṁ vidyād yad yonāvabhijāyate // 147 //

147. The parents mutually give birth to a child with the desire for progeny. The child's birth from mother's womb should be referred to as [sambhūti] biological birth.

आचार्यस्त्वस्य यां जातिं विधिवद् वेदपारगः ।
उत्पादयति सावित्र्या सा सत्या साऽजराऽमरा ॥ 148 ॥

āchāryastvasya yāṁ jātiṁ vidhivad vedapāragaḥ /
utpādayati sāvitrayā sā satyā sā'jarā'marā // 148 //

148. However, [jāti] the true character of the human being, which an Āchārya well-versed in the Vedas instills in him through the Sāvitri (initiating him into knowledge), is real, undecaying, and eternal.

अल्पं वा बहु वा यस्य श्रुतस्यौपकरोति यः ।
तमपीह गुरुं विद्यात्श्रुतौपक्रियया तया ॥ 149 ॥

alpaṁ vā bahu vā yasya śrutasyaupakaroti yaḥ /
tamapīha guruṁ vidyātśrutaupakriyayā tayā // 149 //

149. A person who has [śrutasya upakroti] provided you with any knowledge, however small, should be respected as a Guru [śruta upakriyayā tayā] due to the benefit of that knowledge.

ब्राह्मस्य जन्मनः कर्ता स्वधर्मस्य च शासिता ।
बालोऽपि विप्रो वृद्धस्य पिता भवति धर्मतः ॥ 150 ॥

brāhmasya janmanaḥ kartā svadharmasya cha śāsitā /
bālo'pi vipro vṛddhasya pitā bhavati dharmataḥ // 150 //

150. The scholar who [brāhmasya janmanaḥ] imparts spiritual wisdom and [śāsitā] teaches [svadharmasya] human values becomes, in essence, the father of an older man [dharmataḥ] due to his knowledge, even if he himself is still young.

अध्यापयामास पितृन् शिशुराङ्गिरसः कविः ।
पुत्रका इति हौवाच ज्ञानेन परिगृह्य तान् ॥ 151 ॥

adhyāpayāmāsa pitṝn śiśurāṅgirasaḥ kaviḥ /
putrakā iti hauvācha jñānena parigṛhya tān // 151 //

151. Historical evidence shows that the young scholar, the son of sage Angirā, taught the elderly members of his family. Since he excelled in knowledge, he referred to them as 'Little sons.'

ते तमर्थमपृच्छन्त देवानागतमन्यवः ।
देवाश्चैतान् समेत्यौचुर्न्याय्यं वः शिशुरुक्तवान् ॥ 152 ॥

te tamarthamapṛchchhanta devānāgatamanyavaḥ /
devāśchaitān sametyauchurnyāyyaṁ vaḥ śiśuruktavān // 152

152. They [apṛchchhanta] lodged a complaint with enlightened scholars [tamartham] regarding this matter, [āgata-manyavaḥ] expressing resentment, and a panel of enlightened scholars [nyāyyam] justified the address made by the young scholar.

अज्ञो भवति वै बालः पिता भवति मन्त्रदः ।
अज्ञं हि बालमित्याहुः पितेत्येव तु मन्त्रदम् ॥ 153 ॥

ajño bhavati vai bālaḥ pitā bhavati mantradaḥ /
ajñaṁ hi bālamityāhuḥ pitetyeva tu mantradam // 153 //

153. A person destitute of knowledge is indeed like a child, and he who imparts knowledge is like a father, so an ignorant is often called as child and informed as father.

न हायनैर्न पलितैर्न वित्तेन न बन्धुभिः ।
ऋषयश्चक्रिरे धर्मं योऽनूचानः स नो महान् ॥ 154 ॥

na hāyanairna palitairna vittena na bandhubhiḥ /
ṛṣayaśchakrire dharmaṁ yo'nūchānaḥ sa no mahān // 154 //

154. Greatness is not determined by the [hāyanaiḥ] years, gray hair, wealth, or famous relatives. The ṛṣis have established a principle: "The most knowledgeable among us is truly great."

विप्राणां ज्ञानतो ज्यैष्ठ्यं क्षत्रियाणां तु वीर्यतः ।
वैश्यानां धान्यधनतः शूद्राणामेव जन्मतः ॥ 155 ॥

viprāṇāṁ jñānato jyaiṣṭhyaṁ kṣatriyāṇāṁ tu vīryataḥ /
vaiśyānāṁ dhānyadhanataḥ śūdrāṇāmeva janmataḥ // 155 //

155. The seniority of teachers is assessed based on their knowledge. In contrast, the status of kṣatriyas is determined by their power and authority. For Vaiśyas, seniority is measured by the wealth they have earned or the goods they have produced. Lastly, among uneducated individuals (skilled and unskilled workers) seniority is often judged by their age.

न तेन वृद्धो भवति येनास्य पलितं शिरः ।
यो वै युवाऽप्यधीयानस्तं देवाः स्थविरं विदुः ॥ 156 ॥

na tena vṛddho bhavati yenāsya palitaṁ śiraḥ /
yo vai yuvā'pyadhīyānastaṁ devāḥ sthaviraṁ viduḥ // 156 //

156. A person is not deemed senior simply because they have gray hair; rather, even a knowledgeable young individual is regarded as senior by enlightened scholars.

यथा काष्ठमयो हस्ती यथा चर्ममयो मृगः ।
यश्च विप्रोऽनधीयानस्त्रयस्ते नाम बिभ्रति ॥ 157 ॥

yathā kāṣṭhamayo hastī yathā charmamayo mṛgaḥ /
yaścha vipro'nadhīyānastrayaste nāma bibhrati // 157 //

157. As an elephant made of wood and an antelope made of leather, such is a scholar devoid of knowledge; those three are essentially for nothing but called so for the namesake.

यथा षण्ढोऽफलः स्त्रीषु यथा गौर्गवि चाफला ।
यथा चाज्ञेऽफलं दानं तथा विप्रोऽनृचोऽफलः ॥ 158 ॥

yathā ṣaṇḍho'phalaḥ strīṣu yathā gaurgavi chāphalā /
yathā chājñe'phalaṁ dānaṁ tathā vipro'nṛcho'phalaḥ //

158. As a eunuch is unproductive with women, as a cow with a cow is unprolific, and as a gift made to an ignorant man yields no fruit, even so, is a scholar useless (pseudo-scholar), who is devoid of knowledge.

Code of Conduct for the promotion of Dharma

अहिंसयैव भूतानां कार्यं श्रेयोऽनुशासनम् ।
वाक् चैव मधुरा श्लक्ष्णा प्रयोज्या धर्ममिच्छता ॥ 159 ॥

ahiṁsayaiva bhūtānāṁ kāryaṁ śreyo'nuśāsanam /
vāk chaiva madhurā ślakṣaṇā prayojyā dharmamichchhatā //

159. To promote Dharma (ethical and moral values), one should interact with others without malice and adhere to discipline. Their speech should be sweet and gentle.

यस्य वाङ्मनसी शुद्धे सम्यग् गुप्ते च सर्वदा ।
स वै सर्वमवाप्नोति वेदान्तोपगतं फलम् ॥ 160 ॥

yasya vāṅmanasī śuddhe samyag gupte cha sarvadā /
sa vai sarvamavāpnoti vedāntopagataṁ phalam // 160 //

160. A person whose thoughts and speech are pure and ever perfectly guarded gains everything including mokṣa.

नारुन्तुदः स्यादार्तोऽपि न परद्रोहकर्मधीः ।
ययाऽस्योद्विजते वाचा नालोक्यां तामुदीरयेत् ॥ 161 ॥

nāruntudaḥ syādārto'pi na paradrohakarmadhīḥ /
yayā'syodvijate vāchā nālokyāṁ tāmudīrayet // 161 //

161. Even in pain, one should not make others suffer; one should not harm others in thought or action; one should avoid unusual or unconstitutional words that upset others.

Equanimity under Honour and Dishonour

सम्मानाद् ब्राह्मणो नित्यमुद्विजेत विषादिव ।
अमृतस्येव चाकाङ्क्षेदवमानस्य सर्वदा ॥ 162 ॥

sammānād brāhmaṇo nityamudvijeta viṣādiva /
amṛtasyeva chākāṅkṣedavamānasya sarvadā // 162 //

162. A true scholar should develop an aversion to honors and awards as if they were poison; they should cultivate a liking for dishonors or the absence of honors as if it were nectar.

सुखं ह्यवमतः शेते सुखं च प्रतिबुध्यते ।
सुखं चरति लोकेऽस्मिन्नवमन्ता विनश्यति ॥ 163 ॥

sukhaṁ hyavamataḥ śete sukhaṁ cha pratibudhyate /
sukhaṁ charati loke'sminnavamantā vinaśyati // 163 //

163. Those who are dishonored or criticized seek comfort in sleep, awakening and engaging with others; however, the one who causes dishonor ultimately faces destruction.

Procedure of Study

अनेन क्रमयोगेन संस्कृतात्मा द्विजः शनैः ।
गुरौ वसन् सञ्चिनुयाद् ब्रह्माधिगमिकं तपः ॥ 164 ॥

anena kramayogena saṁskṛtātmā dvijaḥ śanaiḥ /
gurau vasan sañchinuyād brahmādhigamikaṁ tapaḥ // 164 //

164. In this manner, a student [sanskrit-ātmā] who has received the Yajñopavīta (sacred thread) and is living under the guidance of his teacher should gradually accumulate austerity of gaining the Vedic knowledge.

तपोविशेषैर्विविधैर्व्रतैश्च विधिचोदितैः ।
वेदः कृत्स्नोऽधिगन्तव्यः सरहस्यो द्विजन्मना ॥ 165 ॥

tapoviśeṣairvividhairvrataiścha vidhichoditaiḥ /
vedaḥ kṛtsno'dhigantavyaḥ sarahasyo dvijanmanā // 165 //

165. A student must acquire the knowledge of complete Veda together [sarahasyaḥ] with the Upaniṣads, through special austerities and various kinds of observances [vidhi-choditaiḥ] ordained in the Śāstras.

वेदमेव सदाऽभ्यस्येत् तपस्तप्यन् द्विजोत्तमः ।
वेदाभ्यासो हि विप्रस्य तपः परमिहौच्यते ॥ 166 ॥

vedameva sadā'bhyasyet tapastapyan dvijottamaḥ /
vedābhyāso hi viprasya tapaḥ paramihauchyate // 166 //

166. Let a high profile student who desires to perform austerities, repeatedly practice the Veda, becaues the study of

the Veda is declared to be the highest austerity for a student in this world.

आ हैव स नखाग्रेभ्यः परमं तप्यते तपः ।
यः स्रग्व्यपि द्विजोऽधीते स्वाध्यायं शक्तितोऽन्वहम् ॥ 167 ॥

ā haiva sa nakhāgrebhyaḥ paramaṁ tapyate tapaḥ /
yaḥ sragvyapi dvijo'dhīte svādhyāyaṁ śaktito'nvaham // 167

167. A student is deemed to have performed the highest ever austerity till the tip of nails, who, [sragvī api] though wearing a garland, daily takes up the study of Veda to the utmost of his ability.

Note: A student in ancient times was not allowed to wear any garland except upanayana (sacred thread).

योऽनधीत्य द्विजो वेदमन्यत्र कुरुते श्रमम् ।
स जीवन्नेव शूद्रत्वमाशु गच्छति सान्वयः ॥ 168 ॥

yo'nadhītya dvijo vedamanyatra kurute śramam /
sa jīvanneva śūdratvamāśu gachchhati sānvayaḥ // 168 //

168. A [dvijaḥ] student who abandons the study (of the Vedas) and directs his efforts elsewhere remains uneducated (sānvayaḥ) along with his family, and is categorized as a Śudra (uneducated).

Note: This emphasizes that the primary goal of a student's life is the acquisition of knowledge. Those who fail to attain knowledge are referred to as Śudras, or uneducated.

Rules to be Observed by a Student

सेवेतैमांस्तु नियमान् ब्रह्मचारी गुरौ वसन् ।
सन्नियम्यैन्द्रियग्रामं तपोवृद्ध्यर्थमात्मनः ॥ 169 ॥

sevetaimāṁstu niyamān brahmachārī gurau vasan /
sanniyamyaindriyagrāmaṁ tapovṛddhyarthamātmanaḥ //169

169. A student living with their teacher must adhere to a code of conduct, controlling all their senses, to enhance their knowledge and spiritual growth.

नित्यं स्नात्वा शुचिः कुर्याद् देवर्षिपितृतर्पणम् ।

देवताभ्यर्चनं चैव समिदाधानमेव च ॥ 170 ॥

nityaṁ snātvā śuchiḥ kuryād devarṣipitṛtarpaṇam /
devatābhyarchanaṁ chaiva samidādhānameva cha // 170 //

170. Every day, after purifying himself by taking a bath, a student [deva+ṛṣi+pitṛ+tarpaṇan] must conduct himself in a manner that allows him to be free from the debts owed to scholars, seers, and elders. He should also [devatā+abhyarchanam] meditate on Brahman and [samidādhānam] perform Agnihotra.

वर्जयेन् मधुमांसं च गन्धं माल्यं रसान् स्त्रियः ।
शुक्तानि यानि सर्वाणि प्राणिनां चैव हिंसनम् ॥ 171 ॥

varjayen madhumāṁsaṁ cha gandhaṁ mālyaṁ rasān striyaḥ /
śuktāni yāni sarvāṇi prāṇināṁ chaiva hiṁsanam // 171 //

171. A student must avoid intoxicants, meat, perfumes, garlands, condiments, physical contact with the opposite sex, [śuktāni yāni sarvāṇi] all fermented foods, and violence against all living beings.

अभ्यङ्गमञ्जनं चाक्ष्णोरुपानच्छत्रधारणम् ।
कामं क्रोधं च लोभं च नर्तनं गीतवादनम् ॥ 172 ॥

abhyaṅgamañjanaṁ chākṣaṇorupānachchhatradhāraṇam /
kāmaṁ krodhaṁ cha lobhaṁ cha nartanaṁ gītavādanam //

172. A student must also avoid anointing the body parts with creams and oils, applying collyrium into eyes, use of outlandish outfits. A student must avoid lust, anger, greed, public dancing, singing and music.

द्यूतं च जनवादं च परिवादं तथाऽनृतम् ।
स्त्रीणां च प्रेक्षणालम्भमुपघातं परस्य च ॥ 173 ॥

dyūtaṁ cha janavādaṁ cha parivādaṁ tathā'nṛtam /
strīṇāṁ cha prekṣaṇālambhamupaghātaṁ parasya cha //173

173. A student must also avoid gambling, discussion on a particular person, backbiting, lying, [prekṣaṇasm] staring at opposite sex with lustful eyes, [ālambham] embracing a person belonging to opposite sex, and [parasya upaghātam] hurting

others.

एकः शयीत सर्वत्र न रेतः स्कन्दयेत् क्व चित् ।
कामाद् हि स्कन्दयन् रेतो हिनस्ति व्रतमात्मनः ॥ 174 ॥

ēkaḥ śayīta sarvatra na retaḥ skandayet kva chit ।
kāmād hi skandayan reto hinasti vratamātmanaḥ ॥ 174 ॥

174. A student must sleep alone and avoid any sexual stimulation that may lead to ejaculation. If a student allows ejaculation due to sexual urge, he violates the vow of Brahmacharya (celibacy).

स्वप्ने सिक्त्वा ब्रह्मचारी द्विजः शुक्रमकामतः ।
स्नात्वाऽर्कमर्चयित्वा त्रिः पुनर्मामित्यृचं जपेत् ॥ 175 ॥

svapne siktvā brahmachārī dvijaḥ śukramakāmataḥ ।
snātvā'rkamarchayitvā triḥ punarmāmityṛchaṁ japet ॥

175. A student, who has involuntarily wasted his manly strength during sleep, must bathe, [archayitvā] pay respect to [arkam] his learned teacher, and afterwards thrice chant the Ṛk-verse:

पुनर्मामैत्वन्द्रियम् ।

punarmāmaitvandriyam

[Meaning] Again let my strength return to me.

उदकुम्भं सुमनसो गोशकृत्मृत्तिकाकुशान् ।
आहरेद् यावदर्थानि भैक्षं चाहरहश्चरेत् ॥ 176 ॥

udakumbhaṁ sumanaso gośakṛtmṛttikākuśān ।
āhared yāvadarthāni bhaikṣaṁ chāharahaścharet ॥ 176 ॥

176. He should fetch a pot filled with water, flowers, [gośkṛt] cow dung, earth (clay), and Kuśa grass [yāvat arthāni] as required by his teacher, and go daily to beg for food.

वेदयज्ञैरहीनानां प्रशस्तानां स्वकर्मसु ।
ब्रह्मचार्याहरेद् भैक्षं गृहेभ्यः प्रयतोऽन्वहम् ॥ 177 ॥

vedayajñairahīnānāṁ praśastānāṁ svakarmasu ।
brahmachāryāhared bhaikṣaṁ gṛhebhyaḥ
prayato'nvaham ॥177 ॥

177. A student shall bring food each day from the homes of those who have not abandoned the Vedic yajñas and who are well-known for their legitimate occupations.

गुरोः कुले न भिक्षेत न ज्ञातिकुलबन्धुषु ।
अलाभे त्वन्यगेहानां पूर्वं पूर्वं विवर्जयेत् ॥ 178 ॥

guroḥ kule na bhikṣeta na jñātikulabandhuṣu /
alābhe tvanyagehānāṁ pūrvaṁ pūrvaṁ vivarjayet // 178 //

178. He should not beg from his teacher's family or from the families of his own relatives and friends. However, if there are no houses available belonging to strangers, he may approach one of the previously mentioned groups, starting with the last named.

सर्वं वापि चरेद् ग्रामं पूर्वौक्तानामसम्भवे ।
नियम्य प्रयतो वाचमभिशस्तांस्तु वर्जयेत् ॥ 179 ॥

sarvaṁ vāpi chared grāmaṁ pūrvauktānāmasambhave /
niyamya prayato vāchamabhiśastāṁstu varjayet // 179 //

179. If there are no virtuous men as described above, he may visit each house in the village, remaining pure and keeping silent. However, he should avoid [abhiśastān] those accused of pāpa karmas (immoral or unethical actions that can lead to a degradation of a human being).

दूरादाहृत्य समिधः सन्निदध्याद् विहायसि ।
सायं प्रातश्च जुहुयात् ताभिरग्निमतन्द्रितः ॥ 180 ॥

dūrādāhṛtya samidhaḥ sannidadhyād vihāyasi /
sāyaṁ prātaścha juhuyāt tābhiragnimatandritaḥ // 180 //

180. After bringing Samidhās from a distance, [sannidadhyāt] let him place them [vihāyasi] in an airy location, and let him [atandritaḥ] diligently perform Havana with them both morning and evening.

चोदितो गुरुणा नित्यमप्रचोदित एव वा ।
कुर्यादध्ययने यत्नमा[1] चार्यस्य हितेषु च ॥ 181 ॥

---

1 ऽध्ययने योगम्

chodito guruṇā nityamaprachodita ēva vā /
kuryādadhyayane yatnamā chāryasya hiteṣu cha // *181* //

181. Whether inspired by their teachers or not, students should always strive to study and support the charitable efforts of their teachers.

शरीरं चैव वाचं च बुद्धीन्द्रियमनांसि च ।
नियम्य प्राञ्जलिस्तिष्ठेद् वीक्षमाणो गुरोर्मुखम् ॥ 182 ॥

śarīraṁ chaiva vāchaṁ cha buddhīndriyamanāṁsi cha /
niyamya prāñjalistiṣṭhed vīkṣamāṇo gurormukham // *182* //

182. When the teacher is present, a student should stand with folded hands, controlling their body, speech, sense organs, and mind, while respectfully looking at the teacher's face.

नित्यमुद्धृतपाणिः स्यात् साध्वाचारः सुसंवृतः ।
आस्यतामिति चौक्तः सन्नासीताभिमुखं गुरोः ॥ 183 ॥

nityamuddhṛtapāṇiḥ syāt sādhvāchāraḥ susaṁvṛtaḥ /
āsyatāmiti chauktaḥ sannāsītābhimukhaṁ guroḥ // *183* //

183. Students should always keep their right arm uncovered, behave appropriately, and ensure their bodies are well-covered. When addressed with the words, 'Be seated,' they shall sit down facing the teacher.

हीनान्नवस्त्रवेषः स्यात् सर्वदा गुरुसन्निधौ ।
उत्तिष्ठेत् प्रथमं चास्य चरमं चैव संविशेत् ॥ 184 ॥

hīnānnavastraveṣaḥ syāt sarvadā gurusannidhau /
uttiṣṭhet prathamaṁ chāsya charamaṁ chaiva saṁviśet //

184. When in the presence of a teacher, a student should maintain a modest demeanor in both eating and clothing. This means they should eat simply and wear outfits that are less elaborate than those of their teacher. Additionally, students should rise earlier in the morning and go to bed later at night than their teacher.

प्रतिश्रावणसम्भाषे शयानो न समाचरेत् ।
नासीनो न च भुञ्जानो न तिष्ठन्न पराङ्मुखः ॥ 185 ॥

pratiśrāvaṇasambhāṣe śayāno na samācharet /

nāsīno na cha bhuñjāno na tiṣṭhanna parāṅmukhaḥ // *185* //

185. He/She should not answer or converse with his/her teacher while reclining on a bed, sitting, eating, or with an averted face.

आसीनस्य स्थितः कुर्यादभिगच्छंस्तु तिष्ठतः ।
प्रत्युद्गम्य त्वाव्रजतः पश्चाद् धावंस्तु धावतः ॥ 186 ॥

āsīnasya sthitaḥ kuryādabhigachchhaṁstu tiṣṭhataḥ /
pratyudgamya tvāvrajataḥ paśchād dhāvaṁstu dhāvataḥ //

186. Let him or her do that while standing if the teacher is seated. He or she should advance towards the teacher when standing, go to meet the teacher if the teacher advances, and run after the teacher when the teacher runs.

पराङ्मुखस्याभिमुखो दूरस्थस्येत्य चान्तिकम् ।
प्रणम्य तु शयानस्य निदेशे चैव तिष्ठतः ॥ 187 ॥

parāṅmukhasyābhimukho dūrasthasyetya chāntikam /
praṇamya tu śayānasya nideśe chaiva tiṣṭhataḥ // *187* //

187. Approaching the teacher when he is not facing you; getting closer when he is at a distance; bowing low when he is lying down, as well as when he is nearby.

नीचं शय्याऽऽसनं चास्य नित्यं स्याद् गुरुसन्निधौ ।
गुरोस्तु चक्षुर्विषये न यथेष्टासनो भवेत् ॥ 188 ॥

nīchaṁ śayyā''sanaṁ chāsya nityaṁ syād gurusannidhau /
gurostu chakṣurviṣaye na yatheṣṭāsano bhavet // *188* //

188. When close to his teacher, their beds or seats should always be low; and they should not sit comfortably within the sight of his teacher.

नौदाहरेदस्य नाम परोक्षमपि केवलम् ।
न चैवास्यानुकुर्वीत गतिभाषितचेष्टितम् ॥ 189 ॥

naudāharedasya nāma parokṣamapi kevalam /
na chaivāsyānukurvīta gatibhāṣitacheṣṭitam // *189* //

189. Let them not even pronounce their teacher's name (without adding an honorific title) behind their back, and let them not mimic their teachers' gait, speech, and deportment.

गुरोर्यत्र परिवादो निन्दा वाऽपि प्रवर्तते ।
कर्णौ तत्र पिधातव्यौ गन्तव्यं वा ततोऽन्यतः ॥ 190 ॥

guroryatra parivādo nindā vā'pi pravartate /
karṇau tatra pidhātavyau gantavyaṁ vā tato'nyataḥ // 190 //

190. Wherever people falsely reproach, criticize, or defame their teacher, they should cover their ears or leave for another place.

दूरस्थो नार्चयेदेनं न क्रुद्धो नान्तिके स्त्रियाः ।
यानासनस्थश्चैवैनमवरुह्याभिवादयेत् ॥ 191 ॥

dūrastho nārchayedenaṁ na kruddho nāntike striyāḥ /
yānāsanasthaśchaivainamavaruhyābhivādayet // 191 //

191. A student must not wish the teacher from distance, as the teacher may stand aloof, nor when he/she is angry, nor when a woman is near; if a student is seated in a vehicle or on a (raised) seat, he/she must descend and afterwards salute his/her (teacher).

प्रतिवातेऽनुवाते[1] च नासीत गुरुणा सह ।
असंश्रवे चैव गुरोर्न किं चिदपि कीर्तयेत् ॥ 192 ॥

prativāte'nuvāte cha nāsīta guruṇā saha /
asaṁśrave chaiva gurorna kiṁ chidapi kīrtayet // 192 //

192. Students should not sit with their teacher [prativāte] in the direction of the wind blowing from the student to the teacher or [anuvāte] in the direction of the wind blowing from the teacher to the student. Additionally, the student should avoid saying anything [asañśrave] beyond the hearing of their teacher.

गोऽश्वौष्ट्रयानप्रासादप्रस्तरेषु कटेषु च ।
आसीत गुरुणा सार्धं शिलाफलकनौषु च ॥ 193 ॥

go'śvauṣṭrayānaprāsādaprastareṣu kaṭeṣu cha /
āsīta guruṇā sārdhaṁ śilāphalakanauṣu cha // 193 //

193. Students may sit with their teachers in various settings,

---

[1] प्रतिवातानुवाते

such as in vehicles, on carts or carriages pulled by oxen, horses, or camels, [prāsād-prastreṣu] on terraces, [kaṭeṣu] on grass mats, [śilā-phalakeṣu] on rocks, on wooden benches, or in boats and ships.

गुरोर्गुरौ सन्निहिते गुरुवद् वृत्तिमाचरेत् ।
न चानिसृष्टो गुरुणा स्वान् गुरूनभिवादयेत् ॥ 194 ॥

gurorgurau sannihite guruvad vṛttimācharet ।
na chānisṛṣṭo guruṇā svān gurūnabhivādayet ॥ 194 ॥

194. If a student's teacher's teacher is nearby, they should show the same respect they would towards their own teacher. However, when their parents or respected family members are present, the student must not greet their parents or elders [anisṛṣṭaḥ] without seeking permission from their teacher.

विद्यागुरुष्वेवमेव नित्या वृत्तिः स्वयोनिषु ।
प्रतिषेधत्सु चाधर्माद् हितं चोपदिशत्स्वपि ॥ 195 ॥

vidyāguruṣvevameva nityā vṛttiḥ svayoniṣu ।
pratiṣedhatsu chādharmād hitaṁ chopadiśatsvapi ॥ 195 ॥

195. [vṛttiḥ] This behaviour should be [nityā] constantly observed by them towards [vidyāguruṣu] their teachers, [svayoniṣu] their family elders including parents, towards all [adharmāt pratiṣedhatsu] who may restrain them from committing immoral acts or wrongs, or may give them salutary advice to protect their interest.

गुरुपत्नी तु युवतिर्नाभिवाद्यैह पादयोः ।
पूर्णविंशतिवर्षेण गुणदोषौ विजानता ॥ 196 ॥

gurupatnī tu yuvatirnābhivādyaiha pādayoḥ ।
pūrṇaviṁśativarṣeṇa guṇadoṣau vijānatā ॥ 196 ॥

196. Students who have attained the age of twenty years, and know what is becoming and unbecoming, shall not salute a young wife of their teacher (by touching) her feet.

स्वभाव एष नारीणां नराणामिह दूषणम् ।
अतोऽर्थान्न प्रमाद्यन्ति प्रमदासु विपश्चितः ॥ 197 ॥

svabhāva ēṣa nārīṇāṁ narāṇāmiha dūṣaṇam ।
ato'rthānna pramādyanti pramadāsu vipaśchitaḥ ॥ 197 ॥

197. Women naturally attract men; therefore, [vipaśchitaḥ] the wise [na pramādyanti] remain vigilant [pradāsu] in their interactions with them to prevent increasing their attraction.

अविद्वांसमलं लोके विद्वांसमपि वा पुनः ।
प्रमदा ह्युत्पथं नेतुं कामक्रोधवशानुगम् ॥ 198 ॥

avidvāṁsamalaṁ loke vidvāṁsamapi vā punaḥ ।
pramadā hyutpathaṁ netuṁ kāmakrodhavaśānugam ॥ *198*

198. What can be said about an ordinary man enslaved by his desires and anger? [vidvānsam api] Even a learned man, [utpathaṁ netum] can stray [pramadā] in the company of a woman who is not his wife.

मात्रा स्वस्रा दुहित्रा वा न विविक्तासनो भवेत् ।
बलवानिन्द्रियग्रामो विद्वांसमपि कर्षति ॥ 199 ॥

mātrā svasrā duhitrā vā na viviktāsano bhavet ।
balavānindriyagrāmo vidvāṁsamapi karṣati ॥ *199* ॥

199. One should not sit in a lonely place even with one's mother, sister, or daughter; for the senses are unyielding, and may corrupt even a learned man.

कामं तु गुरुपत्नीनां युवतीनां युवा भुवि ।
विधिवद् वन्दनं कुर्यादसावहमिति ब्रुवन् ॥ 200 ॥

kāmaṁ tu gurupatnīnāṁ yuvatīnāṁ yuvā bhuvi ।
vidhivad vandanaṁ kuryādasāvahamiti bruvan ॥ *200* ॥

200. [kāmam] It is proper for [yuvā] a young student [bhuvi vidhivat vandanam kuryā] to kneel before the teacher's young wife, following tradition, [iti bruvan] and say, [asau aham] 'I am so and so.'

विप्रोष्य पादग्रहणमन्वहं चाभिवादनम् ।
गुरुदारेषु कुर्वीत सतां धर्ममनुस्मरन् ॥201 ॥

viproṣya pādagrahaṇamanvahaṁ chābhivādanam ।
gurudāreṣu kurvīta satāṁ dharmamanusmaran ॥*201* ॥

201. On returning from a journey, he must touch the feet of his teacher's wife and salute her daily, considering this as a duty.

यथा खनन् खनित्रेण नरो वार्यधिगच्छति ।
तथा गुरुगतां विद्यां शुश्रूषुरधिगच्छति ॥ 202 ॥

yathā khanan khanitreṇa naro vāryadhigachchhati /
tathā gurugatāṁ vidyāṁ śuśrūṣuradhigachchhati // 202 //

202. As the man who digs with a spade (into the ground) obtains water, even so an obedient (student) obtains the knowledge which lies hidden in their teacher.

मुण्डो वा जटिलो वा स्यादथ वा स्यात्शिखाजटः ।
नैनं ग्रामेऽभिनिम्लोचेत् सूर्यो नाभ्युदियात् क्व चित् ॥ 203 ॥
muṇḍo vā jaṭilo vā syādatha vā syātśikhājaṭaḥ /
nainaṁ grāme'bhinimlochet sūryo nābhyudiyāt kva chit //

203. A student may choose to either [miṇḍaḥ] shave his head (for males), [jaṭilaḥ] braid his hair (for both males and females), or [śikhājaṭaḥ] braid a single lock on the crown of his head (for males only). Additionally, the sun must [na+abhyudayāt] never rise or [abhinimlochet] set [enaṁ grāme] while he/she is in the village or inhabited area.

तं चेदभ्युदियात् सूर्यः शयानं कामचारतः ।
निम्लोचेद् वाऽप्यविज्ञानाज् जपन्नुपवसेद् दिनम् ॥ 204 ॥

taṁ chedabhyudiyāt sūryaḥ śayānaṁ kāmachārataḥ /
nimloched vā'pyavijñānāj japannupavased dinam // 204 //

204. If the sun should rise or set while student is sleeping, be it intentionally or unintentionally, the student shall pass the whole next day studying or, muttering the name of Om.

सूर्येण ह्यभिनिर्मुक्तः शयानोऽभ्युदितश्च यः ।[1]
प्रायश्चित्तमकुर्वाणो युक्तः स्यान् महतेनसा ॥ 205 ॥

sūryeṇa hyabhinirmuktaḥ śayāno'bhyuditaścha yaḥ /
prāyaśchittamakurvāṇo yuktaḥ syān mahatenasā // 205 //

205. For a student who sleeps, while the sun sets or rises, and does not perform propitiatory rite, commits a great mistake.

---

1 ऽभिनिम्लुक्तः

आचम्य प्रयतो नित्यमुभे सन्ध्ये समाहितः ।
शुचौ देशे जपञ्जप्यमुपासीत यथाविधि ॥ 206 ॥

āchamya prayato nityamubhe sandhye samāhitaḥ /
śuchau deśe japañjapyamupāsīta yathāvidhi // 206 //

206. Purified by sipping water, the student shall daily perform Sandhyā during both twilights with a concentrated mind in a clean place, chanting the text to be chanted according to the rule.

यदि स्त्री यद्यवरजः श्रेयः किं चित् समाचरेत् ।
तत् सर्वमाचरेद् युक्तो यत्र चास्य रमेन् मनः ॥ 207 ॥

yadi strī yadyavarajaḥ śreyaḥ kiṁ chit samācharet /
tat sarvamāchared yukto yatra chāsya ramen manaḥ // 207

207. If a female student or a junior one perform anything creditable, let it be diligently followed, as well as (any other permitted act) in which a student finds pleasure.

धर्मार्थावुच्यते श्रेयः कामार्थौ धर्म एव च ।
अर्थ एवैह वा श्रेयस्त्रिवर्ग इति तु स्थितिः ॥ 208 ॥

dharmārthāvuchyate śreyaḥ kāmārthau dharma ēva cha /
artha ēvaiha vā śreyastrivarga iti tu sthitiḥ // 208 //

208. According to some, attaining dharma (moral, ethical values and good education) and artha (material resources) is a creditable job. Others find credit in attaining kāma (the gratification of mundane and spiritual desires) and the artha (material gains), yet others in the attainment of dharma alone, while some stick to attainment of artha alone. However, [iti sthitiḥ] the fact is that attainment of [trivargaḥ] all the three is creditable.

आचार्यश्च पिता चैव माता भ्राता च पूर्वजः ।
नार्तेनाप्यवमन्तव्या ब्राह्मणेन विशेषतः ॥ 209 ॥

āchāryaścha pitā chaiva mātā bhrātā cha pūrvajaḥ /
nārtenāpyavamantavyā brāhmaṇena viśeṣataḥ // 209 //

209. The teacher, the father, the mother, and an elder brother must not be treated with disrespect, especially by a seeker of Brahman, though one be grievously offended (by

them).

आचार्यो ब्रह्मणो मूर्तिः पिता मूर्तिः प्रजापतेः ।
माता पृथिव्या मूर्तिस्तु भ्राता स्वो मूर्तिरात्मनः ॥ 210 ॥

āchāryo brahmaṇo mūrtiḥ pitā mūrtiḥ prajāpateḥ /
mātā pṛthivyā mūrtistu bhrātā svo mūrtirātmanaḥ // 210 //

210. The teacher is the image of Brahman (God before creation), the father is the image of Prajāpati (God after creation), the mother is the image of the earth, and an elder brother is the image of oneself.

यं मातापितरौ क्लेशं सहेते सम्भवे नृणाम् ।
न तस्य निष्कृतिः शक्या कर्तुं वर्षशतैरपि ॥ 211 ॥

yaṁ mātāpitarau kleśaṁ sahete sambhave nṛṇām /
na tasya niṣkṛtiḥ śakyā kartuṁ varṣaśatairapi // 211 //

211. That arduousness and pain which the parents undergo on the birth of (their) children, cannot be compensated even through the service done in hundred years.

तयोर्नित्यं प्रियं कुर्यादाचार्यस्य च सर्वदा ।
तेष्वेव त्रिषु तुष्टेषु तपः सर्वं समाप्यते ॥ 212 ॥

tayornityaṁ priyaṁ kuryādāchāryasya cha sarvadā /
teṣveva triṣu tuṣṭeṣu tapaḥ sarvaṁ samāpyate // 212 //

212. Let a student always do what is agreeable to mother and father and always (what may please) the teacher; when those three are pleased, the student obtains all those rewards which austerities yield.

तेषां त्रयाणां शुश्रूषा परमं तप उच्यते ।
न तैरनभ्यनुज्ञातो धर्ममन्यं समाचरेत् ॥ 213 ॥

teṣāṁ trayāṇāṁ śuśrūṣā paramaṁ tapa uchyate /
na tairanabhyanujñāto dharmamanyaṁ samācharet // 213

213. Taking proper care of those three is declared to be the best (form of) austerity for a student; let him/her not perform other acts deemed to be dharma without their approval.

त एव हि त्रयो लोकास्त एव त्रय आश्रमाः ।
त एव हि त्रयो वेदास्त एवौक्तास्त्रयोऽग्नयः ॥ 214 ॥

ta ēva hi trayo lokāsta ēva traya āśramāḥ ।
ta ēva hi trayo vedāsta ēvauktāstrayo'gnayaḥ ॥ 214 ॥

214. They embody the essence of three realms— Dyauloka (star/sun), Antarikṣa (interveing space) and and Pṛthiviloka (planets/earth), serving as the representatives of the three principal Āśramas. They also symbolize the wisdom found in the three Vedas—Ṛk, Yaju, and Sāma. Furthermore, they stand as the representatives of the three sacred fires: Dakṣiṇāgni, Gārhapatya, and Āhavanīya, which are integral to the Śrauta yajñas.

पिता वै गार्हपत्योऽग्निर्माताऽग्निर्दक्षिणः स्मृतः ।
गुरुराहवनीयस्तु साऽग्नित्रेता गरीयसी ॥ 215 ॥

pitā vai gārhapatyo'gnirmātā'gnirdakṣiṇaḥ smṛtaḥ ।
gururāhavanīyastu sā'gnitretā garīyasī ॥ 215 ॥

215. The father symbolizes the Gārhapatya fire, the mother symbolizes the Dakṣiṇāgni, and the teacher symbolizes the Āhavanīya fire; this triad of fires is highly venerable.

Note: Gārhapatyāgni represents family sanskāras carried forward in family lineage. Mother symbolize the Dakṣiṇāgni, in family life mother delivers the gift of child and teacher symbolises the Āhavanīya agni, due to imparting knowledge to the child.

त्रिष्वप्रमाद्यन्नेतेषु त्रीन् लोकान् विजयेद् गृही ।
दीप्यमानः स्ववपुषा देववद् दिवि मोदते ॥ 216 ॥

triṣvapramādyanneteṣu trīn lokān vijayed gṛhī ।
dīpyamānaḥ svavapuṣā devavad divi modate ॥ 216 ॥

216. A householder who does not neglect those three in life will be successful in the three worlds (human life, divine life and mokṣa) and, radiant in body like a Deva, will enjoy bliss in divinehood.

इमं लोकं मातृभक्त्या पितृभक्त्या तु मध्यमम् ।
गुरुशुश्रूषया त्वेवं ब्रह्मलोकं समश्नुते ॥ 217 ॥

imaṁ lokaṁ mātṛbhaktyā pitṛbhaktyā tu madhyamam ।
guruśuśrūṣayā tvevaṁ brahmalokaṁ samaśnute ॥ 217 ॥

217. Through association with Mother, one thrives in mundane aspects of life; through association with Father, one attains divinehood; but through association with Guru, one achieves Mokṣa.

सर्वे तस्यादृता धर्मा यस्यैते त्रय आदृताः ।
अनादृतास्तु यस्यैते सर्वास्तस्याफलाः क्रियाः ॥ 218 ॥

sarve tasyādṛtā dharmā yasyaite traya ādṛtāḥ ।
anādṛtāstu yasyaite sarvāstasyāphalāḥ kriyāḥ ॥ 218 ॥

218. All duties are fulfilled by those who honour the three; however, for those who do not honour them, all hard work becomes futile.

यावत् त्रयस्ते जीवेयुस्तावन्नान्यं समाचरेत् ।
तेष्वेव नित्यं शुश्रूषां कुर्यात् प्रियहिते रतः ॥ 219 ॥

yāvat trayaste jīveyustāvatnānyaṁ samācharet ।
teṣveva nityaṁ śuśrūṣāṁ kuryāt priyahite rataḥ ॥ 219 ॥

219. As long as those three live, other acts of dharma need not be performed; always take care of them, rejoicing in doing what is agreeable and beneficial to them.

तेषामनुपरोधेन पारत्र्यं यद् यदाचरेत् ।
तत् तन्निवेदयेत् तेभ्यो मनोवचनकर्मभिः ॥ 220 ॥

teṣāmanuparodhena pāratrayaṁ yad yadācharet ।
tat tannivedayet tebhyo manovachanakarmabhiḥ ॥ 220 ॥

220. All actions performed through thought, speech, and action for the benefit of the next life should be done with their [anuparodhena] guidance and permission.

त्रिष्वेतेष्वितिकृत्यं हि पुरुषस्य समाप्यते ।
एष धर्मः परः साक्षादुपधर्मोऽन्य उच्यते ॥ 221 ॥

triṣveteṣvitikṛtyaṁ hi puruṣasya samāpyate ।
ēṣa dharmaḥ paraḥ sākṣādupadharmo'nya uchyate ॥ 221 ॥

221. [itikṛtyam] All duties of human-beings [samāpyate] are concluded [triṣu eteṣu] in the caretaking of these three. This is clearly the highest duty, [anyaḥ] every other act or duty is a [upadharmaḥ] subordinate duty.

Sources of Learning

श्रद्दधानः शुभां विद्यामाददीतावरादपि ।
अन्यादपि परं धर्मं स्त्रीरत्नं दुष्कुलादपि ॥ 222 ॥

śraddadhānaḥ śubhāṁ vidyāmādadītāvarādapi /
anyādapi paraṁ dharmaṁ strīratnaṁ duṣkulādapi // 222 //

222. With a positive attitude, one can receive good learning even from a junior, learn to be dutiful from an outsider, and find an excellent wife even from a corrupt or lowly family.

विषादप्यमृतं ग्राह्यं बालादपि सुभाषितम् ।
अमित्रादपि सद्वृत्तममेध्यादपि काञ्चनम् ॥ 223 ॥

viṣādapyamṛtaṁ grāhyaṁ bālādapi subhāṣitam /
amitrādapi sadvṛttamamedhyādapi kāñchanam // 223 //

223. Nectar may be taken even from poison, good advice even from a child, good conduct even from a foe, and gold even from a heap of rubbish.

स्त्रियो रत्नान्यथो विद्या धर्मः शौचं सुभाषितम् ।
विविधानि च शिल्पानि समादेयानि सर्वतः ॥ 224 ॥

striyo ratnānyatho vidyā dharmaḥ śauchaṁ subhāṣitam /
vividhāni cha śilpāni samādeyāni sarvataḥ // 224 //

224. Excellent wives, ornaments, knowledge, moral and ethical values, purity, good advice, and various arts and technologies may be obtained from everywhere.

अब्राह्मणादध्यापनमापत्काले विधीयते ।
अनुव्रज्या च शुश्रूषा यावदध्यापनं गुरोः ॥ 225 ॥

abrāhmaṇādadhyāpanamāpatkāle vidhīyate /
anuvrajyā cha śuśrūṣā yāvadadhyāpanaṁ guroḥ // 225 //

225. In times of crisis and need, one can learn from the a non-teacher (person other than teaching profession). The non-teacher also deserves to be followed and respected as a Guru, as long as the instruction lasts.

नाब्राह्मणे गुरौ शिष्यो वासमात्यन्तिकं वसेत् ।
ब्राह्मणे वाऽननूचाने काङ्क्षन् गतिमनुत्तमाम् ॥ 226 ॥

nābrāhmaṇe gurau śiṣyo vāsamātyantikaṁ vaset /

brāhmaṇe vā'nanūchāne kāṅkṣan gatimanuttamām // *226*

226. One who seeks to uplift oneself to the superior level shall not stay permanently with a non-teacher, nor with a teacher who is [ananūchāne] not well versed in his subject.

यदि त्वात्यन्तिकं वासं रोचयेत गुरोः कुले ।
युक्तः परिचरेदेनमा शरीरविमोक्षणात् ॥ 227 ॥

yadi tvātyantikaṁ vāsaṁ rochayeta guroḥ kule /
yuktaḥ paricharedenamā śarīravimokṣaṇāt // *227* //

227. But if a student seeks to pass his whole life in the company of a teacher, he must diligently serve him, until he is freed from this body.

न पूर्वं गुरवे किंचिदुपकुर्वीत धर्मवित् ।
स्नास्यंस्तु गुरुणाऽज्ञप्तः शक्त्या गुर्वर्थमाहरेत् ॥ 228 ॥

na pūrvaṁ gurave kiṁchidupakurvīta dharmavit /
snāsyaṁstu guruṇā'jñaptaḥ śaktyā gurvarthamāharet // *228*

228. A student who understands the rules should avoid giving any gifts to their teacher before graduation. However, [snāsyan tu] when preparing for the graduation ceremony, they may offer a present to the teacher, according to their ability and with the teacher's permission.

क्षेत्रं हिरण्यं गामश्वं छत्रौपानहमासनम् ।
धान्यं शाकं च वासांसि गुरवे प्रीतिमावहेत्[1] ॥ 229 ॥

kṣetraṁ hiraṇyaṁ gāmaśvaṁ chhatraupānahamāsanam /
dhānyaṁ śākaṁ cha vāsāṁsi gurave prītimāvahet // *229* //

229. A land, gold, a cow, a horse, a parasol, shoes, a chair, grain, (even) vegetables, or clothes at his pleasure may be gifted to the teacher at the conclusion of the graduation ceremony.

एवं चरति यो विप्रो ब्रह्मचर्यमविप्लुतः ।
स गच्छत्युत्तमस्थानं न चैह जायते पुनः ॥ 230 ॥

---

1 धान्यं वासांसि शाकं वा गुरवे प्रीतिमाहरन्

ēvaṁ charati yo vipro brahmacharyamaviplutaḥ /
sa gachchhatyuttamasthānaṁ na chaiha jāyate punaḥ // 230

230. A scholar who lives his life without breaking his vow of Brahmacharya attains the supreme abode of Mokṣa, never to be born again in this world.

Chapter 3: Duties of Gṛhasthī

The third chapter deals with the choice of a wife and the rules of marriage for all varṇas (professional classes). It explains that one should not marry a woman who has excessive body hair or is completely hairless.

A person with the sanskāras and profession of a Brāhmaṇa (who is spiritually and intellectually elevated) should not marry an uneducated woman. Therefore, marriage should be between individuals of equal merit, temperament, and social and spiritual status to ensure they can progress together.

Manu describes eight types of marriages:

1. Brāhma Marriage: This involves giving away the daughter, dressed in elegant attire and honoured, to a man (bridegroom) who is learned in the Vedas and upholds high moral and ethical values. The bride's parents invite the groom to the marriage.

2. Daiva Marriage: In this type, the daughter is given away, adorned with ornaments, in a marriage ceremony conducted for a bridegroom who excels in performing all duties and yajñas.

3. Ārṣa Marriage: This occurs when the daughter is given to the bridegroom after receiving from him a pair of cows and a bull (or equivalent money thereof) as part of custom.

4. Prājāpatya Marriage: Here, the daughter is given away with respect to a bridegroom after consulting both the bride and bridegroom to mutually agree to enter into Gṛhastha life and its responsibilities.

5. Āsura Marriage: In this case, the bridegroom marries the bride after offering wealth to both her relatives and the bride herself, according to his own choice.

6. Gāndharva Marriage: This is a voluntary union between a bride and bridegroom driven by mutual sexual attraction.

7. Rākṣasa Marriage: This involves the forcible abduction of a maiden from her home while she cries out for help, often after

her relatives have been harmed and their home invaded.

8. Paiśāca Marriage: This is the most immoral type, where a man sexually assaults a girl who is sleeping, intoxicated, in a secluded place, or mentally challenged.

Manu also outlines the merits and demerits of different types of marriages, detailing how many generations of ancestors and descendants can benefit from the virtuous actions of sons born from such unions. He discusses various approaches and timings for a man to engage with his wife sexually, the status of children born from intra-varṇa and inter-varṇa unions, and several categories of women deemed unsuitable for marriage.

Period of Studentship

षट् त्रिंशदाब्दिकं चर्यं गुरौ त्रैवेदिकं व्रतम् ।
तदर्धिकं पादिकं वा ग्रहणान्तिकमेव वा ॥ 1 ॥

ṣaṭ trimśadābdikaṁ charyaṁ gurau traivedikaṁ vratam /
tadardhikaṁ pādikaṁ vā grahaṇāntikameva vā // 1 //

1. The period for the study of the three Vedas under a teacher must be kept maximum for thirty-six years, or for half that time (18 years), or a quarter (9 years), or [grahaṇāntikam eva cha] until the (student) has perfectly learned them.

Proper time of Entry into the Gṛhasthāśrama

वेदानधीत्य वेदौ वा वेदं वाऽपि यथाक्रमम् ।
अविप्लुतब्रह्मचर्यो गृहस्थाश्रममावसेत् ॥ 2 ॥

vedānadhītya vedau vā vedaṁ vā'pi yathākramam /
aviplutabrahmacharyo gṛhasthāśramamāvaset // 2 //

2. (A student) who has studied in due order the three Vedas, or two, or even one only, having never deviated from the vow of Brahmacharya, shall enter the Gṛhastha Aśrama.

गुरुणानुमतः स्नात्वा समावृत्तो यथाविधि ।
उद्वहेत द्विजो भार्यां सवर्णां लक्षणान्विताम् ॥ 3 ॥

guruṇānumataḥ snātvā samāvṛtto yathāvidhi /
udvaheta dvijo bhāryāṁ savarṇāṁ lakṣaṇānvitām // 3 //

3. After graduating and with the teacher's permission, a student may marry a woman of equal sanskāras (merit and temperament), endowed with good character.

Marriageable Girls

असपिण्डा च या मातुरसगोत्रा च या पितुः ।
सा प्रशस्ता द्विजातीनां दारकर्मणि मैथुने[1] ॥ 4 ॥

asapiṇḍā cha yā māturasagotrā cha yā pituḥ /
sā praśastā dvijātīnāṁ dārakarmaṇi maithune // 4 //

4. A woman is considered suitable for marriage and a conjugal union with a student if she does not have a Sapiṇḍa relationship on the student's mother's side, meaning she is not related by blood within six generations (including the mother, maternal grandmother, great-grandmother, and so on). Additionally, she must not belong to the same gotra as the student's father.

महान्त्यपि समृद्धानि गोऽजाविधनधान्यतः ।
स्त्रीसम्बन्धे दशैतानि कुलानि परिवर्जयेत् ॥ 5 ॥

mahāntyapi samṛddhāni go'jāvidhanadhānyataḥ /
strīsambandhe daśaitāni kulāni parivarjayet // 5 //

5. When considering marriage with a woman, he should carefully avoid the following ten families, regardless of their wealth, number of cattle, goats, sheep, grains, or other possessions.

हीनक्रियं निष्पुरुषं निश्छन्दो रोमशार्शसम् ।
क्षय्यामयाव्यपस्मारिश्वित्रिकुष्ठिकुलानि च ॥ 6 ॥

hīnakriyaṁ niṣpuruṣaṁ niśchhando romaśārśasam /
kṣayyāmayāvyapasmāriśvitrikuṣṭhikulāni cha // 6 //

6. The family that neglects yajñas, one which is male-less, one in which the Veda is not studied, one (the members of) which have [romaśa] thick hair on the body, those which are subject to hereditary diseases like [arśasam] piles, [kṣayī]

---

1 मैथिनी

tuberculosis, [āmayāvī] indigestion, [apasmāri] epilepsy, or [śvitri] white or [kuṣṭhi] black leprosy.

नोद्वहेत् कपिलां कन्यां नाधिकाङ्गीं न रोगिणीम् ।
नालोमिकां नातिलोमां न वाचाटां[1] न पिङ्गलाम् ॥ 7 ॥

nodvahet kapilāṁ kanyāṁ nādhikāṅgīṁ na rogiṇīm /
nālomikāṁ nātilomāṁ na vāchāṭāṁ na piṅgalām // 7 //

7. Let him not marry a maiden (with) monkey-colored skin, nor one who has an extra limb, nor one who is sickly, nor one either with no hair or too much nor one who talks nonsense or has yellow pigments on the body,

नर्क्षवृक्षनदीनाम्नीं नान्त्यपर्वतनामिकाम् ।
न पक्ष्यहिप्रेष्यनाम्नीं न च भीषणनामिकाम् ॥ 8 ॥

narkṣavṛkṣanadīnāmnīṁ nāntyaparvatanāmikām /
na pakṣayahipreṣyanāmnīṁ na cha bhīṣaṇanāmikām // 8 //

8. Nor one named after a constellation, a tree, or a river, nor one bearing the name symbolizing a low or mean sense, or of a mountain, nor one named after a bird, a snake, nor one whose name denotes a sense of slavery, nor one whose name is terrifying.

अव्यङ्गाङ्गीं सौम्यनाम्नीं हंसवारणगामिनीम् ।
तनुलोमकेशदशनां मृद्वङ्गीमुद्वहेत् स्त्रियम् ॥ 9 ॥

avyaṅgāṅgīṁ saumyanāmnīṁ haṁsavāraṇagāminīm /
tanulomakeśadaśanāṁ mṛdvaṅgīmudvahet striyam // 9 //

9. Let him wed a female free from deformities, who has a decent/graceful name, the (graceful) gait of a Hansa (goose) or of an elephant, smooth and silky hair on the body and on the head, small teeth, and soft limbs.

The Eight Forms of Marriage

चतुर्णामपि वर्णानां प्रेत्य चैह हिताहितान् ।
अष्टाविमान् समासेन स्त्रीविवाहान्निबोधत ॥ 10 ॥

---

1 वाचालां

chaturṇāmapi varṇānāṁ pretya chaiha hitāhitān /
aṣṭāvimān samāsena strīvivāhānnibodhata // 10 //

10. Now listen to the brief (description of) the following eight types of marriage used by all the four varṇas (professional classes based upon sanskāras) which are both beneficial and harmful here and hereafter.

ब्राह्मो दैवस्तथैवार्षः प्राजापत्यस्तथाऽसुरः ।

गान्धर्वो राक्षसश्चैव पैशाचश्चाष्टमोऽधमः // 11 //
brāhmo daivastathaivārṣaḥ prājāpatyastathā'suraḥ /
gāndharvo rākṣasaśchaiva paiśāchaśchāṣṭamo'dhamaḥ // 11

11. The 8 types of marriages are: the Brāhma, the Daiva, the Ārṣa, the Prājapatya, the Āsura, the Gāndharva, the Rākṣasa, and the 8th and most inferior is the Paiśācha.

Note: The above eight types of marriages are inferior in order. The first one is the most superior type. Everybody is expected to go by the first one. Since, all human beings cannot be superior by nature, temperament, and merit, other forms of marriage are also sanctioned.

आच्छाद्य चार्चयित्वा च श्रुतशीलवते स्वयम् ।
आहूय दानं कन्याया ब्राह्मो धर्मः प्रकीर्तितः ॥ 12 ॥

āchchhādya chārchayitvā cha śrutaśīlavate svayam /
āhūya dānaṁ kanyāyā brāhmo dharmaḥ prakīrtitaḥ // 12 //

12. The Brāhma marriage is the giving away of a daughter, who is dressed beautifully and honored appropriately, to a groom who is knowledgeable in the Vedas and possesses strong moral and ethical values. This ceremony is conducted with the groom being formally invited by the bride's parents for the purpose of marriage.

यज्ञे तु वितते सम्यग् ऋत्विजे कर्म कुर्वते ।
अलङ्कृत्य सुतादानं दैवं धर्मं प्रचक्षते ॥ 13 ॥

yajñe tu vitate samyag ṛtvije karma kurvate /
alaṅkṛtya sutādānaṁ daivaṁ dharmaṁ prachakṣate // 13 //

13. Giving away a daughter who has been adorned with ornaments in a marriage ceremony conducted for the purpose,

to a bridegroom who excels in performing all duties and yajñas, is called Daiva marriage.

एकं गोमिथुनं द्वे वा वरादादाय धर्मतः ।
कन्याप्रदानं विधिवदार्षो धर्मः स उच्यते ॥ 14 ॥

ēkaṁ gomithunaṁ dve vā varādādāya dharmataḥ ।
kanyāpradānaṁ vidhivadārṣo dharmaḥ sa uchyate ॥ 14 ॥

14. When the daughter is given away to the bridegroom after receiving from him a pair of cows and a bull, or two pairs (or eqvivalent money thereof), in accordance with the law, this is called the Ārṣa marriage.

सहौभौ चरतां धर्ममिति वाचाऽनुभाष्य च ।
कन्याप्रदानमभ्यर्च्य प्राजापत्यो विधिः स्मृतः ॥ 15 ॥

sahaubhau charatāṁ dharmamiti vāchā'nubhāṣya cha ।
kanyāpradānamabhyarchya prājāpatyo vidhiḥ smṛtaḥ ॥ 15

15. Giving away their daughter with respect to the bridegroom by the parents, after obtaining consent from both the bride and the bridegroom to enter into Gṛhastha life and fulfill their duties, is referred to as the Prājāpatya marriage.

ज्ञातिभ्यो द्रविणं दत्त्वा कन्यायै चैव शक्तितः ।
कन्याप्रदानं स्वाच्छन्द्यादासुरो धर्म उच्यते ॥ 16 ॥

jñātibhyo draviṇaṁ dattvā kanyāyai chaiva śaktitaḥ ।
kanyāpradānaṁ svāchchhandyādāsuro dharma uchyate ॥16

16. When the bridegroom receives a bride after giving as much wealth as he can afford to both the bride's relatives and the bride herself, according to his own will, this union is called the Āsura marriage.

इच्छयाऽन्योन्यसंयोगः कन्यायाश्च वरस्य च ।
गान्धर्वः स तु विज्ञेयो मैथुन्यः कामसम्भवः ॥ 17 ॥

ichchhayā'nyonyasaṁyogaḥ kanyāyāścha varasya cha ।
gāndharvaḥ sa tu vijñeyo maithunyaḥ kāmasambhavaḥ ॥17

17. The Gāndharva marriage is a voluntary union between a bride and groom based on mutual attraction.

हत्वा छित्त्वा च भित्त्वा च क्रोशन्तीं रुदतीं गृहात् ।

प्रसह्य कन्याहरणं राक्षसो विधिरुच्यते ॥ 18 ॥

hatvā chhittvā cha bhittvā cha krośantīṁ rudatīṁ gṛhāt /
prasahya kanyāharaṇaṁ rākṣaso vidhiruchyate // 18 //

18. The forced abduction of a young woman from her home, while she cries and weeps, after her relatives have been slain or wounded and their houses broken into, is called the Rākśasa marriage.

सुप्तां मत्तां प्रमत्तां वा रहो यत्रोपगच्छति ।
स पापिष्ठो विवाहानां पैशाचश्चाष्टमोऽधमः[1] ॥ 19 ॥

suptāṁ mattāṁ pramattāṁ vā raho yatropagachchhati /
sa pāpiṣṭho vivāhānāṁ paiśāchaśchāṣṭamo'dhamaḥ // 19 //

19. When a man outrages the modesty of a woman who is sleeping, intoxicated, or located in a deserted or secluded place, or who is mentally challenged, this is referred to as the eighth and most immoral type of marriage, known as Paiśācha marriage.

ब्राह्मादिषु विवाहेषु चतुर्ष्वेवानुपूर्वशः ।
ब्रह्मवर्चस्विनः[2] पुत्रा जायन्ते शिष्टसम्मताः ॥ 20 ॥

brāhmādiṣu vivāheṣu chaturṣvevānupūrvaśaḥ /
brahmavarchasvinaḥ putrā jāyante śiṣṭasammatāḥ // 20 //

20. Progeny born from the four marriages, beginning with the Brāhma marriage, is often radiant with knowledge of the Vedas and benefits from the company of [śiṣṭas] enlightened persons.

रूपसत्त्वगुणोपेता धनवन्तो यशस्विनः ।
पर्याप्तभोगा धर्मिष्ठा जीवन्ति च शतं समाः ॥ 21 ॥

rūpasattvaguṇopetā dhanavanto yaśasvinaḥ /
paryāptabhogā dharmiṣṭhā jīvanti cha śataṁ samāḥ // 21 //

21. Endowded with the qualities of beauty and goodness,

---

1 पैशाचः प्रथितोऽधमः

2 ब्रह्मवर्चसिनः

possessing wealth and fame, obtaining as many enjoyments as they desire and being most righteous, they will live a hundred years.

इतरेषु तु शिष्टेषु नृशंसाऽनृतवादिनः ।
जायन्ते दुर्विवाहेषु ब्रह्मधर्मद्विषः सुताः ॥ 22 ॥

itareṣu tu śiṣṭeṣu nṛśaṁsā'nṛtavādinaḥ /
jāyante durvivāheṣu brahmadharmadviṣaḥ sutāḥ // 22 //

22. But progeny begot from the remaining (four) blamable marriages is often cruel, speaker of untruth, and hater of the Vedic dharma (laws and duties instructed in the Vedas).

अनिन्दितैः स्त्रीविवाहैरनिन्द्या भवति प्रजा ।
निन्दितैर्निन्दिता नृणां तस्मान्निन्द्यान् विवर्जयेत् ॥ 23 ॥
aninditaiḥ strīvivāhairanindyā bhavati prajā /
ninditairninditā nṛṇāṁ tasmānnindyān vivarjayet //23 //

23. Blameless marriages produce blameless children, while blamable marriages result in blamable offspring. Therefore, one should avoid blamable forms of marriage.

Duties of Marital life

ऋतुकालाभिगामी स्यात् स्वदारनिरतः सदा ।
पर्ववर्जं व्रजेच्चैनां तद्व्रतो रतिकाम्यया ॥ 24 ॥

ṛtukālābhigāmī syāt svadāraniratah sadā /
parvavarjaṁ vrajechchaināṁ tadvrato ratikāmyayā // 24 //

24. A husband should approach his wife at the right time, remaining devoted to her. He may express his desire for conjugal union any day, except on the Parvans (the full moon and new moon days).

ऋतुः स्वाभाविकः स्त्रीणां रात्रयः षोडश स्मृताः ।
चतुर्भिरितरैः सार्धमहोभिः सद्विगर्हितैः ॥ 25 ॥
ṛtuḥ svābhāvikaḥ strīṇāṁ rātrayaḥ ṣoḍaśa smṛtāḥ /
chaturbhiritaraiḥ sārdhamahobhiḥ sadvigarhitaiḥ //25 //

25. The natural period for women to cohabit lasts sixteen nights, starting from the onset of menstruation. The first four days of menstruation are prohibited by experts.

तासामाद्याश्चतस्रस्तु निन्दितैकादशी च या ।
त्रयोदशी च शेषास्तु प्रशस्ता दशरात्रयः ॥ 26 ॥

tāsāmādyāśchatasrastu ninditaikādaśī cha yā /
trayodaśī cha śeṣāstu praśastā daśarātrayaḥ // *26* //

26. Among these, the first four nights, the eleventh, and the thirteenth are declared forbidden; the remaining nights are recommended.

युग्मासु पुत्रा जायन्ते स्त्रियोऽयुग्मासु रात्रिषु ।
तस्माद् युग्मासु पुत्रार्थी संविशेदार्तवे स्त्रियम् ॥ 27 ॥

yugmāsu putrā jāyante striyo'yugmāsu rātriṣu /
tasmād yugmāsu putrārthī saṁviśedārtave striyam // *27* //

27. Male children are conceived on even days, and female children on uneven days; therefore, someone who desires a son should engage with their wife on the even days of her cycle.

पुमान् पुंसोऽधिके शुक्रे स्त्री भवत्यधिके स्त्रियाः ।
समेऽपुमान् पुंस्त्रियौ वा क्षीणेऽल्पे च विपर्ययः ॥ 28 ॥
pumān puṁso'dhike śukre strī bhavatyadhike striyāḥ /
same'pumān puṁstriyau vā kṣīṇe'lpe cha viparyayaḥ //*28* //

28. A male child is conceived when the sperm is strong, while a female child is conceived when the ovum is strong. If both are equally strong, it may result in either an impotent boy or a barren girl. However, if both the sperm and ovum are weak or deficient in quantity, conception may fail altogether.

निन्द्यास्वष्टासु चान्यासु स्त्रियो रात्रिषु वर्जयन् ।
ब्रह्मचार्येव भवति यत्र तत्राश्रमे वसन् ॥ 29 ॥

nindyāsvaṣṭāsu chānyāsu striyo rātriṣu varjayan /
brahmachāryeva bhavati yatra tatrāśrame vasan // *29* //

29. One who avoids women on the six forbidden nights and eight others is considered equal to a Brahmachārī, even while living the married life (Gṛhastha Āśrama).

Note: In a typical menstrual cycle of one month, only 16 days starting from menstruation are considered suitable for cohabitation. Among these 16 days, the first four nights of menstruation, as well as the 11th and 13th days, are prohibited for cohabitation. From the remaining 10 days, if a married man avoids cohabitation with his wife for 8 days, he will be regarded as a Brahmachārī.

Rules Regarding Marriage

न कन्यायाः पिता विद्वान् गृह्णीयात् शुल्कमण्वपि ।
गृह्णंशुल्कं हि लोभेन स्यान्नरोऽपत्यविक्रयी ॥ 30 ॥

na kanyāyāḥ pitā vidvān gṛhṇīyāt śulkamaṇvapi /
gṛhṇaṁśulkaṁ hi lobhena syānnaro'patyavikrayī // 30 //

30. The girl's father, if wise, should not accept any dowery from the family of the bridegroom; by accepting money out of greed, he becomes a child seller.

स्त्रीधनानि तु ये मोहादुपजीवन्ति बान्धवाः ।
नारीयानानि वस्त्रं वा ते पापा यान्त्यधोगतिम् ॥ 31 ॥

strīdhanāni tu ye mohādupajīvanti bāndhavāḥ /
nārīyānāni vastraṁ vā te pāpā yāntyadhogatim // 31 //

31. The bridegroom's family members who, through folly, live upon the bride's properties—even the bride's vehicles (conveyances) and clothes- commit pāpa (evil) and fall into the lower species.

आर्षे गोमिथुनं शुल्कं के चिदाहुर्मृषैव तत् ।
अल्पोऽप्येवं महान् वाऽपि विक्रयस्तावदेव सः[1] ॥ 32 ॥

ārṣe gomithunaṁ śulkaṁ ke chidāhurmṛṣaiva tat /
alpo'pyevaṁ mahān vā'pi vikrayastāvadeva saḥ // 32 //

32. Some people call the pair of cows or the bulls given at an Ārṣa wedding 'a dowery;' (but) that is wrong, since (the acceptance of) a dowery, be it small or great, is a sale (of the daughter).

यासां नाददते शुल्कं ज्ञातयो न स विक्रयः ।
अर्हणं तत् कुमारीणामानृशंस्यं च केवलम् ॥ 33 ॥

yāsāṁ nādadate śulkaṁ jñātayo na sa vikrayaḥ /
arhaṇaṁ tat kumārīṇāmānṛśaṁsyaṁ cha kevalam // 33 //

---

[1] *तावानेव स विक्रयः*

33. When the relatives do not appropriate (for their use) the gratuity (given), it is not a sale; (in that case) the (gift) is only a token of respect and of kindness towards the maidens.

पितृभिर्भ्रातृभिश्चैताः पतिभिर्देवरैस्तथा ।
पूज्या भूषयितव्याश्च बहुकल्याणमीप्सुभिः ॥ 34 ॥

pitṛbhirbhrātṛbhiśchaitāḥ patibhirdevaraistathā ।
pūjyā bhūṣayitavyāścha bahukalyāṇamīpsubhiḥ ॥ 34 ॥

34. Women must be honoured and adorned by their fathers, brothers, husbands, and brothers-in-law, who desire (their own) welfare.

यत्र नार्यस्तु पूज्यन्ते रमन्ते तत्र देवताः ।
यत्रैतास्तु न पूज्यन्ते सर्वास्तत्राफलाः क्रियाः ॥ 35 ॥

yatra nāryastu pūjyante ramante tatra devatāḥ ।
yatraitāstu na pūjyante sarvāstatrāphalāḥ kriyāḥ ॥ 35 ॥

35. The families that honour women are blessed with happiness and prosperity, but those that do not honor them will find no good work bears fruit.

शोचन्ति जामयो यत्र विनश्यत्याशु तत् कुलम् ।
न शोचन्ति तु यत्रैता वर्धते तद् हि सर्वदा ॥ 36 ॥

śochanti jāmayo yatra vinaśyatyāśu tat kulam ।
na śochanti tu yatraitā vardhate tad hi sarvadā ॥ 36 ॥

36. Where females live in grief, the family soon perishes; but a family where they are not unhappy always thrives.

जामयो यानि गेहानि शपन्त्यप्रतिपूजिताः ॥
तानि कृत्याहतानीव विनश्यन्ति समन्ततः ॥ 37 ॥

jāmayo yāni gehāni śapantyapratipūjitāḥ ॥
tāni kṛtyāhatānīva vinaśyanti samantataḥ ॥ 37 ॥

37. The houses where females are not duly honored are cursed and perish ultimately as if destroyed by occult science.

तस्मादेताः सदा पूज्या भूषणाच्छादनाशनैः ।
भूतिकामैर्नरैर्नित्यं सत्कारेषूत्सवेषु च ॥ 38 ॥

tasmādetāḥ sadā pūjyā bhūṣaṇāchchhādanāśanaiḥ ।
bhūtikāmairnarairnityaṁ satkāreṣūtsaveṣu cha ॥ 38 ॥

38. Hence, men seeking prosperity should honor women during holidays and festivals with gifts of ornaments, clothing, and fine food.

सन्तुष्टो भार्यया भर्ता भर्त्रा भार्या तथैव च ।
यस्मिन्नेव कुले नित्यं कल्याणं तत्र वै ध्रुवम् ॥ 39 ॥

santuṣṭo bhāryayā bhartā bhartrā bhāryā tathaiva cha /
yasminneva kule nityaṁ kalyāṇaṁ tatra vai dhruvam // 39

39. In a family where both the husband and wife are pleased with each other, their happiness will surely last.

यदि हि स्त्री न रोचेत पुमांसं न प्रमोदयेत् ।
अप्रमोदात् पुनः पुंसः प्रजनं न प्रवर्तते ॥ 40 ॥

yadi hi strī na rocheta pumāṁsaṁ na pramodayet /
apramodāt punaḥ puṁsaḥ prajanaṁ na pravartate // 40 //

40. If a wife fails to attract her partner, he will not be happy with her, and thus, his instinct for having children may diminish.

स्त्रियां तु रोचमानायां सर्वं तद् रोचते कुलम् ।
तस्यां त्वरोचमानायां सर्वमेव न रोचते ॥ 41 ॥

striyāṁ tu rochamānāyāṁ sarvaṁ tad rochate kulam /
tasyāṁ tvarochamānāyāṁ sarvameva na rochate // 41 //

41. If a wife is happy with her partner, the whole family will be happy. However, if she is unhappy, everything will seem dismal.

Duties of a Gṛhastha: Pañchamahāyajña

वैवाहिकेऽग्नौ कुर्वीत गृह्यं कर्म यथाविधि ।
पञ्चयज्ञविधानं च पक्तिं चान्वाहिकीं गृही ॥ 42 ॥

vaivāhike'gnau kurvīta gṛhyaṁ karma yathāvidhi /
pañchayajñavidhānaṁ cha paktiṁ chānvāhikīṁ gṛhī // 42 //

42. With the gārhapatya fire, kindled at the wedding, a householder shall perform according to the law the gṛhya sanskāras and the five (great) sacrifices, and (with that) he shall daily cook his food.

Note: Gārhapatya fire is the fire kindled at the wedding. A

Gṛhasthi is required to perform all sanskāras with that fire. Dakṣiṇāgni or Anvāhārya Pachana is also part of the Gārhaptya fire where daily food is cooked. In yajñas, Dakṣiṇāgni or Anvāhārya Pachana fire is used to make food to be eaten as Dakṣiṇā.

पञ्च सूना गृहस्थस्य चुल्ली पेषण्युपस्करः ।
कण्डनी चौदकुम्भश्च बध्यते[1] यास्तु वाहयन् ॥ 43 ॥

pañcha sūnā gṛhasthasya chullī peṣaṇyupaskaraḥ /
kaṇḍanī chaudakumbhaścha badhyate yāstu vāhayan // 43 //

43. A householder has five [sūnā] places where they commit violence viz. the hearth, the grinding stone, the broom, the pestle and mortar, and the water-vessel, by using which he commits pāpas (downgrading act).

तासां क्रमेण सर्वासां निष्कृत्यर्थं महर्षिभिः ।
पञ्च क्लृप्ता महायज्ञाः प्रत्यहं गृहमेधिनाम् ॥ 44 ॥

tāsāṁ krameṇa sarvāsāṁ niṣkṛtyarthaṁ maharṣibhiḥ /
pañcha kḷptā mahāyajñāḥ pratyahaṁ gṛhamedhinām // 44 //

44. In order to successively expiate the pāpās committed by means of all these five, the great sages have prescribed for householders the daily performance of the five great yajñas.

अध्यापनं ब्रह्मयज्ञः पितृयज्ञस्तु तर्पणम् ।
होमो दैवो बलिर्भौतो नृयज्ञोऽतिथिपूजनम् ॥ 45 ॥

adhyāpanaṁ brahmayajñaḥ pitṛyajñastu tarpaṇam /
homo daivo balirbhauto nṛyajño'tithipūjanam // 45 //

45. Teaching (and studying) is called Brahmayajña, providing proper care to elderly persons in the family through food and drinkable items, often called Tarpaṇa or Pitṛyajña, offering oblations in Agnihotra is called Devayajña, providing food to the living beings (human beings and animals) dependant on you in or around your house is called Balivaiśvadevayajña, and the hospitable reception of scholars or

---

[1] वध्यते

Saṁnyāsīs is called Nṛyajña (Atithiyajña).

पञ्चैतान् यो महाऽयज्ञान्न हापयति शक्तितः ।
स गृहेऽपि वसन्नित्यं सूनादोषैर्न लिप्यते ॥ 46 ॥

pañchaitān yo mahā'yajñānna hāpayati śaktitaḥ /
sa gṛhe'pi vasannityaṁ sūnādoṣairna lipyate // 46 //

46. He who [na hāpayati] does not neglect these five great yajñas, while he is able to perform them, is not tainted by the pāpas committed in the five places of violence while being in the Gṛhasthāśram.

देवताऽतिथिभृत्यानां पितॄणामात्मनश्च यः ।
न निर्वपति पञ्चानामुच्छ्वसन्न स जीवति ॥ 47 ॥

devatā'tithibhṛtyānāṁ pitṝṇāmātmanaścha yaḥ /
na nirvapati pañchānāmuchchhvasanna sa jīvati // 47 //

47. He who does not perform the five great yajñās should not be considered truly alive, even if he breathes.

अहुतं च हुतं चैव तथा प्रहुतमेव च ।
ब्राह्म्यं हुतं प्राशितं च पञ्चयज्ञान् प्रचक्षते ॥ 48 ॥

ahutaṁ cha hutaṁ chaiva tathā prahutameva cha /
brāhmyaṁ hutaṁ prāśitaṁ cha pañchayajñān prachakṣate //

48. They call (these) five yajñas also, Ahuta, Huta, Prahuta, Brāhmya-huta, and Prāśita.

जपोऽहुतो हुतो होमः प्रहुतो भौतिको बलिः ।
ब्राह्म्यं हुतं द्विजाग्र्यार्चा प्राशितं पितृतर्पणम् ॥ 49 ॥

japo'huto huto homaḥ prahuto bhautiko baliḥ /
brāhmyaṁ hutaṁ dvijāgryārchā prāśitaṁ pitṛtarpaṇam //

49. Ahuta (not offered in the fire) Japa (study of Vedic texts) is called Brahmayajña; Huta (oblations offered to the fire of yajña) is called Devayajña; Prahuta (offered by distributing or scattering on the ground) [bhautikaḥ baliḥ] is the Balivaiśvadeva yajña or Bhūtayajnā; Brāhmya-huta (offering hospitality to scholars or saṁnyāsīs) is the respectful reception of scholars or saṁnyāsīs; and Pāśita (taking care of elderly persons in the family by providing food etc.) is called Pitṛ-tarpaṇa.

स्वाध्याये नित्ययुक्तः स्याद् दैवे चैवैह कर्मणि ।
दैवकर्मणि युक्तो हि बिभर्तीदं चराचरम् ॥ 50 ॥

svādhyāye nityayuktaḥ syād daive chaivaiha karmaṇi /
daivakarmaṇi yukto hi bibhartīdaṁ charācharam // 50 //

50. Every man should dedicate himself daily to the study of the Śāstras and Vedas, as well as to the Devayajña (Agnihotra). One who diligently performs Agnihotra while living in this world supports both the living and non-living realms.

अग्नौ प्रास्ताऽहुतिः सम्यगादित्यमुपतिष्ठते ।
आदित्याज् जायते वृष्टिर्वृष्टेरन्नं ततः प्रजाः ॥ 51 ॥

agnau prāstā'hutiḥ samyagādityamupatiṣṭhate /
ādityāj jāyate vṛṣṭirvṛṣṭerannaṁ tataḥ prajāḥ // 51 //

51. An offering made to the fire reaches the sun, which then causes rain to fall on the earth by vaporizing water from the earth's bodies through radiation heating. From the rain, food is produced, providing sustenance for living creatures.

यथा वायुं समाश्रित्य वर्तन्ते सर्वजन्तवः[1] ।
तथा गृहस्थमाश्रित्य वर्तन्ते सर्व आश्रमाः[2] ॥ 52 ॥

yathā vāyuṁ samāśritya vartante sarvajantavaḥ /
tathā gṛhasthamāśritya vartante sarva āśramāḥ // 52 //

52. As all living creatures subsist by receiving support from the air, even so (the members of) all Āśramas subsist by receiving support from the Gṛhastha (householder).

यस्मात् त्रयोऽप्याश्रमिणो दानेनान्नेन चान्वहम् ।
गृहस्थेनैव धार्यन्ते तस्माज् ज्येष्ठाश्रमो गृही ॥ 53 ॥

yasmāt trayo'pyāśramiṇo dānenānnena chānvaham /
gṛhasthenaiva dhāryante tasmāj jyeṣṭhāśramo gṛhī // 53 //

53. Since all three Āśramas are daily supported by householders through charity and food, the Gṛhasthāśrama

---

1 सर्वे जीवन्ति जन्तवः

2 वर्तन्त इतराश्रमः

(order of householders) is the most excellent order.

स सन्धार्यः प्रयत्नेन स्वर्गमक्षयमिच्छता ।
सुखं चेहेच्छताऽत्यन्तं योऽधार्यो दुर्बलेन्द्रियैः ॥ 54 ॥

sa sandhāryaḥ prayatnena svargamakṣayamichchhatā /
sukhaṁ chehechchhatā'tyantaṁ yo'dhāryo durbalendriyaiḥ //

54. This Gṛhasthāśrama which cannot be practised by weak personss, must be carefully practised by those who [svargam akṣayam ichchhatā] desire imperishable bliss in mokṣa, and [sukham ichchhatā] constant happiness in this life.

ऋषयः पितरो देवा भूतान्यतिथयस्तथा ।
आशासते कुटुम्बिभ्यस्तेभ्यः कार्यं विजानता ॥ 55 ॥

ṛṣayaḥ pitaro devā bhūtānyatithayastathā /
āśāsate kuṭumbibhyastebhyaḥ kāryaṁ vijānatā // 55 //

55. The sages, the elderly persons, enlightened persons, the animals and poors, and scholars and saṁnyāsīs [āśāsate] depend upon the householders (for charities and foods); hence [vijānatā] a householder who knows his duty, [tebhyaḥ kāryam] must help them.

स्वाध्यायेनार्चयेतऋषीन् होमैर्देवान् यथाविधि ।
पितृंश्राद्धैश्च नृनन्नैर्भूतानि बलिकर्मणा ॥ 56 ॥

svādhyāyenārchayetaṛṣīn homairdevān yathāvidhi /
pitṝṁśrāddhaiścha nṝnannairbhūtāni balikarmaṇā // 56 //

56. By studying Śāstras and Vedas, we pay due respect to the seers; through Agnihotra, we do Devapūjā [take care of the environment], through śṛāddha [taking care of elders with a positive attitude] we show respect to the elderly persons in the family, by providing food, we pay respect to the visiting scholars and saṁnyāsīs, and the by distributing and scattering food on ground, we take care of poor and animals.

कुर्यादहरहः[1] श्राद्धमन्नाद्येनोदकेन वा ।
पयोमूलफलैर्वाऽपि पितृभ्यः प्रीतिमावहन् ॥ 57 ॥

---

[1] दद्यादहरहः

kuryādaharahaḥ śrāddhamannādyenodakena vā /
payomūlaphalairvā'pi pitṛbhyaḥ prītimāvahan // 57 //

57. A person should provide [pitṛbhyaḥ] elderly members of the family and community with food, drinkable water, milk, roots, and fruits [prītimāvahan] affectionately each day, to keep them happy.

वैश्वदेवस्य सिद्धस्य गृह्येऽग्नौ विधिपूर्वकम् ।
आभ्यः कुर्याद् देवताभ्यो ब्राह्मणो होममन्वहम् ॥ 58 ॥

vaiśvadevasya siddhasya gṛhye'gnau vidhipūrvakam /
ābhyaḥ kuryād devatābhyo brāhmaṇo homamanvaham 58

58. An educated person shall duly offer an oblation of portion of the [siddhasya] cooked food [gṛhye agnau] prepared in the kitchen [viśvadevasya] for the poor and animals to [ābhyaḥ devatābhyaḥ] the following deities:

अग्नेः सोमस्य चैवादौ तयोश्चैव समस्तयोः ।
विश्वेभ्यश्चैव देवेभ्यो धन्वन्तरय एव च ॥ 59 ॥

agneḥ somasya chaivādau tayośchaiva samastayoḥ /
viśvebhyaśchaiva devebhyo dhanvantaraya ēva cha // 59 //

59. First oblation to Agni, and (next) to Soma, then to both these deities conjointly, further to Viśvedevāḥ, and then to Dhanvantari chanting mantras addressed to them. For instance,

ओं अग्नये स्वाहा।

ओं सोमाय स्वाहा।

ओम् अग्नीषोमाभ्यां स्वाहा।

ओं विश्वेभ्यः देवेभ्यः स्वाहा।

कुह्वै चैवानुमत्यै च प्रजापतय एव च ।
सह द्यावापृथिव्योश्च तथा स्विष्टकृतेऽन्ततः ॥ 60 ॥

kuhvai chaivānumatyai cha prajāpataya ēva cha /
saha dyāvāpṛthivyoścha tathā sviṣṭakṛte'ntataḥ // 60 //

60. Further to Kuhu (the new-moon day), to Anumati (the full-moon day), to Prajāpati (galaxy), to Dyau loka (sun) and Pṛthivī loka (earth) conjointly, and finally to Sviṣṭakṛt (for fullfilment of desire) chanting mantras concerned with them.

For instance,

ओं कुह्वै स्वाहा।

ओम् अनुमत्यै स्वाहा।

ओं प्रजापतये स्वाहा।

ओं द्यावा-पृथिवीभ्यां स्वाहा।

ओं स्विष्टकृते स्वाहा।

एवं सम्यग् हविर्हुत्वा सर्वदिक्षु प्रदक्षिणम् ।
इन्द्रान्तकाप्पतीन्दुभ्यः सानुगेभ्यो बलिं हरेत् ॥ 61 ॥

ēvaṁ samyag havirhutvā sarvadikṣu pradakṣiṇam /
indrāntakāppatīndubhyaḥ sānugebhyo baliṁ haret // 61 //

61. After offering the oblations duly, place food for animals in all directions from the right (east) to the left (south), chanting mantras addressed to deities: [indra+antaka+appapati+indubhyaḥ] Indra, Yama, Varuṇa, and Soma with their concerned mantras [sānugebhyaḥ] prefixed with 'sānuga'. The mantras are as under:

ओं सानुगायेन्द्राय नमः। In the east direction

ओं सानुगाय यमाय नमः। In the south direction

ओं सानुगायवरुणाय नमः। In the west direction

ओं सानुगाय सोमाय नमः। In the north direction

मरुद्भ्य इति तु द्वारि क्षिपेदप्स्वद्भ्य इत्यपि ।
वनस्पतिभ्य इत्येवं मुसलोलूखले हरेत् ॥ 62 ॥

marudbhya iti tu dvāri kṣipedapsvadbhya ityapi /
vanaspatibhya ityevaṁ musalolūkhale haret // 62 //

62. Chanting mantra of Maruts, place some near the door; and put (some) in water, chanting mantra addressed to Adbhyaḥ; place some near the pestle and the mortar with mantra addressed to Vanaspati. For instance,

ओं मरुदभ्यो नमः। Place near door

ओम् अदम्यो नमः। Put in water

ओं वनस्पतिभ्यो नमः। Place near the pestle and the mortar

उच्छीर्षके श्रियै कुर्याद् भद्रकाल्यै च पादतः ।
ब्रह्मवास्तोष्पतिभ्यां तु वास्तुमध्ये बलिं हरेत् ॥ 63 ॥

uchchhīrṣake śriyai kuryād bhadrakālyai cha pādataḥ /
brahmavāstoṣpatibhyāṁ tu vāstumadhye baliṁ haret // 63 //

63. By chanting mantra ओं श्रियै नमः, place food in the northeast direction; by ओं भद्रकाल्यै नमः, in the southwest direction; by chanting ओं ब्रह्मपतये नमः, ओं वास्तोष्पतये नमः place food in the centre of the outer area of house.

विश्वेभ्यश्चैव देवेभ्यो बलिमाकाश उत्क्षिपेत् ।
दिवाचरेभ्यो भूतेभ्यो नक्तञ्चारिभ्य एव च ॥ 64 ॥

viśvebhyaśchaiva devebhyo balimākāśa utkṣipet /
divācharebhyo bhūtebhyo naktañchāribhya ēva cha // 64 //

64. Let him place food on the roof of the house in open sky by chanting mantras ओं विश्वेभ्यः देवेभ्यः नमः for birds; by chanting ओं दिवाचरेभ्यो भूतेभ्यः for creatures roaming about by day; and by ओं नक्तंचारिम्यो भूतेभ्यो नमः for creatures roaming at night.

पृष्ठवास्तुनि कुर्वीत बलिं सर्वात्मभूतये[1] ।
पितृभ्यो बलिशेषं तु सर्वं दक्षिणतो हरेत् ॥ 65 ॥

pṛṣṭhavāstuni kurvīta baliṁ sarvātmabhūtaye /
pitṛbhyo baliśeṣaṁ tu sarvaṁ dakṣiṇato haret // 65 //

65. In the backyard of the house let him place a portion of food for [sarvātmabhūtaye] Brahman, omnipresent in all creatures, by chanting a mantra ओं सर्वात्मभूतये नमः. The remaining food should be served to [pitṛbhyaḥ] the elderly persons present in the southern part of the house by chanting a mantra ओं पितृभ्यः स्वधायिभ्यः स्वधा नमः ।

शूनां च पतितानां च श्वपचां पापरोगिणाम् ।
वयसानां[2] कृमीणां च शनकैर्निर्वपेद् भुवि ॥ 66 ॥

śūnāṁ cha patitānāṁ cha śvapachāṁ pāparogiṇām /
vayasānāṁ kṛmīṇāṁ cha śanakairnirvaped bhuvi // 66 //

---

[1] सर्वान्नभूतये

[2] वयसां च

66. Let one [śanakaiḥ] gently [nirvipet] place [bhuvi] on the ground (some portion of food) for dogs, [patitānām] those fallen from the vow of Brahmacharya, [śvapachām] dog-keepers or dog-feeders, [pāparogiṇām] those afflicted with diseases developed due to the pāpakarmas of the previous life, [vayasānām] birds and [kṛmīṇām] insects like ants.

कृत्वैतद् बलिकर्मैवमतिथिं पूर्वमाशयेत् ।
भिक्षां च भिक्षवे दद्याद् विधिवद् ब्रह्मचारिणे ॥ 67 ॥

kṛtvaitad balikarmaivamatithiṁ pūrvamāśayet /
bhikṣāṁ cha bhikṣave dadyād vidhivad brahmachāriṇe //67

67. After performing this Balivaiśvadeva yajña, one should first serve food to a visiting scholar or saṁnyāsī, and then provide alms in a proper manner to a student.

वैश्वदेवे तु निर्वृत्ते यद्यन्योऽतिथिराव्रजेत् ।
तस्याप्यन्नं यथाशक्ति प्रदद्यान्न बलिं हरेत् ॥ 68 ॥

vaiśvadeve tu nirvṛtte yadyanyo'tithirāvrajet /
tasyāpyannaṁ yathāśakti pradadyānna baliṁ haret // 68 //

68. Nonetheless, if another guest arrives after the Vaiśvadeva offering has been completed, the householder must provide him food according to his means, but he should not repeat the Bali offering by placing a portion of food at different locations.

सम्प्राप्ताय त्वतिथये प्रदद्यादासनौदके ।
अन्नं चैव यथाशक्ति सत्कृत्य विधिपूर्वकम् ॥ 69 ॥

samprāptāya tvatithaye pradadyādāsanaudake /
annaṁ chaiva yathāśakti satkṛtya vidhipūrvakam // 69 //

69. An individual should offer, in an appropriate manner, a seat, water, and food to a visiting scholar or saṁnyāsī who has come voluntarily, according to one's ability.

तृणानि भूमिरुदकं वाक् चतुर्थी च सूनृता ।
एतान्यपि सतां गेहे नोच्छिद्यन्ते कदा चन ॥ 70 ॥

tṛṇāni bhūmirudakaṁ vāk chaturthī cha sūnṛtā /
ētānyapi satāṁ gehe nochchhidyante kadā chana // 70 //

70. Mats for seating, room (for resting), water, and fourthly

a kind word; these (things) never fail in the homes of good men.

एकरात्रं तु निवसन्नतिथिर्ब्राह्मणः स्मृतः ।
अनित्यं हि स्थितो यस्मात् तस्मादतिथिरुच्यते ॥ 71 ॥

ēkarātraṁ tu nivasannatithirbrāhmaṇaḥ smṛtaḥ /
anityaṁ hi sthito yasmāt tasmādatithiruchyate // 71 //

71. But a scholar or saṁnyāsī who stays one night only is called a visitor; because his arrival and departure are not [anityam] fixed, he is called atithi (visitor).

नैकग्रामीणमतिथिं विप्रं साङ्गतिकं तथा ।
उपस्थितं गृहे विद्याद् भार्या यत्राग्नयोऽपि वा ॥ 72 ॥

naikagrāmīṇamatithiṁ vipraṁ sāṅgatikaṁ tathā /
upasthitaṁ gṛhe vidyād bhāryā yatrāgnayo'pi vā // 72 //

72. One must not regard [vipram] a scholar who [ekagrāmiṇam] dwells in the same village, nor [sāṅgatikam] a friend who is married and performs five great yajñas, [atithim] as a visitor when they arrive at a household.

उपासते ये गृहस्थाः परपाकमबुद्धयः ।
तेन ते प्रेत्य पशुतां व्रजन्त्यन्नादिदायिनः ॥ 73 ॥

upāsate ye gṛhasthāḥ parapākamabuddhayaḥ /
tena te pretya paśutāṁ vrajantyannādidāyinaḥ // 73 //

73. Those foolish Gṛhasthis (householders) who constantly seek to live on the food of others, in consequence, after death, become animals in the house of those who give them food.

अप्रणोद्योऽतिथिः सायं सूर्यौढो गृहमेधिना ।
काले प्राप्तस्त्वकाले वा नास्यानश्नन् गृहे वसेत् ॥ 74 ॥

apraṇodyo'tithiḥ sāyaṁ sūryauḍho gṛhamedhinā /
kāle prāptastvakāle vā nāsyānaśnan gṛhe vaset // 74 //

74. [gṛhamedhinā] A householder must ensure that a [atithiḥ] scholar or saṁnyāsī (renunciant) who arrives at the house [sūroḍhaḥ] after sunset should not be [apraṇodya] turned away. Additionally, the visitor must not leave without being offered food, regardless of whether they arrive at an appropriate

or inconvenient time.

न वै स्वयं तदश्नीयादतिथिं यन्न भोजयेत् ।
धन्यं यशस्यमायुष्यं स्वर्ग्यं वाऽतिथिपूजनम् ॥ 75 ॥

na vai svayaṁ tadaśnīyādatithiṁ yanna bhojayet /
dhanyaṁ yaśasyamāyuṣyaṁ svargyaṁ vā'tithipūjanam //75

75. Householders should not eat any food that they do not offer to their Atithis [visiting scholars and renunciates). Welcoming atithis, brings wealth, fame, long life, and spiritual happiness.

इतरानपि सख्यादीन् सम्प्रीत्या गृहमागतान् ।
प्रकृत्यान्नं यथाशक्ति भोजयेत् सह भार्यया ॥ 76 ॥

itarānapi sakhyādīn samprītyā gṛhamāgatān /
prakṛtyānnaṁ yathāśakti bhojayet saha bhāryayā // 76 //

76. He may provide food to personal friends and their wives who visit his house out of affection, according to his means.

सुवासिनीः कुमारीश्च रोगिणो गर्भिणीः स्त्रियः ।
अतिथिभ्योऽग्र एवैतान्[1] भोजयेदविचारयन् ॥ 77 ॥

suvāsinīḥ kumārīścha rogiṇo garbhiṇīḥ striyaḥ /
atithibhyo'gra ēvaitān bhojayedavichārayan // 77 //

77. He may give food without hesitation to the following persons: newly-married women, infants, the sick, and pregnant women, even before his venerable atithis.

भुक्तवत्स्वथ विप्रेषु स्वेषु भृत्येषु चैव हि ।
भुञ्जीयातां ततः पश्चादवशिष्टं तु दम्पती ॥ 78 ॥
bhuktavatsvatha vipreṣu sveṣu bhṛtyeṣu chaiva hi /
bhuñjīyātāṁ tataḥ paśchādavaśiṣṭaṁ tu dampatī // 78 //

78. After the scholars, renunciates, kinsmen, and servants have dined, the householder and his wife may eat what remains.

अघं स केवलं भुङ्क्ते यः पचत्यात्मकारणात् ।
यज्ञशिष्टाशनं ह्येतत् सतामन्नं विधीयते ॥ 79 ॥
aghaṁ sa kevalaṁ bhuṅkte yaḥ pachatyātmakāraṇāt /

---

1 अतिथिभ्योऽन्वगेवैतान्

yajñaśiṣṭāśanaṁ hyetat satāmannaṁ vidhīyate // *79* //

79. He who prepares food only for himself eats nothing but [pāpa] sin; for it is ordained that a gentleman should eat after performing five great yajñas.

विघसाशी भवेन्नित्यं नित्यं वाऽमृतभोजनः ।
विघसो भुक्तशेषं तु यज्ञशेषं तथाऽमृतम् ॥ 80 ॥

vighasāśī bhavennityaṁ nityaṁ vā'mṛtabhojanaḥ /
vighaso bhuktaśeṣaṁ tu yajñaśeṣaṁ tathā'mṛtam // *80* //

80. Let him partake daily of the [vighasa] Vighas food (what remains after it has been consumed by elderly members of the family, visiting scholars, or renunciates) and [amrita] amṛta food (what is consumed after performing yajñās). Vighasa refers to the food that remains after serving these respected individuals, while amrita is what we eat after conducting yajñas.

एतद् वोऽभिहितं सर्वं विधानं पाञ्चयज्ञिकम् ।
द्विजातिमुख्यवृत्तीनां विधानं श्रूयतामिति ॥ 81 ॥

ētad vo'bhihitaṁ sarvaṁ vidhānaṁ pāñchayajñikam /
dvijātimukhyavṛttīnāṁ vidhānaṁ śrūyatāmiti // *81* //

81. All ordinances regarding the 'Five Great Yajñas' have been declared to you. Now, listen to the law concerning the primary duties and means of livelihood suitable for educated householders.

Chapter 4: Duties of Householders and Suitable Means of Livelihood

The fourth chapter discusses the appropriate lifestyle for educated persons. Manu outlines the responsibilities of a householder. An educated householder should consistently perform the Agnihotra at sunrise and sunset, as Agni is seen as the bridge between humans and the divine. When offerings (havya) are made to Agni, they reach Lord Indra and please him.

Scholars are advised not to accept gifts from those who derive their livelihood from immoral sources. Additionally, a scholar should practice generosity through yajñas and charitable works according to his means, provided there are deserving recipients.

At the conclusion of this chapter, Manu emphasizes the importance of meditation. He encourages educated persons to reflect on what is beneficial for their souls, stating that those who meditate in solitude can achieve supreme bliss. Therefore, Manu has laid out guidelines for how an educated householder should live and sustain himself.

The Age of Gṛhasthāśrama (Household Life)

चतुर्थमायुषो भागमुषित्वाऽद्यं गुरौ द्विजाः ।
द्वितीयमायुषो भागं कृतदारो गृहे वसेत् ॥1॥

chaturthamāyuṣo bhāgamuṣitvā'dyaṁ gurau dvijāḥ |
dvitīyamāyuṣo bhāgaṁ kṛtadāro gṛhe vaset ||1||

1. After spending the quarter part of life (first 25 years of life) with a teacher, a student will live in his own home during the second quarter of the next 25 years (from age 25 to 50) after marrying a wife.

Note: The statement above suggests that Manu believes the average human lifespan is 100 years. After graduating, a student is considered dvija, or "twice-born," which signifies that they have received an education. Every educated individual experiences two forms of birth: the biological birth that occurs in the mother's womb and the spiritual birth that takes place during their education under a teacher. Therefore, the term "dvija" in the Manusmṛti is used to refer to educated individuals.

Rules for Earning livelyhood

अद्रोहेणैव भूतानामल्पद्रोहेण वा पुनः ।
या वृत्तिस्तां समास्थाय विप्रो जीवेदनापदि ॥2॥

adroheṇaiva bhūtānāmalpadroheṇa vā punaḥ ।
yā vṛttistāṁ samāsthāya vipro jīvedanāpadi ॥2॥

2. [vipraḥ] A scholar must [smāsthāya] seek a means of [vṛttiḥ] subsistence which either causes no or at least little pain to the creatures or fellow beings and live by that except in emergent circumstances.

Purpose of accumulation of Wealth

यात्रामात्रप्रसिद्ध्यर्थं स्वैः कर्मभिरगर्हितैः ।
अक्लेशेन शरीरस्य कुर्वीत धनसञ्चयम् ॥3॥

yātrāmātraprasiddhyarthaṁ svaiḥ karmabhiragarhitaiḥ ।
akleśena śarīrasya kurvīta dhanasañchayam ॥3॥

3. For the purpose of basic life maintenance, let a gṛhastha accumulate wealth by engaging in irreproachable occupations that do not cause unnecessary harm to the body.

सन्तोषं परमास्थाय सुखार्थी संयतो भवेत् ।
सन्तोषमूलं हि सुखं दुःखमूलं विपर्ययः ॥4॥

santoṣaṁ paramāsthāya sukhārthī saṁyato bhavet ।
santoṣamūlaṁ hi sukhaṁ duḥkhamūlaṁ viparyayaḥ ॥4॥

4. To achieve happiness, one must practice contentment and avoid obsessing over wealth, as true happiness is rooted in contentment, while the desire for money leads to unhappiness.

Dos and Don'ts for a Gṛhasthī (Householder)

अतोऽन्यतमया वृत्त्या जीवंस्तु स्नातको द्विजः ।
स्वर्गायुष्ययशस्यानि व्रताणीमानि धारयेत् ॥5॥

ato'nyatamayā vṛttyā jīvaṁstu snātako dvijaḥ ।

svargāyuṣyayaśasyāni vratāṇīmāni dhārayet //5 //

5. An educated gṛhastha, living by the prescribed means of livelihood (professions), must observe the following vows securing spiritual bliss, long life, and fame.

वेदोदितं स्वकं कर्म नित्यं कुर्यादतन्द्रितः ।
तद् हि कुर्वन् यथाशक्ति प्राप्नोति परमां गतिम् ॥6॥

vedoditaṁ svakaṁ karma nityaṁ kuryādatandritaḥ /
tad hi kurvan yathāśakti prāpnoti paramāṁ gatim //6 //

6. Let a gṛhasthi (householder) carry out the nitya karmas prescribed for him in the Veda without exhaustion; for he who performs these according to his capacity achieves the highest state (mokṣa).

नैहेतार्थान् प्रसङ्गेन न विरुद्धेन कर्मणा ।
न विद्यमानेष्वर्थेषु[1] नार्त्यामपि यतस्ततः ॥7॥

naihetārthān prasaṅgena na viruddhena karmaṇā /
na vidyamāneṣvartheṣu nārtyāmapi yatastataḥ //7 //

7. Whether he be rich or even in distress, let him not [Īhet] seek [arthān] wealth [prasaṅena] through addicted activities like singing, music, and dancing, nor by contrary acts (prohibited activities), nor especially [vidyamāneṣu artheṣu] when sufficient means of living already exist.

Note: Medhātithi defines prasaṅga as activities that people become addicted to, such as singing, music, and dancing.

इन्द्रियार्थेषु सर्वेषु न प्रसज्येत कामतः ।
अतिप्रसक्तिं चैतेषां मनसा संनिवर्तयेत् ॥8॥

indriyārtheṣu sarveṣu na prasajyeta kāmataḥ /
atiprasaktiṁ chaiteṣāṁ manasā saṁnivartayet //8 //

8. Let a gṛhasthī not attach himself to any sensory objects due to a desire for enjoyment, and let him carefully avoid excessive attachment to them, if present.

सर्वान् परित्यजेदर्थान् स्वाध्यायस्य विरोधिनः ।

---

[1] कल्पमानेष्वर्थेषु

यथा तथाऽध्यापयंस्तु सा ह्यस्य कृतकृत्यता ॥9॥

sarvān parityajedarthān svādhyāyasya virodhinaḥ ।
yathā tathā'dhyāpayaṁstu sā hyasya kṛtakṛtyatā ॥9॥

9. Let a householder avoid all means of acquiring wealth that hinder the study (of the Veda and other Śāstras); let him find time in any way for the study (teaching oneself), for that pursuit brings him luck.

बुद्धिवृद्धिकराण्याशु धन्यानि च हितानि च ।
नित्यं शास्त्राण्यवेक्षेत निगमांश्चैव वैदिकान् ॥10॥

buddhivṛddhikarāṇyāśu dhanyāni cha hitāni cha ।
nityaṁ śāstrāṇyavekṣeta nigamāṁśchaiva vaidikān ॥10॥

10. He should refer daily to the Śāstras (scientifically explained texts) that enhance wisdom, promote both spiritual and material prosperity, and are beneficial for his personal growth. He should also study the Nigamas that explain the Vedas.

यथा यथा हि पुरुषः शास्त्रं समधिगच्छति ।
तथा तथा विजानाति विज्ञानं चास्य रोचते ॥11॥

yathā yathā hi puruṣaḥ śāstraṁ samadhigachchhati ।
tathā tathā vijānāti vijñānaṁ chāsya rochate ॥11॥

11. As a human being studies Śāstras (scientifically explained treatises), he begins to understand them more deeply and develops an interest in scientific topics and spiritual practices.

Pañcha-Mahāyajñas

ऋषियज्ञं देवयज्ञं भूतयज्ञं च सर्वदा ।
नृयज्ञं पितृयज्ञं च यथाशक्ति न हापयेत् ॥12॥

ṛṣiyajñaṁ devayajñaṁ bhūtayajñaṁ cha sarvadā ।
nṛyajñaṁ pitṛyajñaṁ cha yathāśakti na hāpayet ॥12॥

12. He should never neglect the following duties if he can perform them:

1. Ṛṣiyajña (the study of Śastras)

2. Devayajña (performing Agnihotra)

3. Bhūtayajña (caring for the poor and feeding animals)

4. Nṛyajña (hosting visiting Vedic scholars and renunciates)

5. Pitṛyajña (taking care of elder members of the family and community).

Agnihotra and Darśa-Pūrṇamāsa

अग्निहोत्रं च जुहुयादाद्यन्ते द्युनिशोः सदा ।
दर्शेन चार्धमासान्ते पौर्णमासेन चैव हि ॥13 ॥

agnihotraṁ cha juhuyādādyante dyuniśoḥ sadā /
darśena chārdhamāsānte paurṇamāsena chaiva hi //13 //

13. A gṛhasthī (householder) should always perform the Agnihotra at the beginning or at the end of the day and night, and the Darśa (New Moon) and Paurṇamāsa (Full Moon) yajñas (iṣṭis) at the end of each half-month.

New Harvest (Navasasyeśṭi) Yajña

सस्यान्ते नवसस्येष्ट्या तथार्त्वन्ते द्विजोऽध्वरैः ।
पशुना त्वयनस्यादौ समान्ते[1] सौमिकैर्मखैः ॥14 ॥

sasyānte navasasyeṣṭyā tathārtvante dvijo'dhvaraiḥ /
paśunā tvayanasyādau samānte saumikairmakhaiḥ //14 //

14. At the end of the previous crop, an educated Gṛhasthī should perform Navasasyeṣṭi (New-Harvest yajña) with the grain of the new crop. (Holi and Deepawali are examples of Navasasyeṣṭis in India); at the end of the (three) seasons [adhvara] the Chāturmāsya yajña should be performed; at the beginning of Ayanas (Soltices), [paśuyajña] solar and geothermal energy harnessing jobs should be done, e.g. at the beginning of Uttarāyaṇa (21 March), Aśvamedha yāga (solar energy harnessing job) should be initiated which will persist till 22 Septermber and at the beginning of Dakṣiṇāyaṇa (23 Sept.), Gomedha yāga (geothermal energy harvesting job) should be

[1] यनान्ते तु समान्ते

initiated which will persist till 21 March; and at the end of the year [saumikhaiḥ makhaiḥ] Soma-yāgas like Agniṣṭoma yāgas should be conducted.

Note: For more details of Paśuyāgas and Somayāgas, refer to the present author's books 'Science of Śrauta Yāgas' and 'Energy in the Vedas'.

Hosting Vedic Scholars and Renunciates (Atithi-yajña)

आसनाशनशय्याभिरद्भिर्मूलफलेन वा ।
नास्य कश्चिद् वसेद् गेहे शक्तितोऽनर्चितोऽतिथिः ॥15 ॥

āsanāśanaśayyābhiradbhirmūlaphalena vā /
nāsya kaśchid vased gehe śaktito'narchito'tithiḥ //15 //

15. No visiting Vedic scholar or Saṁnyāsī (renunciate) must stay in gṛhasthī's house without being honoured, to the best of his ability, with a seat, food, a bed, water, or roots and fruits.

पाषण्डिनो विकर्मस्थान् बैडालव्रतिकान् शठान् ।
हैतुकान् बकवृत्तींश्च वाङ्मात्रेणापि नार्चयेत् ॥16 ॥

pāṣaṇḍino vikarmasthān baiḍālavratikān śaṭhān /
haitukān bakavṛttīṁścha vāṅmātreṇāpi nārchayet //16 //

16. Let him not honour, even by a greeting, those [pāṣaṇḍinaḥ] who have recourse to such life conditions as are opposed to the Vedas and Śāstras, who [vikarmasthāna] perform activities prohibited in the Śāstras, men who behave like cats, rogues, [haitukān] who raise doubts about everything and those who behave like herons.

वेदविद्याव्रतस्नातांश्रोत्रियान् गृहमेधिनः ।
पूजयेद् हव्यकव्येन विपरीतांश्च वर्जयेत् ॥17 ॥

vedavidyāvratasnātāṁśrotriyān gṛhamedhinaḥ /
pūjayed havyakavyena viparītāṁścha varjayet //17 //

17. Those who have completed their graduation after fulfilling their commitment to studying the Vedas, who are householders, and who are Śrotriyas (scholars well-versed in the four Vedas) should be honoured by offering them [havyas]—food that can be prepared as an oblation for the yajña fire—as well as [kavyas]—gifts that are appropriate for kavis (scholars);

and must avoid those who are different.

शक्तितोऽपचमानेभ्यो दातव्यं गृहमेधिना ।
संविभागश्च भूतेभ्यः कर्तव्योऽनुपरोधतः ॥18 ॥

śaktito'pachamānebhyo dātavyaṁ gṛhamedhinā ।
saṁvibhāgaścha bhūtebhyaḥ kartavyo'nuparodhataḥ ॥*18* ॥

18. [gṛhamedhinā] A householder should provide as much food as they can spare to those who are unable to cook for themselves, such as brahmachārīs and saṁnyāsīs. Additionally, [saṁvibhāgaḥ bhūtebhyaḥ kartavyaḥ] they should distribute any other surplus items to those in need, [anuparodhataḥ] ensuring that their own family does not suffer as a result.

Note: Manu uses the term 'gṛhamedhī' to refer to a householder. The literal meaning of 'gṛhamedhī' is an individual who performs the 'gṛhamedha yāga' through marriage.

Maintenance of Personal Hygiene

क्लृप्तकेशनखश्मश्रुर्दान्तः शुक्लाम्बरः शुचिः ।
स्वाध्याये चैव युक्तः स्यान्नित्यमात्महितेषु च ॥19 ॥

kḷptakeśanakhaśmaśrurdāntaḥ śuklāmbaraḥ śuchiḥ ।
svādhyāye chaiva yuktaḥ syānnityamātmahiteṣu cha ॥*19* ॥

19. To maintain his well-being, he should keep his hair, nails, and beard neatly trimmed. He should control his desires through discipline, wear white garments, and stay pure. Additionally, he should engage in the study of the Veda and other Śāstras, and consistently participate in actions that contribute to his welfare.

नेक्षेतोद्यन्तमादित्यं नास्तं यान्तं कदा चन ।
नोपसृष्टं न वारिस्थं न मध्यं नभसो गतम् ॥20 ॥

nekṣetodyantamādityaṁ nāstaṁ yāntaṁ kadā chana ।
nopasṛṣṭaṁ na vāristhaṁ na madhyaṁ nabhaso gatam ॥*20*

20. He should never gaze at the sun during an eclipse, whether it is rising, setting, reflected in water, or positioned high in the sky.

नोपगच्छेत् प्रमत्तोऽपि स्त्रियमार्तवदर्शने ।
समानशयने चैव न शयीत तया सह ॥21॥

nopagachchhet pramatto'pi striyamārtavadarśane /
samānaśayane chaiva na śayīta tayā saha //21//

21. Although he has an irresistible urge, let him not approach his wife during her menstrual period, nor should he sleep in the same bed with her.

रजसाऽभिप्लुतां नारीं नरस्य ह्युपगच्छतः ।
प्रज्ञा तेजो बलं चक्षुरायुश्चैव प्रहीयते ॥22॥

rajasā'bhiplutāṁ nārīṁ narasya hyupagachchhataḥ /
prajñā tejo balaṁ chakṣurāyuśchaiva prahīyate //22//

22. For the wisdom, energy, strength, sight, and vitality of a man, approaching a woman covered with menstrual excretions, utterly perish.

तां विवर्जयतस्तस्य रजसा समभिप्लुताम् ।
प्रज्ञा तेजो बलं चक्षुरायुश्चैव प्रवर्धते ॥23॥

tāṁ vivarjayatastasya rajasā samabhiplutām /
prajñā tejo balaṁ chakṣurāyuśchaiva pravardhate //23//

23. If he avoids her during that time, his wisdom, energy, strength, sight, and vitality will increase.

नाञ्जयन्तीं स्वके नेत्रे न चाभ्यक्तामनावृताम् ।
न पश्येत् प्रसवन्तीं च तेजस्कामो द्विजोत्तमः ॥24॥

nāñjayantīṁ svake netre na chābhyaktāmanāvṛtām /
na paśyet prasavantīṁ cha tejaskāmo dvijottamaḥ //24//

24. An wise person who desires energy must not look at a woman applying a collyrium to her eyes, anointing herself uncovered or bringing forth (a child).

नान्नमद्यादेकवासा न नग्नः स्नानमाचरेत् ।
न मूत्रं पथि कुर्वीत न भस्मनि न गोव्रजे ॥25॥

nānnamadyādekavāsā na nagnaḥ snānamācharet /
na mūtraṁ pathi kurvīta na bhasmani na govraje //25//

25. Let him not eat, dressed with one garment only; let him not bathe naked; let him not void urine on a road, on ashes, or

in a cow-pen,

न फालकृष्टे न जले न चित्यां न च पर्वते ।
न जीर्णदेवायतने न वल्मीके कदा चन ॥26॥

na phālakṛṣṭe na jale na chityāṁ na cha parvate ।
na jīrṇadevāyatane na valmīke kadā chana ॥26॥

26. Nor on ploughed land, in water, on an altar of bricks, on a mountain, on the ruins of a temple, nor ever on an ant-hill,

न ससत्त्वेषु गर्तेषु न गच्छन्नपि न स्थितः ।
न नदीतीरमासाद्य न च पर्वतमस्तके ॥27॥

na sasattveṣu garteṣu na gachchhannapi na sthitaḥ ।
na nadītīramāsādya na cha parvatamastake ॥27॥

27. Nor in holes inhabited by living creatures, nor while he walks or stands, nor on reaching the bank of a river, nor on the top of a mountain.

तिरस्कृत्योच्चरेत् काष्ठलोष्ठपत्रतृणादिना[1] ।
नियम्य प्रयतो वाचं संवीताङ्गोऽवगुण्ठितः ॥28॥

tiraskṛtyochcharet kāṣṭhaloṣṭhapatratṛṇādinā ।
niyamya prayato vāchaṁ saṁvītāṅgo'vaguṇṭhitaḥ ॥28॥

28. He may position himself in a place covered with sticks, clods, leaves, grass, and similar materials, restraining his speech, wrapping up his body, and covering himself.

नाप्सु मूत्रं पुरीषं वा ष्ठीवनं वा समुत्सृजेत् ।
अमेध्यलिप्तमन्यद् वा लोहितं वा विषाणि वा ॥29॥

nāpsu mūtraṁ purīṣaṁ vā ṣṭhīvanaṁ vā samutsṛjet ।
amedhyaliptamanyad vā lohitaṁ vā viṣāṇi vā ॥29॥

29. Let him not discharge into water urine or faeces, or saliva, or anything contaminated by impure things, or blood, or poison or poisonous things.

नाधर्मिके वसेद् ग्रामे न व्याधिबहुले भृशम् ।

---

[1] तृणादि च

नैकः प्रपद्येताध्वानं न चिरं पर्वते वसेत् ॥30॥

nādharmike vased grāme na vyādhibahule bhṛśaṁ ।
naikaḥ prapadyetādhvānaṁ na chiraṁ parvate vaset ॥30॥

30. Do not dwell in a place where dharma is ignored, nor stay long where diseases are common; do not travel alone, nor remain for an extended time on a mountain.

न शूद्रराज्ये निवसेन्नाधार्मिकजनावृते ।
न पाषण्डिगणाक्रान्ते नोपस्सृटेऽन्त्यजैर्नृभिः ॥31॥

na śūdrarājye nivasennādhārmikajanāvṛte ।
na pāṣaṇḍigaṇākrānte nopassṛṭe'ntyajairnṛbhiḥ ॥31॥

31. Let him not dwell in a country where the rulers are uneducated, in one surrounded by unrighteous men, in one inhabited by those not following Vedas, nor in one swarming with men of mean acts.

न भुञ्जीतोद्धृतस्नेहं नातिसौहित्यमाचरेत् ।
नातिप्रगे नातिसायं न सायं प्रातराशितः ॥32॥

na bhuñjītoddhṛtasnehaṁ nātisauhityamācharet ।
nātiprage nātisāyaṁ na sāyaṁ prātarāśitaḥ ॥32॥

32. He should avoid [bhuñjīta+uddṛta+sneham] eating anything from which the oil has been extracted. He should not [atisauhityam] overeat, nor should he eat [atiprage] too early in the morning or [atisāyam] too late in the evening. Additionally, if he has overeaten in the morning, he should refrain from eating in the evening.

न कुर्वीत वृथाचेष्टां न वार्यञ्जलिना पिबेत् ।
नोत्सङ्गे भक्षयेद् भक्ष्यान्न जातु स्यात् कुतूहली ॥33॥

na kurvīta vṛthācheṣṭāṁ na vāryañjalinā pibet ।
notsaṅge bhakṣayed bhakṣayānna jātu syāt kutūhalī ॥33॥

33. Let him not exert himself without purpose; let him not drink water from his joined palms; let him not eat food placed in his lap; let him never be overly curious.

न नृत्येदथ वा गायेन्न वादित्राणि वादयेत्[1]।
नास्फोटयेन्न च क्ष्वेडेन्न च रक्तो विरावयेत्[2] ॥34॥

na nṛtyedatha vā gāyenna vāditrāṇi vādayet ।
nāsphoṭayenna cha kṣaveḍenna cha rakto virāvayet ॥34॥

34. Let him avoid dancing, singing, playing musical instruments, or making excessive noises due to attachment.

न पादौ धावयेत् कांस्ये कदा चिदपि भाजने ।
न भिन्नभाण्डे भुञ्जीत न भावप्रतिदूषिते ॥35॥

na pādau dhāvayet kāṁsye kadā chidapi bhājane ।
na bhinnabhāṇḍe bhuñjīta na bhāvapratidūṣite ॥35॥

35. He should never wash his feet in a white brass vessel; he should not eat from a broken earthen dish or from a vessel he dislikes.

उपानहौ च वासश्च धृतमन्यैर्न धारयेत् ।
उपवीतमलङ्कारं स्रजं करकमेव च ॥36॥

upānahau cha vāsaścha dhṛtamanyairna dhārayet ।
upavītamalaṅkāraṁ srajaṁ karakameva cha ॥36॥

36. He should not use shoes, clothing, a sacred thread, ornaments, a garland, or a water container that have been used by others.

न विगर्ह्य कथां कुर्याद्[3] बहिर्माल्यं न धारयेत् ।
गवां च यानं पृष्ठेन सर्वथैव विगर्हितम् ॥37॥

na vigarhya kathāṁ kuryād bahirmālyaṁ na dhārayet ।
gavāṁ cha yānaṁ pṛṣṭhena sarvathaiva vigarhitam ॥37॥

37. Let him avoid engaging in contentious conversations and not wear a garland. Riding on the backs of cows or rooftop of vehicles is completely discouraged.

अद्वारेण च नातीयाद् ग्रामं वा वेश्म वाऽवृतम् ।

---

[1] नृत्येन्नैव गायेच्च न वादित्राणि वादयेत्

[2] च रक्तो विरोधयेत्

[3] न विगृह्य कथां कुर्याद्

रात्रौ च वृक्षमूलानि दूरतः परिवर्जयेत् ॥38॥

advāreṇa cha nātīyād grāmaṁ vā veśma vā'vṛtam /
rātrau cha vṛkṣamūlāni dūrataḥ parivarjayet //38//

38. He should not enter a walled village or house except through the gate, and at night, he should stay far away from the bases of trees.

सर्वं च तिलसम्बद्धं नाद्यादस्तमिते रवौ ।
न च नग्नः शयीतैह न चोच्छिष्टः क्व चिद् व्रजेत् ॥39॥

sarvaṁ cha tilasambaddhaṁ nādyādastamite ravau /
na cha nagnaḥ śayītaiha na chochchhiṣṭaḥ kva chid vrajet //

39. Let him not eat after sunset any (food) containing sesamum grains; let him never sleep naked, nor go anywhere with mouth unwashed after meals.

आर्द्रपादस्तु भुञ्जीत नार्द्रपादस्तु संविशेत् ।
आर्द्रपादस्तु भुञ्जानो दीर्घमायुरवाप्नुयात् ॥40॥

ārdrapādastu bhuñjīta nārdrapādastu saṁviśet /
ārdrapādastu bhuñjāno dīrghamāyuravāpnuyāt //40//

40. Let him eat while his feet are still wet from ablution, but he should not go to bed with wet feet. Eating with wet feet, one would attain a long life.

अचक्षुर्विषयं दुर्गं न प्रपद्येत कर्हि चित् ।
न विण्मूत्रमुदीक्षेत न बाहुभ्यां नदीं तरेत् ॥41॥

achakṣurviṣayaṁ durgaṁ na prapadyeta karhi chit /
na viṇmūtramudīkṣeta na bāhubhyāṁ nadīṁ taret //41//

41. He must avoid places that are difficult to access and not within his line of sight; he shall not observe [vit+mūtram] urine or feces; nor shall he cross a river while carrying anything in his arms.

अधितिष्ठेन्न केशांस्तु न भस्मास्थिकपालिकाः ।
न कार्पासास्थि न तुषान् दीर्घमायुर्जिजीविषुः ॥42॥

adhitiṣṭhenna keśāṁstu na bhasmāsthikapālikāḥ /
na kārpāsāsthi na tuṣān dīrghamāyurjijīviṣuḥ //42//

42. One desirous of living long shall not step on hair, ashes,

bones, and [kapālikāḥ] potsherds or [kārpāsāsthi] on cotton seed or [tuṣān]chaff.

न संवसेच्च पतितैर्न चाण्डालैर्न पुल्कसैः ।
न मूर्खैर्नावलिप्तैश्च नान्त्यैर्नान्त्यावसायिभिः ॥43 ॥

na saṁvasechcha patitairna chāṇḍālairna pulkasaiḥ /
na mūrkhairnāvaliptaiścha nāntyairnāntyāvasāyibhiḥ //43 //

43. Never [saṁvaset] set friednly relations with those fallen from dharma, Chaṇḍalas, Pulkasas (nomadic people), fools, haughty, mlechchhas and Antyavasāyins (peole with mean objectives).

न संहताभ्यां पाणिभ्यां कण्डूयेदात्मनः शिरः ।
न स्पृशेच्चैतदुच्छिष्टो न च स्नायाद् विना ततः ॥44 ॥

na saṁhatābhyāṁ pāṇibhyāṁ kaṇḍūyedātmanaḥ śiraḥ /
na spṛśechchaitaduchchhiṣṭo na cha snāyād vinā tataḥ //44

44. Do not scratch your head with both hands together; avoid touching it unless your hands are washed, and do not bathe until your head has been washed first.

Note: For taking bath, water should be poured on head first.

केशग्रहान् प्रहारांश्च शिरस्येतान् विवर्जयेत् ।
शिरःस्नातश्च तैलेन नाङ्गं किं चिदपि स्पृशेत् ॥45 ॥

keśagrahān prahārāṁścha śirasyetān vivarjayet /
śiraḥsnātaścha tailena nāṅgaṁ kiṁ chidapi spṛśet //45 //

45. Avoid catching hair and striking the head. If oil has been applied to the head, avoid touching other body parts with the same oily hands.

Routine Duties

ब्राह्मे मुहूर्ते बुध्येत धर्मार्थौ चानुचिन्तयेत् ।
कायक्लेशांश्च तन्मूलान् वेदतत्त्वार्थमेव च ॥46 ॥

brāhme muhūrte budhyeta dharmārthau chānuchintayet /
kāyakleśāṁścha tanmūlān vedatattvārthameva cha //46 //

46. Let him wake in the Brahma Muhurta (one hour 36 minutes before sunrise) and think of dharma and means of acquiring artha (material resources), whether those means are

acquired as per dharma or not; also of the bodily ailments and their causes, and the true meaning of the Veda.

Note: One muhurta is equal to 48 minutes.

उत्थायावश्यकं कृत्वा कृतशौचः समाहितः ।
पूर्वां सन्ध्यां जपंस्तिष्ठेत् स्वकाले चापरां चिरम् ॥47 ॥

utthāyāvaśyakaṁ kṛtvā kṛtaśauchaḥ samāhitaḥ /
pūrvāṁ sandhyāṁ japaṁstiṣṭhet svakāle chāparāṁ chiram

47. After getting out of bed, completing the daily routine, and refreshing himself with a focused mind, he should perform the morning and evening Sandhyā at the appropriate times.

ऋषयो दीर्घसन्ध्यत्वाद् दीर्घमायुरवाप्नुयुः ।
प्रज्ञां यशश्च कीर्तिं च ब्रह्मवर्चसमेव च ॥48 ॥

ṛṣayo dīrghasandhyatvād dīrghamāyuravāpnuyuḥ /
prajñāṁ yaśaścha kīrtiṁ cha brahmavarchasameva cha //

48. Through consistent long practice of Sandhyās, the sages attained longevity, wisdom, respect, fame, and excellence in Vedic knowledge.

Company to be Avoided

वैरिणं नोपसेवेत सहायं चैव वैरिणः ।
अधार्मिकं तस्करं च परस्यैव च योषितम् ॥49 ॥

vairiṇaṁ nopaseveta sahāyaṁ chaiva vairiṇaḥ /
adhārmikaṁ taskaraṁ cha parasyaiva cha yoṣitam //49 //

49. Let him not maintain relationship with an enemy, the friend of an enemy, a wicked person, a thief, or another man's wife.

न हीदृशमनायुष्यं लोके किं चन विद्यते ।
यादृशं पुरुषस्येह परदारोपसेवनम् ॥50 ॥

na hīdṛśamanāyuṣyaṁ loke kiṁ chana vidyate /
yādṛśaṁ puruṣasyeha paradāropasevanam //50 //

50. In this world, nothing is more harmful to a long life than maintaining relationships with another man's wife.

Other Duties

नात्मानमवमन्येत पूर्वाभिरसमृद्धिभिः ।
आ मृत्योः श्रियमन्विच्छेन्नैनां मन्येत दुर्लभाम् ॥51॥

nātmānamavamanyeta pūrvābhirasamṛddhibhiḥ ।
ā mṛtyoḥ śriyamanvichchhennaināṁ manyeta durlabhām ॥

51. He should not look down on himself because of past failures; he must seek fortune until death, without losing hope of achieving it.

सत्यं ब्रूयात् प्रियं ब्रूयान्न ब्रूयात् सत्यमप्रियम् ।
प्रियं च नानृतं ब्रूयादेष धर्मः सनातनः ॥52॥

satyaṁ brūyāt priyaṁ brūyānna brūyāt satyamapriyam ।
priyaṁ cha nānṛtaṁ brūyādeṣa dharmaḥ sanātanaḥ ॥52॥

52. Let him speak what is true, let him speak what is pleasing, let him not speak a displeasing truth, and let him not speak a pleasing falsehood; that is the eternal duty.

भद्रं भद्रमिति ब्रूयाद् भद्रमित्येव वा वदेत् ।
शुष्कवैरं विवादं च न कुर्यात् केन चित् सह ॥53॥

bhadraṁ bhadramiti brūyād bhadramityeva vā vadet ।
śuṣkavairaṁ vivādaṁ cha na kuryāt kena chit saha ॥53॥

53. Always tell what is beneficial, regardless of others' feelings. Avoid unnecessary conflict or disputes with anyone.

हीनाङ्गानतिरिक्ताङ्गान् विद्याहीनान् वयोऽधिकान्[1] ।
रूपद्रविणहीनांश्च[2] जातिहीनांश्च नाक्षिपेत् ॥54॥

hīnāṅgānatiriktāṅgān vidyāhīnān vayo'dhikān ।
rūpadraviṇahīnāṁścha jātihīnāṁścha nākṣipet ॥54॥

54. Do not insult those with extra limbs, those lacking limbs, or the uninformed. Avoid disrespecting the elderly, those without beauty or wealth, and individuals of low birth.

मङ्गलाचारयुक्तः स्यात् प्रयतात्मा जितेन्द्रियः ।

---

1 वयो'अतिगान्

2 रूपद्रव्यहीनांश्च

जपेच्च जुहुयाच्चैव नित्यमग्निमतन्द्रितः ॥55॥

maṅgalāchārayuktaḥ syāt prayatātmā jitendriyaḥ ।
japechcha juhuyāchchaiva nityamagnimatandritaḥ ॥55॥

55. Let him engage in welfare activities, strive for his material and spiritual progress, and control all his sense organs. He should always study the Vedas and Śāstras tirelessly and perform Agnihotra daily.

मङ्गलाचारयुक्तानां नित्यं च प्रयतात्मनाम् ।
जपतां जुह्वतां चैव विनिपातो न विद्यते ॥56॥

maṅgalāchārayuktānāṁ nityaṁ cha prayatātmanām ।
japatāṁ juhvatāṁ chaiva vinipāto na vidyate ॥56॥

56. Those who are engaged in welfare activities, strive for their material and spiritual progress, and control all their senses are never downgraded to lower species.

वेदमेवाभ्यसेन्नित्यं[1] यथाकालमतन्द्रितः ।
तं ह्यस्याहुः परं धर्ममुपधर्मोऽन्य उच्यते ॥57॥

vedamevābhyasennityaṁ yathākālamatandritaḥ ।
taṁ hyasyāhuḥ paraṁ dharmamupadharmo'nya uchyate ॥

57. Daily study the Vedas and Śāstras, which are written according to the Vedas, tirelessly; this is considered the primary duty, while all other duties are secondary.

वेदाभ्यासेन सततं शौचेन तपसैव च ।
अद्रोहेण च भूतानां जातिं स्मरति पौर्विकीम् ॥58॥

vedābhyāsena satataṁ śauchena tapasaiva cha ।
adroheṇa cha bhūtānāṁ jātiṁ smarati paurvikīm ॥58॥

58. Through consistent practice of studying the Vedas and Śāstras, maintaining spiritual and physical purity, practicing yoga and austerities, and harboring no enmity towards living beings, one can attain the ability to remember past lives.

पौर्विकीं संस्मरन् जातिं ब्रह्मैवाभ्यस्यते पुनः ।

---

[1] वेदमेव जपेन्

ब्रह्माभ्यासेन चाजस्रमनन्तं सुखमश्नुते ॥59॥

paurvikīṁ saṁsmaran jātiṁ brahmaivābhyasyate punaḥ ।
brahmābhyāsena chājasramanantaṁ sukhamaśnute ॥59॥

59. Those who remember their former lives and continue to practice the study of the Veda attain the bliss of mokṣa through continuous study of the Veda.

अभिवादयेद् वृद्धांश्च दद्याच्चैवासनं स्वकम् ।
कृताञ्जलिरुपासीत गच्छतः पृष्ठतोऽन्वियात् ॥60॥

abhivādayed vṛddhāṁścha dadyāchchaivāsanaṁ svakam ।
kṛtāñjalirupāsīta gachchhataḥ pṛṣṭhato'nviyāt ॥60॥

60. Greet elders, give them your seat, and sit near them with folded hands. When they leave, walk behind them.

श्रुतिस्मृत्योदितं सम्यग् निबद्धं स्वेषु कर्मसु ।
धर्ममूलं निषेवेत सदाचारमतन्द्रितः ॥61॥

śrutismṛtyoditaṁ samyaga nibaddhaṁ sveṣu karmasu ।
dharmamūlaṁ niṣeveta sadāchāramatandritaḥ ॥61॥

61. In all his actions, a gṛhasthī (householder) must diligently adhere to good conduct, which serves as the foundation of dharma as outlined in the Vedas and smṛtis.

आचारात्लभते ह्यायुराचारादीप्सिताः प्रजाः ।
आचाराद् धनमक्षय्यमाचारो हन्त्यलक्षणम् ॥62॥

āchārātlabhate hyāyurāchārādīpsitāḥ prajāḥ ।
āchārād dhanamakṣayyamāchāro hantyalakṣaṇam ॥62॥

62. By practicing good moral conduct, a gṛhasthī (householder) achieves long life; through good conduct, he attains desirable offspring; good conduct leads to lasting wealth; and good conduct mitigates the effects of bad sanskāras.

दुराचारो हि पुरुषो लोके भवति निन्दितः ।
दुःखभागी च सततं व्याधितोऽल्पायुरेव च ॥63॥

durāchāro hi puruṣo loke bhavati ninditaḥ ।
duḥkhabhāgī cha satataṁ vyādhito'lpāyureva cha ॥63॥

63. A man of immoral conduct is criticized by others, often facing misfortunes, suffering from illnesses, and living a short

life.

सर्वलक्षणहीनोऽपि यः सदाचारवान्नरः ।
श्रद्दधानोऽनसूयश्च शतं वर्षाणि जीवति ॥64॥

sarvalakṣaṇahīno'pi yaḥ sadāchāravānnaraḥ ।
śraddadhāno'nasūyaścha śataṁ varṣāṇi jīvati ॥64॥

64. A man who practices good moral conduct, maintains a positive attitude, and is free from envy can live a hundred years, even if he lacks good sanskāras.

यद् यत् परवशं कर्म तत् तद् यत्नेन वर्जयेत् ।
यद् यदात्मवशं तु स्यात् तत् तत् सेवेत यत्नतः ॥65॥

yad yat paravaśaṁ karma tat tad yatnena varjayet ।
yad yadātmavaśaṁ tu syāt tat tat seveta yatnataḥ ॥65॥

65. Avoid carefully all endeavors dependent on others; pursue those reliant on yourself.

सर्वं परवशं दुःखं सर्वमात्मवशं सुखम् ।
एतद् विद्यात् समासेन लक्षणं सुखदुःखयोः ॥66॥

sarvaṁ paravaśaṁ duḥkhaṁ sarvamātmavaśaṁ sukham ।
ētad vidyāt samāsena lakṣaṇaṁ sukhaduḥkhayoḥ ॥66॥

66. Everything that relies on others causes pain; everything that relies on oneself brings pleasure. This is the concise definition of pleasure and pain.

यत् कर्म कुर्वतोऽस्य स्यात् परितोषोऽन्तरात्मनः ।
तत् प्रयत्नेन कुर्वीत विपरीतं तु वर्जयेत् ॥67॥

yat karma kurvato'sya syāt paritoṣo'ntarātmanaḥ ।
tat prayatnena kurvīta viparītaṁ tu varjayet ॥67॥

67. When an action brings you joy, you should perform it diligently; however, you should avoid actions that do not.

आचार्यं च प्रवक्तारं पितरं मातरं गुरुम् ।
न हिंस्याद् ब्राह्मणान् गाश्च सर्वांश्चैव तपस्विनः ॥68॥

āchāryaṁ cha pravaktāraṁ pitaraṁ mātaraṁ gurum ।
na hiṁsyād brāhmaṇān gāścha sarvāṁśchaiva tapasvinaḥ ॥

68. One should never offend the teacher who initiated him,

nor the one who explained the Veda, nor his father and mother, nor any other Guru, nor cows, nor scholars, nor anyone performing austerities.

नास्तिक्यं वेदनिन्दां च देवतानां च कुत्सनम् ।
द्वेषं दम्भं च[1] मानं च क्रोधं तैक्ष्ण्यं च वर्जयेत् ॥69॥

nāstikyaṁ vedanindāṁ cha devatānāṁ cha kutsanam /
dveṣaṁ dambhaṁ cha mānaṁ cha krodhaṁ taikṣaṇyaṁ cha varjayet //69 //

69. He should avoid atheism, criticism of the Vedas, disrespecting [devatā] those who contribute to the society and nation, hatred, lack of modesty, pride, anger, and harshness.

परस्य दण्डं नोद्यच्छेत् क्रुद्धो नैनं निपातयेत् ।
अन्यत्र पुत्राच्छिष्याद् वा शिष्ट्यर्थं ताडयेत्तु तौ ॥70॥

parasya daṇḍaṁ nodyachchhet kruddho nainaṁ nipātayet
anyatra putrātśiṣyād vā śiṣṭyarthaṁ tāḍayettu tau //70 //

70. When angry, one should not raise a stick against another man or strike anyone except for his son or pupil; those two he may beat to correct them.

अधार्मिको नरो यो हि यस्य चाप्यनृतं धनम् ।
हिंसारतश्च[2] यो नित्यं नैहासौ सुखमेधते ॥71॥

adhārmiko naro yo hi yasya chāpyanṛtaṁ dhanam /
hiṁsārataścha yo nityaṁ naihāsau sukhamedhate //71 //

71. A man who does not adhere to dharma (moral and ethical values, and fails to perform his duties diligently), similarly, those who acquire wealth through deceit and those who consistently engage in violence—whether through their words, thoughts, or actions against others—will never attain spiritual happiness in this world.

न सीदन्नपि धर्मेण मनोऽधर्मे निवेशयेत् ।

---

[1] द्वेषं स्तम्भं च

[2] हिंसारतिश्

अधार्मिकानां पापानामाशु पश्यन् विपर्ययम् ॥72॥

na sīdannapi dharmeṇa mano'dharme niveśayet /
adhārmikānāṁ pāpānāmāśu paśyan viparyayam //72 //

72. Although one may suffer for following dharma, he should never let his heart turn to adharma, [paśyan] knowing that immoral and unethical people will face their destruction sooner or later.

Note: Dharma here means moral and ethical values and adharma immoral and unethical values.

नाधर्मश्चरितो लोके सद्यः फलति गौरिव ।
शनैरावर्त्यमानस्तु कर्तुर्मूलानि कृन्तति ॥73॥

nādharmaścharito loke sadyaḥ phalati gauriva /
śanairāvartyamānastu karturmūlāni kṛntati //73 //

73. Adharma practiced in this world does not immediately bear fruit, like a cow; instead, it gradually cuts off the roots of those who commit it.

यदि नात्मनि पुत्रेषु न चेत् पुत्रेषु नप्तृषु ।
न त्वेव तु कृतोऽधर्मः[1] कर्तुर्भवति निष्फलः ॥74॥

yadi nātmani putreṣu na chet putreṣu naptṛṣu /
na tveva tu kṛto'dharmaḥ karturbhavati niṣphalaḥ //74 //

74. If the punishment for adharma does not fall on the offender himself, it falls on his sons. If not on the sons, then at least on his grandsons; but adharma, once committed, never fails to produce consequences.

अधर्मेणैधते तावत् ततो भद्राणि पश्यति ।
ततः सपत्नान् जयति समूलस्तु विनश्यति ॥75॥

adharmeṇaidhate tāvat tato bhadrāṇi paśyati /
tataḥ sapatnān jayati samūlastu vinaśyati //75 //

75. The perpetrator of adharma may prosper temporarily, achieving great wealth and defeating his foes, but ultimately he

[1] कृतो धर्मः

is doomed to perish from his very foundations.

सत्यधर्मार्यवृत्तेषु शौचे चैवारमेत् सदा ।
शिष्यांश्च शिष्याद् धर्मेण वाक्बाहूदरसंयतः ॥76 ॥

satyadharmāryavṛtteṣu śauche chaivāramet sadā /
śiṣyāṁścha śiṣyād dharmeṇa vākbāhūdarasaṁyataḥ //76 //

76. Let him always take joy in true dharma, uphold noble conduct, and maintain purity both internally and externally. Let him teach his students true dharma. Let him keep his words, actions, and desires under control.

परित्यजेदर्थकामौ यौ स्यातां धर्मवर्जितौ ।
धर्मं चाप्यसुखोदर्कं लोकसङ्क्रुष्टमेव च ॥77 ॥

parityajedarthakāmau yau syātāṁ dharmavarjitau /
dharmaṁ chāpyasukhodarkaṁ lokasaṅkruṣṭameva cha 77

77. A person should avoid seeking material wealth and desires if they are obtained through unethical means (adharma). They should also refrain from pursuing wealth and fulfilling desires that, although achieved through ethical means (dharma), lead to future problems or threaten the well-being of humanity as a whole.

न पाणिपादचपलो न नेत्रचपलोऽनृजुः ।
न स्याद् वाक्चपलश्चैव न परद्रोहकर्मधीः ॥78 ॥

na pāṇipādachapalo na netrachapalo'nṛjuḥ /
na syād vākchapalaśchaiva na paradrohakarmadhīḥ //78 //

78. One should not be overly active with their hands, feet, or eyes, nor engage in deceitful behaviour, be excessively talkative, or focus one's mind on actions that harm others.

येनास्य पितरो याता येन याताः पितामहाः ।
तेन यायात् सतां मार्गं तेन गच्छन्न रिष्यति ॥79 ॥

yenāsya pitaro yātā yena yātāḥ pitāmahāḥ /
tena yāyāt satāṁ mārgaṁ tena gachchhanna riṣyati //79 //

79. Let him follow the path of holy men that his ancestors followed; as long as he adheres to it, he will not suffer harm.

ऋत्विक्पुरोहिताचार्यैर्मातुलातिथिसंश्रितैः ।

बालवृद्धातुरैर्वैद्यैर्ज्ञातिसम्बन्धिबान्धवैः ॥80 ॥
मातापितृभ्यां जामीभिर्भ्रात्रा पुत्रेण भार्यया ।
दुहित्रा दासवर्गेण विवादं न समाचरेत् ॥81 ॥

ṛtvikpurohitāchāryairmātulātithisaṁśritaiḥ /
bālavṛddhāturairvaidyairjñātisambandhibāndhavaiḥ //80 //
mātāpitṛbhyāṁ jāmībhirbhrātrā putreṇa bhāryayā /
duhitrā dāsavargeṇa vivādaṁ na samācharet //81 //

80-81. A person should avoid quarrelling with the following individuals: an officiating priest, a domestic priest, an Āchārya (teacher or mentor), a maternal uncle, visiting Vedic scholars, renunciates, dependents, infants, the elderly, sick individuals, physicians, paternal relatives, in-laws, friends, as well as close family members such as a father, mother, sister, brother, son, wife, daughter, and workers.

प्रतिग्रहसमर्थोऽपि प्रसङ्गं तत्र वर्जयेत् ।
प्रतिग्रहेण ह्यस्याशु ब्राह्मं तेजः प्रशाम्यति ॥82 ॥

pratigrahasamartho'pi prasaṅgaṁ tatra varjayet /
pratigraheṇa hyasyāśu brāhmaṁ tejaḥ praśāmyati //82 //

82. Although he may be entitled to accept gifts due to his learning and sanctity, he should not become overly attached to this habit; for accepting too many gifts can soon extinguish the divine light within him.

न द्रव्याणामविज्ञाय विधिं धर्म्यं प्रतिग्रहे ।
प्राज्ञः प्रतिग्रहं कुर्यादवसीदन्नपि क्षुधा ॥83 ॥

na dravyāṇāmavijñāya vidhiṁ dharmyaṁ pratigrahe /
prājñaḥ pratigrahaṁ kuryādavasīdannapi kṣudhā //83 //

83. Without complete knowledge of the proper procedure outlined in the Śāstras for accepting gifts, a wise person should refrain from taking anything, even if they are desperately suffering from hunger.

अतपास्त्वनधीयानः प्रतिग्रहरुचिर्द्विजः ।
अम्भस्यश्मप्लवेनैव सह तेनैव मज्जति ॥84 ॥

atapāstvanadhīyānaḥ pratigraharuchirdvijaḥ /
ambhasyaśmaplavenaiva saha tenaiva majjati //84 //

84. A Vedic scholar who does not engage in austerities or study the Vedas, yet takes pleasure in receiving gifts, ultimately suffers the consequences of those donations. This is similar to a person attempting to cross the water in a boat made of stone, who will sink along with the boat.

तस्मादविद्वान् बिभियाद् यस्मात् तस्मात् प्रतिग्रहात् ।
स्वल्पकेनाप्यविद्वान् हि पङ्के गौरिव सीदति ॥85॥

tasmādavidvān bibhiyād yasmāt tasmāt pratigrahāt /
svalpakenāpyavidvān hi paṅke gauriva sīdati //85//

85. Therefore, an ignorant person should be cautious about accepting any gifts; for even a small gift makes a fool sink into lower species, just as a cow can sink into a swamp.

न वार्यपि प्रयच्छेत् तु बैडालव्रतिके द्विजे ।
न बकव्रतिके पापे नावेदविदि धर्मवित् ॥86॥

na vāryapi prayachchhet tu baiḍālavratike dvije /
na bakavratike pāpe nāvedavidi dharmavit //86//

86. (A man) who knows dharma should not offer even water to a scholar (pseudo scholar) who acts like a cat, nor to one who acts like a heron, nor to one who is unacquainted with the Veda.

त्रिष्वप्येतेषु दत्तं हि विधिनाऽप्यर्जितं धनम् ।
दातुर्भवत्यनर्थाय परत्रादातुरेव च ॥87॥

triṣvapyeteṣu dattaṁ hi vidhinā'pyarjitaṁ dhanam /
dāturbhavatyanarthāya paratrādātureva cha //87//

87. Wealth earned in accordance with dharma, when given to the three mentioned persons, becomes useless for the donor and brings suffering to the recipient in the next life.

यथा प्लवेनोपलेन निमज्जत्युदके तरन् ।
तथा निमज्जतोऽधस्तादज्ञौ दातृप्रतीच्छकौ ॥88॥
yathā plavenopalena nimajjatyudake taran /
tathā nimajjato'dhastādajñau dātṛpratīchchhakau //88//

88. Just as someone who attempts to cross the water in a stone boat sinks to the bottom, an ignorant donor and an ignorant [pratīchchhakau] donee also sink to a lower species.

धर्मध्वजी सदा लुब्धश्छाद्मिको लोकदम्भकः ।
बैडालव्रतिको ज्ञेयो हिंस्रः सर्वाभिसन्धकः ॥89 ॥

dharmadhvajī sadā lubdhaśchhādmiko lokadambhakaḥ ।
baiḍālavratiko jñeyo hiṁsraḥ sarvābhisandhakaḥ ॥89 ॥

89. A man who is always greedy, yet pretends to uphold the principles of dharma, is a hypocrite and a deceiver of the people. He is causing harm and forms alliances with everyone, regardless of their merits or faults. Such a person can be described as "behaving like a cat."

अधोदृष्टिर्नैष्कृतिकः स्वार्थसाधनतत्परः ।
शठो मिथ्याविनीतश्च बकव्रतचरो द्विजः ॥90 ॥

adhodṛṣṭirnaiṣkṛtikaḥ svārthasādhanatatparaḥ ।
śaṭho mithyāvinītaścha bakavratacharo dvijaḥ ॥90 ॥

90. The scholar, who looks downcast and has a cruel disposition, solely intent on achieving his selfish motives, dishonest and falsely gentle is called 'acting like a heron'.

ये बकव्रतिनो विप्रा ये च मार्जारलिङ्गिनः ।
ते पतन्त्यन्धतामिस्रे तेन पापेन कर्मणा ॥91 ॥

ye bakavratino viprā ye cha mārjāraliṅginaḥ ।
te patantyandhatāmisre tena pāpena karmaṇā ॥91 ॥

91. Those pseudo-scholars who act like herons and those who display the characteristics of cats fall in consequence of their pāpa karmas into lower species (in next life) enveloped with the darkness of ignorance.

न धर्मस्यापदेशेन पापं कृत्वा व्रतं चरेत् ।
व्रतेन पापं प्रच्छाद्य कुर्वन् स्त्रीशूद्रदम्भनम् ॥92 ॥

na dharmasyāpadeśena pāpaṁ kṛtvā vrataṁ charet ।
vratena pāpaṁ prachchhādya kurvan strīśūdradambhanam

92. A person who commits pāpa under the guise of dharma, and deceives innocent women and labourers, should not take a vow of gaining spiritual merit, thus hiding his pāpa under the pretext of a vow.

अलिङ्गी लिङ्गिवेषेण यो वृत्तिमुपजीवति ।

स लिङ्गिनां हरत्येनस्तिर्यग्योनौ च जायते ॥93॥

aliṅgī liṅgiveṣeṇa yo vṛttimupajīvati /
sa liṅgināṁ haratyenastiryagyonau cha jāyate //93//

93. One who lacks the necessary qualifications but earns a living by showcasing those qualifications bears the guilt of all who are truly qualified and is reborn in the form of an animal.

परकीयनिपानेषु न स्नायाद् हि कदा चन[1] ।
निपानकर्तुः स्नात्वा तु दुष्कृतांशेन लिप्यते ॥94॥

parakīyanipāneṣu na snāyād hi kadā chana /
nipānakartuḥ snātvā tu duṣkṛtāṁśena lipyate //94//

94. A person should never bathe in the tanks used by others; if he does, he will contract the same infections as previous users.

नदीषु देवखातेषु तडागेषु सरःसु च ।
स्नानं समाचरेन्नित्यं गर्तप्रस्रवणेषु च ॥95॥

nadīṣu devakhāteṣu taḍāgeṣu sarahsu cha /
snānaṁ samācharennityaṁ gartaprasravaṇeṣu cha //95//

95. One should always bathe in rivers, ponds, lakes, and springs made by nature.

यमान् सेवेत सततं न नित्यं नियमान् बुधः ।
यमान् पतत्यकुर्वाणो नियमान् केवलान् भजन् ॥96॥

yamān seveta satataṁ na nityaṁ niyamān budhaḥ /
yamān patatyakurvāṇo niyamān kevalān bhajan //96//

96. A wise person should continuously practice yamas (social discipline), though he may neglect niyamas (self-discipline); for he who does not practice social discipline while obeying self-discipline will experience downfall.

Note: A human being is inherently a social creature. To facilitate personal and societal upliftment, the rules of yamas (social discipline) and niyamas (self-discipline) have been established by ancient sages, including Manu and Patañjali, the author of Yagadarśana. As social beings, it is essential for every

---

[1] स्नायाच्च कदा चन

individual to adhere to yamas to maintain law and order within society, which is crucial for the progress of all.

For personal spiritual development, niyamas are recommended. It is important to strictly follow these rules of yamas to prevent any disruption in the social structure, even though one might feel tempted to neglect niyamas at times.

The five yamas are:

1. Non-violence (Ahimsa)

2. Truthfulness (Satya)

3. Non-stealing (Asteya)

4. Celibacy (Brahmacharya)

5. Non-hoarding (Aparigraha) – not accumulating wealth beyond what is necessary.

Similarly, the five niyamas are:

1. Internal purity and external cleanliness (Śaucha)

2. Contentment (Santoṣa)

3. Study of the Vedas and scriptures (Svādhyāya)

4. Yoga and austerities (Tapas)

5. Meditation on God or surrendering to the divine (Ishvara Pranidhana).

By adhering to these principles, individuals can contribute to both their own spiritual growth and the well-being of society as a whole.

Charitable works

दानधर्मं निषेवेत नित्यमैष्टिकपौर्तिकम् ।
परितुष्टेन भावेन पात्रमासाद्य शक्तितः ॥97 ॥

dānadharmaṁ niṣeveta nityamaiṣṭikapaurtikam /
parituṣṭena bhāvena pātramāsādya śaktitaḥ //97 //

97. A person should always perform dhārmika and charitable works, such as organizing yajñas and constructing

wells and ponds, according to their ability and with a joyful heart if they find a worthy recipient.

सर्वेषामेव दानानां ब्रह्मदानं विशिष्यते ।
वार्यन्नगोमहीवासस्तिलकाञ्चनसर्पिषाम् ॥98॥

sarveṣāmeva dānānāṁ brahmadānaṁ viśiṣyate /
vāryannagomahīvāsastilakāñchanasarpiṣām //98 //

98. The knowledge of the Veda is the greatest gift, surpassing the gifts of water, food, cows, land, clothes, sesame, gold, and clarified butter.

धर्मं शनैः सञ्चिनुयाद्[1] वल्मीकमिव पुत्तिकाः ।
परलोकसहायार्थं सर्वभूतान्यपीडयन् ॥99॥

nāmutra hi sahāyārthaṁ pitā mātā cha tiṣṭhataḥ /
na putradāraṁ na jñātirdharmastiṣṭhati kevalaḥ //99 //

99. Without causing pain to any creature, let a person gradually accumulate dharma to secure a companion for the next life, just as the white ant slowly builds its ant-hill.

नामुत्र हि सहायार्थं पिता माता च तिष्ठतः ।
न पुत्रदारं न ज्ञातिर्धर्मस्तिष्ठति केवलः ॥100॥

nāmutra hi sahāyārthaṁ pitā mātā cha tiṣṭhataḥ /
na putradāraṁ na jñātirdharmastiṣṭhati kevalaḥ //100 //

100. In the next life, neither father, mother, wife, sons, nor relatives will remain as companions; only dharma will accompany you.

एकः प्रजायते जन्तुरेक एव प्रलीयते ।
एकोऽनुभुङ्क्ते सुकृतमेक एव च दुष्कृतम् ॥101॥

ēkaḥ prajāyate jantureka ēva pralīyate /
ēko'nubhuṅkte sukṛtameka ēva cha duṣkṛtam //101 //

101. Each being is born alone, lives alone, and dies alone; each one experiences the outcomes of its good or bad karmas alone.

---

[1] सञ्चिनुयाद्

मृतं शरीरमुत्सृज्य काष्ठलोष्टसमं क्षितौ ।
विमुखा बान्धवा यान्ति धर्मस्तमनुगच्छति ॥102॥

mṛtaṁ śarīramutsṛjya kāṣṭhaloṣṭasamaṁ kṣitau ।
vimukhā bāndhavā yānti dharmastamanugachchhati ॥102॥

102. Leaving the dead body on the ground like a log or a clod of earth, the relatives depart with averted faces; however, dharma follows the soul.

तस्माद् धर्मं सहायार्थं नित्यं सञ्चिनुयात्शनैः ।
धर्मेण हि सहायेन तमस्तरति दुस्तरम् ॥103॥

tasmād dharmaṁ sahāyārthaṁ nityaṁ sañchinuyātśanaiḥ ।
dharmeṇa hi sahāyena tamastarati dustaram ॥103॥

103. Thus, individuals gradually accumulate dharma as their companion after death; with dharma by their side, they will navigate through the challenging darkness.

धर्मप्रधानं पुरुषं तपसा हतकिल्बिषम् ।
परलोकं नयत्याशु भास्वन्तं खशरीरिणम् ॥ 104 ॥

dharmapradhānaṁ puruṣaṁ tapasā hatakilbiṣam ।
paralokaṁ nayatyāśu bhāsvantaṁ khaśarīriṇam ॥ 104 ॥

104. That companion (dharma) speedily carries the man devoted to dharma and has effaced his bad sanskāras by yogic practice and austerities, to the next life, radiant and clothed with a subtle body.

उत्तमैरुत्तमैर्नित्यं सम्बन्धानाचरेत्[1] सह ।
निनीषुः कुलमुत्कर्षमधमानधमांस्त्यजेत् ॥ 105 ॥

uttamairuttamairnityaṁ sambandhānācharet saha ।
ninīṣuḥ kulamutkarṣamadhamānadhamāṁstyajet ॥ 105 ॥

105. For individuals who wish to elevate their family's status, it is important to connect with those of high value and avoid those with low values.

दृढकारी मृदुर्दान्तः क्रूराचारैरसंवसन् ।

---

1 सम्भन्धान्

अहिंस्रो दमदानाभ्यां जयेत् स्वर्गं तथाव्रतः ॥ 106 ॥

dṛḍhakārī mṛdurdāntaḥ krūrāchārairasaṁvasan /
ahiṁsro damadānābhyāṁ jayet svargaṁ tathāvrataḥ // 106

106. Persons who are persevering, gentle, patient, avoid the company of those who behave cruelly and does not harm living beings- by consistently living this way, restraining their senses, and helping those in need, they attain divine bliss.

योऽन्यथा सन्तमात्मानमन्यथा सत्सु भाषते ।
स पापकृत्तमो लोके स्तेन आत्मापहारकः ॥107 ॥

yo'nyathā santamātmānamanyathā satsu bhāṣate /
sa pāpakṛttamo loke stena ātmāpahārakaḥ //107 //

107. A person who gives his false introduction to virtuous (men), is the most evil person in this world; he is a thief who deceives himself.

वाच्यर्था नियताः सर्वे वाङ्मूला वाग्विनिःसृताः ।
तांस्तु[1] यः स्तेनयेद् वाचं स सर्वस्तेयकृन्नरः ॥108 ॥

vāchyarthā niyatāḥ sarve vāṅmūlā vāgviniḥsṛtāḥ /
tāṁstu yaḥ stenayed vāchaṁ sa sarvasteyakṛnnaraḥ //108 //

108. All behavior is shaped by speech; the nature of all people is defined by it. However, a person who is dishonest in speech is dishonest in everything.

महर्षिपितृदेवानां गत्वाऽनृण्यं यथाविधि ।
पुत्रे सर्वं समासज्य वसेन् माध्यस्थ्यमाश्रितः[2] ॥109 ॥

maharṣipitṛdevānāṁ gatvā'nṛṇyaṁ yathāvidhi /
putre sarvaṁ samāsajya vasen mādhyasthyamāśritaḥ //109 //

109. Once a householder (gṛhasthī) has freed himself from the debts of the sages (ṛṣi-ṛṇa), ancestors (pitṛ-ṛṇa), and nature (deva-ṛṇa), he should properly hand over all his possessions to his heirs. He should then dwell in his home without worrying about worldly concerns before transitioning to the Vānaprastha

---

[1] तान् तु

[2] आस्थितः

Āśrama.

एकाकी चिन्तयेन्नित्यं विविक्ते हितमात्मनः[1] ।
एकाकी चिन्तयानो हि परं श्रेयोऽधिगच्छति ॥110 ॥

ēkākī chintayennityaṁ vivikte hitamātmanaḥ /
ēkākī chintayāno hi paraṁ śreyo'dhigachchhati //110 //

110. Let a person meditate alone in solitude on what is good for him, for he who does so attains spiritual bliss.

एषौदिता गृहस्थस्य वृत्तिर्विप्रस्य शाश्वती ।
स्नातकव्रतकल्पश्च सत्त्ववृद्धिकरः शुभः ॥111 ॥

ēṣauditā gṛhasthasya vṛttirviprasya śāśvatī /
snātakavratakalpaścha sattvavṛddhikaraḥ śubhaḥ //111 //

111. Thus, the daily routine of an educated Gṛhasthī (householder) has been outlined, along with the principles for a graduate gṛhasthī, aimed at enhancing his sattvaguṇa.

अनेन विप्रो वृत्तेन वर्तयन् वेदशास्त्रवित् ।
व्यपेतकल्मषो नित्यं ब्रह्मलोके महीयते ॥112 ॥

anena vipro vṛttena vartayan vedaśāstravit /
vyapetakalmaṣo nityaṁ brahmaloke mahīyate //112 //

112. A learned scholar, well-versed in the Vedas, who consistently follows this routine and diligently eradicates bad sanskāras, will attain Brahmaloka (mokṣa).

---

[1] इतमात्मनि

Chapter 5: Food Habits and Purifications

The fifth chapter addresses hospitality, food habits, and various restrictions. In this section, Manu explains why a person should never consume the flesh of animals. He asserts that meat can only be obtained by causing harm to living beings, and that harm to sentient creatures is detrimental to achieving spiritual elevation. Therefore, one should avoid eating meat.

Prohibited Foods

लशुनं गृञ्जनं चैव पलाण्डुं कवकानि च ।
अभक्ष्याणि द्विजातीनाममेध्यप्रभवानि च ॥1॥

laśunaṁ gṛñjanaṁ chaiva palāṇḍuṁ kavakāni cha /
abhakṣayāṇi dvijātīnāmamedhyaprabhavāni cha //1 //

1. Garlic, turnip and onions, mushrooms and (all plants), growing at impure places, are unfit to be eaten by human beings.

Note: The word dvija is used by Manu for educated persons and dvijāti is used for all human beings.

अनिर्दशाया गोः क्षीरमौष्ट्रमैकशफं तथा ।
आविकं सन्धिनीक्षीरं[1] विवत्सायाश्च गोः पयः ॥2॥

anirdaśāyā goḥ kṣīramauṣṭramaikaśaphaṁ tathā /
āvikaṁ sandhinīkṣīraṁ vivatsāyāścha goḥ payaḥ //2 //

2. The milk of a [anirdiśāyāḥ] cow within ten days after calving, that of camels, one-hoofed animals, sheep, [sandhinī] cow in heat, or that of a [vivitsāyāḥ] calf which has died.

आरण्यानां च सर्वेषां मृगाणां माहिषं विना ।
स्त्रीक्षीरं चैव वर्ज्यानि सर्वशुक्तानि चैव हि ॥3॥

āraṇyānāṁ cha sarveṣāṁ mṛgāṇāṁ māhiṣaṁ vinā /
strīkṣīraṁ chaiva varjyāni sarvaśuktāni chaiva hi //3 //

3. The milk of all wild animals, except buffalo, that of

---

[1] सन्धिनीक्षीरं

women, and all sour substances should be avoided.

दधि भक्ष्यं च शुक्तेषु सर्वं च दधिसम्भवम्[1] ।
यानि चैवाभिषूयन्ते पुष्पमूलफलैः शुभैः ॥4॥

dadhi bhakṣayaṁ cha śukteṣu sarvaṁ cha dadhisambhavam
yāni chaivābhiṣūyante puṣpamūlaphalaiḥ śubhaiḥ ॥4॥

4. Among soured substances, the curd is fit for consumption, along with everything prepared from it, as well as all that is extracted from pure flowers, roots, and fruits.

यत् किं चित् स्नेहसंयुक्तं भक्ष्यं भोज्यमगर्हितम् ।
तत् पर्युषितमप्याद्यं हविःशेषं च यद् भवेत् ॥5॥

yat kiṁ chit snehasaṁyuktaṁ bhakṣayaṁ
bhojyamagarhitam ।
tat paryuṣitamapyādyaṁ haviḥśeṣaṁ cha yad bhavet ॥5॥

5. Such foods and eat-worthy food items as mixed with oils may be consumed, even if stale, as long as they are unspoiled. Yajña offerings may also be eaten.

Note: Here, meat is not worth eating.

चिरस्थितमपि त्वाद्यमस्नेहाक्तं द्विजातिभिः ।
यवगोधूमजं सर्वं पयसश्चैव विक्रिया ॥6॥

chirasthitamapi tvādyamasnehāktaṁ dvijātibhiḥ ।
yavagodhūmajaṁ sarvaṁ payasaśchaiva vikriyā ॥6॥

6. All items made from barley and wheat, as well as all milk products, may be consumed by human beings without being mixed with oils, even if they have been stored for a long time.

योऽहिंसकानि भूतानि हिनस्त्यात्मसुखैच्छया ।
स जीवंश्च मृतश्चैव न क्व चित् सुखमेधते ॥7॥

yo'hiṁsakāni bhūtāni hinastyātmasukhaichchhayā ।
sa jīvaṁścha mṛtaśchaiva na kva chit sukhamedhate ॥7॥

7. Those who kill harmless creatures for their own pleasure never find happiness, either in life or after death.

---

[1] दधिसम्भवम्

यो बन्धनवधक्लेशान् प्राणिनां न चिकीर्षति ।
स सर्वस्य हितप्रेप्सुः सुखमत्यन्तमश्नुते ॥8॥

yo bandhanavadhakleśān prāṇināṁ na chikīrṣati /
sa sarvasya hitaprepsuḥ sukhamatyantamaśnute //8 //

8. Those who do not seek to capture, slaughter, or inflict suffering on living beings are well-wishers of all and attain endless bliss.

यद् ध्यायति यत् कुरुते रतिं बध्नाति यत्र च ।
तदवाप्नोत्ययत्नेन यो हिनस्ति न किं चन ॥9॥

yad dhyāyati yat kurute ratiṁ badhnāti yatra cha /
tadavāpnotyayatnena yo hinasti na kiṁ chana //9 //

9. Those who do not harm any creature effortlessly achieve whatever they think, success in their endeavors, and fulfill their aspirations.

नाकृत्वा प्राणिनां हिंसां मांसमुत्पद्यते क्व चित् ।
न च प्राणिवधः स्वर्ग्यस्तस्मान् मांसं विवर्जयेत् ॥10॥

nākṛtvā prāṇināṁ hiṁsāṁ māṁsamutpadyate kva chit /
na cha prāṇivadhaḥ svargyastasmān māṁsaṁ vivarjayet //10

10. Meat cannot be obtained without causing harm to living beings, and harming sentient creatures prevents the attainment of divine bliss; therefore, one should avoid consuming meat.

समुत्पत्तिं च मांसस्य वधबन्धौ च देहिनाम् ।
प्रसमीक्ष्य निवर्तेत सर्वमांसस्य भक्षणात् ॥11॥

samutpattiṁ cha māṁsasya vadhabandhau cha dehinām /
prasamīkṣaya nivarteta sarvamāṁsasya bhakṣaṇāt //11 //

11. After carefully considering the origins of meat, fettering and slaughtering of living beings, one should refrain from consuming all types of meat.

अनुमन्ता विशसिता निहन्ता क्रयविक्रयी ।
संस्कर्ता चोपहर्ता च खादकश्चेति घातकाः ॥12॥

anumantā viśasitā nihantā krayavikrayī /
saṁskartā chopahartā cha khādakaścheti ghātakāḥ //12 //

12. Anyone involved in the process of slaughtering an

animal—whether by permitting it, cutting it up, killing it, buying or selling the meat, cooking it, serving it, or eating it—should all be considered a slayer of the animal.

स्वमांसं परमांसेन यो वर्धयितुमिच्छति ।
अनभ्यर्च्य पितॄन् देवांस्ततोऽन्यो नास्त्यपुण्यकृत् ॥13 ॥

svamāṁsaṁ paramāṁsena yo vardhayitumichchhati /
anabhyarchya pitṝn devāṁstato'nyo nāstyapuṇyakṛt //13 //

13. There is no greater cruel than the man who, while neglecting elderly family members and failing to perform Devayajña (Agnihotra), seeks to nourish his own flesh at the expense of the flesh of other beings.

वर्षे वर्षेऽश्वमेधेन यो यजेत शतं समाः ।
मांसानि च न खादेद् यस्तयोः पुण्यफलं समम् ॥14 ॥

varṣe varṣe'śvamedhena yo yajeta śataṁ samāḥ /
māṁsāni cha na khāded yastayoḥ puṇyaphalaṁ samam //14 //

14. Both the one who offers a Aśvamedha-yāga every year for a hundred years and the one who abstains completely from meat eating receive the same rewards for their virtuous actions.

फलमूलाशनैर्मेध्यैर्मुन्यन्नानां च भोजनैः ।
न तत् फलमवाप्नोति यत्मांसपरिवर्जनात् ॥15 ॥

phalamūlāśanairmedhyairmunyannānāṁ cha bhojanaiḥ /
na tat phalamavāpnoti yatmāṁsaparivarjanāt //15 //

15. One does not gain as much reward from subsisting on pure fruit and roots, or from eating food suitable for ascetics in the forest, as one does by entirely avoiding the use of flesh.

मां स भक्षयिताऽमुत्र यस्य मांसमिहाद्म्यहम् ।
एतत्मांसस्य मांसत्वं प्रवदन्ति मनीषिणः ॥16 ॥

māṁ sa bhakṣayitā'mutra yasya māṁsamihādmyaham /
ētatmāṁsasya māṁsatvaṁ pravadanti manīṣiṇaḥ //16 //

16. [maṁ sah] 'Me he will' [admi] devour in the next life, whose flesh I eat in this life; the wise declare this (to be) the real meaning of the word [māṁsa] 'flesh'.

Impurity Due to Death

प्रेतशुद्धिं प्रवक्ष्यामि द्रव्यशुद्धिं तथैव च ।
चतुर्णामपि वर्णानां यथावदनुपूर्वशः ॥17 ॥

pretaśuddhiṁ pravakṣayāmi dravyaśuddhiṁ tathaiva cha /
chaturṇāmapi varṇānāṁ yathāvadanupūrvaśaḥ //17 //

17. I will now in due order explain the purification on death and the purification of things, as prescribed for the four varṇas (professional classes based on sanskāras).

दन्तजातेऽनुजाते च कृतचूडे च संस्थिते ।
अशुद्धा बान्धवाः सर्वे सूतके च तथौच्यते ॥18 ॥

dantajāte'nujāte cha kṛtachūḍe cha saṁsthite /
aśuddhā bāndhavāḥ sarve sūtake cha tathauchyate //18 //

18. When a child dies after teething, or before teaching or if it has received the tonsure (chūḍākaraṇa) sanskāra, all relatives become impure. The same rule applies to the birth of a child.

दशाहं शावमाशौचं सपिण्डेषु विधीयते ।
अर्वाक् सञ्चयनादस्थ्नां त्र्यहमेकाहमेव वा ॥19 ॥

daśāhaṁ śāvamāśauchaṁ sapiṇḍeṣu vidhīyate /
arvāk sañchayanādasthnāṁ trayahamekāhameva vā //19 //

19. It is stated that among sapiṇḍas (blood relations) the impurity on account of death lasts ten days, or until the bones have been collected, or three days or only one day.

Difference between Sapiṇḍa and Samānodaka Relationship

सपिण्डता तु पुरुषे सप्तमे विनिवर्तते ।
समानोदकभावस्तु जन्मनाम्नोरवेदने ॥20 ॥

sapiṇḍatā tu puruṣe saptame vinivartate /
samānodakabhāvastu janmanāmnoravedane //20 //

20. The sapiṇḍa relationship (blood relationship) ends at the seventh generation in descending order, while the Samānodaka relationship ceases when the birth and name are unknown.

यथैदं शावमाशौचं सपिण्डेषु विधीयते ।
जननेऽप्येवमेव स्यान्निपुणं शुद्धिमिच्छताम् ॥21॥

yathaidaṁ śāvamāśauchaṁ sapiṇḍeṣu vidhīyate /
janane'pyevameva syānnipuṇaṁ śuddhimichchhatām //21//

21. Since the impurity caused by death applies to all Sapiṇḍas, it should also be accepted on the occasion of a birth [śuddhim ichchhatām] by those who wish to remain completely pure.

सर्वेषां शावमाशौचं मातापित्रोस्तु सूतकम् ।
सूतकं मातुरेव स्यादुपस्पृश्य पिता शुचिः ॥22॥

sarveṣāṁ śāvamāśauchaṁ mātāpitrostu sūtakam /
sūtakaṁ mātureva syādupaspṛśya pitā śuchiḥ //22//

22. While the impurity resulting from a death affects all Sapiṇḍas, that caused by a birth applies only to the parents—specifically, to the mother alone—while the father can become pure by bathing.

Other forms of Impurity

निरस्य तु पुमांशुक्रमुपस्पृस्यैव शुध्यति ।
बैजिकादभिसम्बन्धादनुरुन्ध्यादघं त्र्यहम् ॥23॥

nirasya tu pumāṁśukramupaspṛsyaiva śudhyati /
baijikādabhisambandhādanurundhyādaghaṁ trayaham //23

23. [śukraṁ nirasya] After nightfall, a man is purified simply [upaspṛsya eva] by bathing; [baijikāt abhisambandhāt] after sexual intercourse, [anurudgyāt agham] he shall remain in a state of impurity [trayaham] for three days.

अह्ना चैकेन रात्र्या च त्रिरात्रैरेव च त्रिभिः ।
शवस्पृशो विशुध्यन्ति त्र्यहादुदकदायिनः ॥24॥

ahnā chaikena rātrayā cha trirātraireva cha tribhiḥ /
śavaspṛśo viśudhyanti trayahādudakadāyinaḥ //24//

24. Those who have touched a corpse are purified after ten days: one day added to three nights multiplied by three. Those who give libations of water are purified after three days.

गुरोः प्रेतस्य शिष्यस्तु पितृमेधं समाचरन् ।

प्रेतहारैः[1] समं तत्र दशरात्रेण शुध्यति ॥25॥

guroḥ pretasya śiṣyastu pitṛmedhaṁ samācharan /
pretahāraiḥ samaṁ tatra daśarātreṇa śudhyati //25//

25. A pupil who performs the Pitṛimedha (cremation) for his deceased teacher becomes pure after ten days, along with those who carry the corpse to the cremation ground.

रात्रिभिर्मासतुल्याभिर्गर्भस्रावे विशुध्यति ।
रजस्युपरते साध्वी स्नानेन स्त्री रजस्वला ॥26॥

rātribhirmāsatulyābhirgarbhasrāve viśudhyati /
rajasyuparate sādhvī snānena strī rajasvalā //26//

26. A woman is considered purified after a miscarriage for the same number of days as the months since conception, while a menstruating female becomes pure by bathing after her menstruation ends.

ज्ञानं तपोऽग्निराहारो मृत्मनो वार्युपाञ्जनम् ।
वायुः कर्मार्ककालौ च शुद्धेः कर्तृणि देहिनाम् ॥27॥

jñānaṁ tapo'gnirāhāro mṛtmano vāryupāñjanam /
vāyuḥ karmārkakālau cha śuddheḥ kartṝṇi dehinām //27//

27. Knowledge, yoga (austerities), fire, sāttvika food, earth, restraint of the mind, water, smearing with cow dung, wind, yajña, sun, and time purify living beings.

सर्वेषामेव शौचानामर्थशौचं परं स्मृतम् ।
योऽर्थे शुचिर्हि स शुचिर्न मृद्वारिशुचिः शुचिः ॥28॥

sarveṣāmeva śauchānāmarthaśauchaṁ paraṁ smṛtam /
yo'rthe śuchirhi sa śuchirna mṛdvāriśuchiḥ śuchiḥ //28//

28. Among all modes of purification, purity in (the acquisition of) wealth is declared to be the best; for a person is said to be pure who earns wealth with clean hands, not he who purifies himself with earth and water.

---

[1] प्रेताहारैः

क्षान्त्या शुध्यन्ति[1] विद्वांसो दानेनाकार्यकारिणः ।
प्रच्छन्नपापा जप्येन तपसा वेदवित्तमाः ॥29॥

kṣāntyā śudhyanti vidvāṁso dānenākāryakāriṇaḥ ।
prachchhannapāpā japyena tapasā vedavittamāḥ ॥29॥

29. The learned are purified through forgiveness; those who have committed forbidden actions are purified by charity. People who commit immoral acts in secret are purified by the study of Śāstras, and those who best understand the Vedas achieve this through yoga (austerities).

मृत्तोयैः शुध्यते शोध्यं नदी वेगेन शुध्यति ।
रजसा स्त्री मनोदुष्टा संन्यासेन द्विजोत्तमाः ॥30॥

mṛttoyaiḥ śudhyate śodhyaṁ nadī vegena śudhyati ।
rajasā strī manoduṣṭā saṁnyāsena dvijottamāḥ ॥30॥

30. Things can be cleaned by earth and water, a river by its current, mood swing of a woman is treated by the menstrual secretion, a Vedic scholar by taking saṁnyāsa.

अद्भिर्गात्राणि शुध्यन्ति मनः सत्येन शुध्यति ।
विद्यातपोभ्यां भूतात्मा बुद्धिर्ज्ञानेन शुध्यति[2] ॥31॥

adbhirgātrāṇi śudhyanti manaḥ satyena śudhyati ।
vidyātapobhyāṁ bhūtātmā buddhirjñānena śudhyati ॥31॥

31. The body is cleansed by water, the mind is purified by truthfulness, the individual soul by spiritual knowledge and yoga, the buddhi (intellect) by true knowledge.

एष शौचस्य वः प्रोक्तः शरीरस्य विनिर्णयः ।
नानाविधानां द्रव्याणां शुद्धेः श्रृणुत निर्णयम् ॥32॥

ēṣa śauchasya vaḥ proktaḥ śarīrasya vinirṇayaḥ ।
nānāvidhānāṁ dravyāṇāṁ śuddheḥ śṛṇuta nirṇayam ॥32॥

32. Thus the rules for the purification of the body have been stated to you; hear now the rule regarding the purification of

---

1 शुद्ध्यन्ति

2 शुद्ध्यति

the various things.

तैजसानां मणीनां च सर्वस्याश्ममयस्य च ।
भस्मनाऽद्भिर्मृदा चैव शुद्धिरुक्ता मनीषिभिः ॥33 ॥

taijasānāṁ maṇīnāṁ cha sarvasyāśmamayasya cha /
bhasmanā'dbhirmṛdā chaiva śuddhiruktā manīṣibhiḥ //33 //

33. The wise ordain that all (objects) made of metal, gems, and anything made of stone are to be cleansed with ashes, earth, and water.

निर्लेपं काञ्चनं भाण्डमद्भिरेव विशुध्यति[1] ।
अब्जमश्ममयं चैव राजतं चानुपस्कृतम् ॥34 ॥

nirlepaṁ kāñchanaṁ bhāṇḍamadbhireva viśudhyati /
abjamaśmamayaṁ chaiva rājataṁ chānupaskṛtam //34 //

34. A golden vessel that shows no stains becomes pure with water alone. Likewise, [abjam] what is produced in water, such as shells and coral, [aśma-mayam] what is made of stone, and an [anupaskṛtam] uncarved silver vessel.

अपामग्नेश्च संयोगाद् हैमं रौप्यं च निर्बभौ ।
तस्मात् तयोः स्वयोन्यैव निर्णेको गुणवत्तरः ॥35 ॥

apāmagneścha saṁyogād haimaṁ raupyaṁ cha nirbabhau
tasmāt tayoḥ svayonyaiva nirṇeko guṇavattaraḥ //35 //

35. Gold and silver originate from the union of water and fire, so vessels made from these metals are [nirṇeko] best purified using both fire and water, [svayonyā eva] their original sources.

ताम्रायस्कांस्यरैत्यानां त्रपुणः सीसकस्य च ।
शौचं यथार्हं कर्तव्यं क्षाराम्लोदकवारिभिः ॥36 ॥

tāmrāyaskāṁsyaraityānāṁ trapuṇaḥ sīsakasya cha /
śauchaṁ yathārhaṁ kartavyaṁ kṣārāmlodakavāribhiḥ //36 //

36. Copper, iron, brass, [raityānām] pewter, tin, and lead must be cleansed, as may be suitable, by alkaline (substances),

---

[1] विशुद्ध्यति

acids or water.

द्रवाणां चैव सर्वेषां शुद्धिरुत्पवनं स्मृतम् ।
प्रोक्षणं संहतानां च दारवाणां च तक्षणम् ॥37 ॥

dravāṇāṁ chaiva sarveṣāṁ śuddhirutpavanaṁ smṛtam /
prokṣaṇaṁ saṁhatānāṁ cha dāravāṇāṁ cha takṣaṇam //37

37. The purification of all types of liquids should be done by [utpavanam] straining them. Solid objects should be cleaned [prokṣaṇam] by wiping them with water, and wooden items can be treated [takṣaṇam] by scraping them.

मार्जनं यज्ञपात्राणां पाणिना यज्ञकर्मणि ।
चमसानां ग्रहाणां च शुद्धिः प्रक्षालनेन तु ॥38 ॥

mārjanaṁ yajñapātrāṇāṁ pāṇinā yajñakarmaṇi /
chamasānāṁ grahāṇāṁ cha śuddhiḥ prakṣālanena tu //38 //

38. At vessels used for yajña like chamasas and grahas can be cleaned by [mārjanam] rubbing them [pāṇinā] with the hand, and [prakṣālanena] rinsing them with water.

चरूणां स्रुक्स्रुवाणां च शुद्धिरुष्णेन वारिणा ।
स्फ्यशूर्पशकटानां च मुसलौलूखलस्य च ॥39 ॥

charūṇāṁ sruksruvāṇāṁ cha śuddhiruṣṇena vāriṇā /
sphyaśūrpaśakaṭānāṁ cha musalaulūkhalasya cha //39 //

39. The [chrūṇām] cooking pans and [sruk-sruvāṇām] the spoons called sruk and sruvā, likewise [sphya] the wooden sword, [śurpa] the winnowing-basket, [śakaṭa] the cart for bringing the grain, the pestle and the mortar must be cleaned with hot water.

अद्भिस्तु प्रोक्षणं शौचं बहूनां धान्यवाससाम् ।
प्रक्षालनेन त्वल्पानामद्भिः शौचं विधीयते ॥40 ॥

adbhistu prokṣaṇaṁ śauchaṁ bahūnāṁ dhānyavāsasām /
prakṣālanena tvalpānāmadbhiḥ śauchaṁ vidhīyate //40 //

40. The manner of purifying large quantities of grain and of cloth is to soaking them into water; but the purification of small quantities is prescribed (to take place) by washing them.

चैलवच्चर्मणां शुद्धिर्वैदलानां तथैव च ।

शाकमूलफलानां च धान्यवत्शुद्धिरिष्यते ॥41॥

chailavachcharmaṇāṁ śuddhirvaidalānāṁ tathaiva cha /
śākamūlaphalānāṁ cha dhānyavatśuddhiriṣyate //41//

41. [charmaṇām] Leather items, and [vaidalānām] objects made of split cane must be cleaned [chailavat] like clothes; vegetables, roots, and fruit can be cleaned like grain.

कौशेयाविकयोरूषैः कुतपानामरिष्टकैः ।
श्रीफलैरंशुपट्टानां क्षौमाणां गौरसर्षपैः ॥42॥

kauśeyāvikayorūṣaiḥ kutapānāmariṣṭakaiḥ /
śrīphalairaṁśupaṭṭānāṁ kṣaumāṇāṁ gaurasarṣapaiḥ //42//

42. [kauṣeya] Silk and [āvika] woollen stuffs are cleaned by means [ūṣaiḥ] of saline earth; [kutapānām] blankets with Ariṣṭa (soap-berries); [Aṅśupaṭṭānām] fibrous clothes with Bel fruit; [kṣaumāṇām] linen cloth with a paste of yellow mustard.

क्षौमवत्शङ्खश्रृङ्गाणामस्थिदन्तमयस्य च ।
शुद्धिर्विजानता कार्या गोमूत्रेणौदकेन वा ॥43॥

kṣaumavatśaṅkhaśṛṅgāṇāmasthidantamayasya cha /
śuddhirvijānatā kāryā gomūtreṇaudakena vā //43//

43. [vijānatā] An expert should clean the objects made of [śaṅkha] conch-shells, [śṛṅga] horn, [asthi] bone and [danta] ivory like linen cloth, or with a mixture of cow's urine and water.

प्रोक्षणात् तृणकाष्ठं च पलालं चैव शुध्यति ।
मार्जनौपाञ्जनैर्वेश्म पुनःपाकेन मृण्मयम् ॥44॥

prokṣaṇāt tṛṇakāṣṭhaṁ cha palālaṁ chaiva śudhyati /
mārjanaupāñjanairveśma punaḥpākena mṛṇmayam //44//

44. Objects made of grass, wood, and straw become pure by being soaked in water and wiped, a house by sweeping and [upāñjanaiḥ] smearing it with cowdung or whitewash, an earthen vessel by rebaking.

मद्यैर्मूत्रैः पुरीषैर्वा ष्ठीवनैः पूयशोणितैः ।
संस्पृष्टं नैव शुद्ध्येत पुनःपाकेन मृत्मयम् ॥45॥

madyairmūtraiḥ purīṣairvā ṣṭhīvanaiḥ pūyaśoṇitaiḥ /

saṁspṛṣṭaṁ naiva śuddhyeta punaḥpākena mṛtmayam //45

45. An earthen vessel which has been defiled by alcohol, urine, stool, saliva, pus or blood cannot be purified by rebaking.

संमार्जनौपाञ्जनेन सेकेनौल्लेखनेन च ।
गवां च परिवासेन भूमिः शुध्यति[1] पञ्चभिः ॥46 ॥

saṁmārjanaupāñjanena sekenaullekhanena cha /
gavāṁ cha parivāsena bhūmiḥ śudhyati pañchabhiḥ //46 //

46. The land is purified by five methods: sweeping, smearing with cow dung, sprinkling with cow urine or milk, scraping, and allowing cows to stay on it day and night.

यावन्नापेत्यमेध्याक्ताद् गन्धो लेपश्च तत्कृतः ।
तावन् मृद्वारि चादेयं सर्वासु द्रव्यशुद्धिषु ॥47 ॥

yāvannāpetyamedhyāktād gandho lepaścha tatkṛtaḥ /
tāvan mṛdvāri chādeyaṁ sarvāsu dravyaśuddhiṣu //47 //

47. [yāvat] As long as [gandhaḥ] the smell [na apaiti] does not leave an [amedhya+aktāt] object defiled by impure substances, and [lepaḥ] the stain [tatkṛtaḥ] caused by them does not disappear, [tāvan] so long must [mṛt] earth and [vāri] water [ādeyam] be applied [dravyaśuddhiṣu] in cleansing things.

---

1 शुद्ध्यति

Chapter 6: Duties of Vānaprastha and Saṁnyāsa

The sixth chapter addresses the responsibilities associated with Vānaprastha Āśram. When a householder notices his skin wrinkling and his hair turning grey, and observes the arrival of his grandchildren, he is prompted to retreat to the forest. Once in the forest, he should meditate to understand the subtle nature of the supreme soul and its presence within all living beings, from the highest to the lowest. Manu outlines the virtues of contentment, forgiveness, self-control, abstaining from the wrongful appropriation of anything, purification, wisdom, knowledge of the supreme soul, and restraint from anger. A scholar who studies and follows these laws will achieve the highest state of existence.

Time for Vānaprastha Āśrama

एवं गृहाश्रमे स्थित्वा विधिवत् स्नातको द्विजः ।
वने वसेत् तु नियतो यथावद् विजितैन्द्रियः ॥1॥

ēvaṁ gṛhāśrame sthitvā vidhivat snātako dvijaḥ /
vane vaset tu niyato yathāvad vijitaindriyaḥ //1 //

1. After graduation, a student who has lived in Gṛhasthāśrama (the householder's life) and has fulfilled his duties properly may, with a firm resolution and by restraining his senses, choose to dwell in the forest while duly observing the rules outlined below.

गृहस्थस्तु यथा पश्येद् वलीपलितमात्मनः ।
अपत्यस्यैव चापत्यं तदाऽरण्यं समाश्रयेत् ॥2॥

gṛhasthastu yathā paśyed valīpalitamātmanaḥ /
apatyasyaiva chāpatyaṁ tadā'raṇyaṁ samāśrayet //2 //

2. When a householder notices his wrinkled skin and white hair, and sees his grandchildren, he may consider retreating to the forest.

सन्त्यज्य ग्राम्यमाहारं सर्वं चैव परिच्छदम् ।
पुत्रेषु भार्यां निक्षिप्य वनं गच्छेत् सहैव वा ॥3॥

santyajya grāmyamāhāraṁ sarvaṁ chaiva parichchhadam /
putreṣu bhāryāṁ nikṣipya vanaṁ gachchhet sahaiva vā //3 //

3. Leaving behind all cultivated food and personal belongings, he may enter the forest, either entrusting his wife to his sons or going with her.

अग्निहोत्रं समादाय गृह्यं चाग्निपरिच्छदम् ।
ग्रामादरण्यं निःसृत्य निवसेन्नियतेन्द्रियः ॥4 ॥

agnihotraṁ samādāya gṛhyaṁ chāgniparichchhadam /
grāmādaraṇyaṁ niḥsṛtya nivasenniyatendriyaḥ //4 //

4. He should take the necessary implements for Agnihotra and proceed from the village to the forest, where he can reside while properly controlling his senses.

Routine of Vānaprasthī (Forest Dweller)

मुन्यन्नैर्विविधैर्मेध्यैः शाकमूलफलेन वा ।
एतानेव महायज्ञान्निर्वपेद् विधिपूर्वकम् ॥5 ॥

munyannairvividhairmedhyaiḥ śākamūlaphalena vā /
ētāneva mahāyajñānnirvaped vidhipūrvakam //5 //

5. Let him offer those five great yajñās following proper procedure, with various kinds [medhyaiḥ] of pure [muni+annaiḥ] food fit for ascetics, or with herbs, roots, and fruit.

वसीत चर्म चीरं वा सायं स्नायात् प्रगे तथा ।
जटाश्च बिभृयान्नित्यं श्मश्रुलोमनखानि च ॥6 ॥

vasīta charma chīraṁ vā sāyaṁ snāyāt prage tathā /
jaṭāścha bibhṛyānnityaṁ śmaśrulomanakhāni cha //6 //

6. Let him wear woollen or cotton clothes, as needed; bathe in the evening and the morning; and always wear matted locks, as well as hair on his body, beard, and nails.

यद्भक्ष्यं[1] स्याद् ततो दद्याद् बलिं भिक्षां च शक्तितः ।

---

[1] यद्भक्षः

अब्मूलफलभिक्षाभिरर्चयेदाश्रमागतान्[1] ॥7॥

yadbhakṣayaṁ syād tato dadyād baliṁ bhikṣāṁ cha śaktitaḥ
abmūlaphalabhikṣābhirarchayedāśramāgatān ॥7॥

7. Let him feed the animals surrounding him with the same food he eats and give alms according to his ability. Let him honour those who come to his hermitage by offering them alms consisting of water, roots, and fruit.

स्वाध्याये नित्ययुक्तः स्याद् दान्तो मैत्रः समाहितः ।
दाता नित्यमनादाता सर्वभूतानुकम्पकः ॥8॥

svādhyāye nityayuktaḥ syād dānto maitraḥ samāhitaḥ ।
dātā nityamanādātā sarvabhūtānukampakaḥ ॥8॥

8. He should consistently engage in Vedic studies, practice self-restraint over his senses, maintain a friendly attitude towards everyone, focus his mind, be actively involved in charitable deeds, avoid accepting gifts, and show compassion towards all living beings.

वैतानिकं च जुहुयादग्निहोत्रं यथाविधि ।
दर्शमस्कन्दयन् पर्व पौर्णमासं च योगतः ॥9॥

vaitānikaṁ cha juhuyādagnihotraṁ yathāvidhi ।
darśamaskandayan parva paurṇamāsaṁ cha yogataḥ ॥9॥

9. He should properly perform the Agnihotra, ensuring to [askandayan] never omit the Darśa (new-moon) and Pūrṇamāśa (full-moon) yajñas at the appropriate times.

ऋक्षेष्ट्याग्रयणं[2] चैव चातुर्मास्यानि चाहरेत् ।
तुरायणं च क्रमशो दक्षस्यायनमेव[3] च ॥10॥

ṛkṣeṣṭyāgrayaṇaṁ chaiva chāturmāsyāni chāharet ।
turāyaṇaṁ cha kramaśo dakṣasyāyanameva cha ॥10॥

---

[1] आश्रमागतं

[2] दर्शेष्ट्य् ।आग्रयणं

[3] दाक्षस्यायनं

10. He should also perform the Nakṣatreṣṭi, the Āgrayaṇa (new harvest yajña), and the Chāturmāsya yajñas (yajñas conducted at the beginning of each of the four seasons). Additionally, he should properly observe the Turāyaṇa (Uttarāyaṇa, which occurs around March 21) and the Dakṣāyaṇa (Dakṣiṇāyana, which occurs around September 23) in due order.

Note: The concepts of Uttarāyaṇa and Dakṣiṇāyana in Manusmṛti differ from our current understanding. Today, we recognize Uttarāyaṇa as beginning on December 21 and Dakṣiṇāyana on June 21. This shift is largely due to Bharat's geographical location, which is currently situated at approximately 8 degrees north of the Equator in the Northern Hemisphere. As a result, the definitions of Uttarāyaṇa and Dakṣiṇāyana have evolved accordingly.

In contrast, during Manu's time, Bharat was located along the Equator. So, Manu had a different perspective on these periods. According to the continental drift theory, the Indian plate was positioned near the Equator about 120 million (12 crore) years ago. This supports the notion that Manu existed on Earth around the beginning of the present Vaivasvata Manvantara (12 crore years ago).

वासन्तशारदैर्मेध्यैर्मुन्यन्नैः स्वयमाहृतैः ।
पुरोडाशांश्चरूंश्चैव विधिवन्निर्वपेत् पृथक् ॥11॥

vāsantaśāradairmedhyairmunyannaiḥ svayamāhṛtaiḥ ।
puroḍāśāṁścharūṁśchaiva vidhivannirvapet pṛthak ॥11॥

11. The individual should prepare puroḍāsas (cakes made of rice or barley) and charu (cakes made of pulses) as offerings for the yajña. These offerings should be made with pure grains suitable for ascetics, which grow in the spring and autumn, and that he has personally collected, following the prescribed method.

देवताभ्यस्तु तद् हुत्वा वन्यं मेध्यतरं हविः ।
शेषमात्मनि युञ्जीत लवणं च स्वयं कृतम् ॥12॥

devatābhyastu tad hutvā vanyaṁ medhyataraṁ haviḥ ।

śeṣamātmani yuñjīta lavaṇaṁ cha svayaṁ kṛtam ॥12 ॥

12. After offering [medyataram] the purest oblations from the forest's produce to the devatās in the yajñā, he may use the remaining portion for himself, mixed with salt, prepared by himself.

स्थलजौदकशाकानि पुष्पमूलफलानि च ।
मेध्यवृक्षोद्भवान्यद्यात् स्नेहांश्च फलसम्भवान् ॥13 ॥

sthalajaudakaśākāni puṣpamūlaphalāni cha ।
medhyavṛkṣodbhavānyadyāt snehāṁścha phalasambhavān

13. He should consume the vegetables that grow on land and in water, as well as flowers, roots, fruits, and products from pure trees, including oils derived from fruits.

वर्जयेन् मधु मांसं च भौमानि कवकानि च ।
भूस्तृणं शिग्रुकं चैव श्लेश्मातकफलानि च ॥14 ॥

varjayen madhu māṁsaṁ cha bhaumāni kavakāni cha ।
bhūstṛṇaṁ śigrukaṁ chaiva śleśmātakaphalāni cha ॥14 ॥

14. Let him avoid honey, flesh, and mushrooms growing on the ground, [Bhustṛṇa] the broad-leaved turpentine grass (Andropogon Schoenanthus), [Śigruka] pot-herb, and [Sleśmātaka phalāni] the fruit of Assyrian Plum plant (Cordia Myxa).

त्यजेदाश्वयुजे मासि मुन्यन्नं पूर्वसञ्चितम् ।
जीर्णानि चैव वासांसि शाकमूलफलानि च ॥15 ॥

tyajedāśvayuje māsi munyannaṁ pūrvasañchitam ।
jīrṇāni chaiva vāsāṁsi śākamūlaphalāni cha ॥15 ॥

15. Let him throw away in the month of Āśvina the food of ascetics, which he formerly collected, likewise his worn-out clothes and his vegetables, roots, and fruit.

न फालकृष्टमश्नीयादुत्सृष्टमपि केन चित् ।
न ग्रामजातान्यार्तोऽपि मूलाणि च फलानि च[1] ॥16 ॥

---

[1] पुष्पानि च फलानि च

na phālakṛṣṭamaśnīyādutsṛṣṭamapi kena chit /
na grāmajātānyārto'pi mūlāṇi cha phalāni cha //16 //

16. He should not eat anything grown on ploughed land, even if it has been left by someone, nor should he eat roots and fruits grown in a village, even if he is extremely hungry.

अप्रयत्नः सुखार्थेषु ब्रह्मचारी धराऽऽशयः ।
शरणेष्वममश्चैव वृक्षमूलनिकेतनः ॥17 ॥

aprayatnaḥ sukhārtheṣu brahmachārī dharā''śayaḥ /
śaraṇeṣvamamaśchaiva vṛkṣamūlaniketanaḥ //17 //

17. Making no effort to procure things that bring pleasure, living chaste, sleeping on bare ground, not caring for shelter, and dwelling at the roots of trees.

एताश्चान्याश्च सेवेत दीक्षा विप्रो वने वसन् ।
विविधाश्चौपनिषदीरात्मसंसिद्धये श्रुतीः ॥18 ॥

ētāśchānyāścha seveta dīkṣā vipro vane vasan /
vividhāśchaupaniṣadīrātmasaṁsiddhaye śrutīḥ //18 //

18. These and other observances must be diligently practiced by a Vānaprasthī dwelling in the forest. In order to attain complete union with the supreme Soul, he must study various sacred texts of the Upaniṣads.

ऋषिभिर्ब्राह्मणैश्चैव गृहस्थैरेव सेविताः ।
विद्यातपोविवृद्ध्यर्थं शरीरस्य च शुद्धये ॥19 ॥

ṛṣibhirbrāhmaṇaiśchaiva gṛhasthaireva sevitāḥ /
vidyātapovivṛddhyarthaṁ śarīrasya cha śuddhaye //19 //

19. He should follow those practices that have been observed by the sages (Rishis) and householder-scholars to enhance their knowledge of Brahman, increase their austerity, and sanctify their bodies.

Saṁnyāsa Āśrama

वनेषु च विहृत्यैवं तृतीयं भागमायुषः ।
चतुर्थमायुषो भागं त्यक्त्वा सङ्गान् परिव्रजेत् ॥20 ॥

vaneṣu cha vihṛtyaivaṁ tṛtīyaṁ bhāgamāyuṣaḥ /

chaturthamāyuṣo bhāgaṁ tyakvā saṅgān parivrajet //20 //

20. Having spent the third part of his life in the forest, he may live as a privrājaka (ascetic) during the fourth part of his existence after abandoning all attachment to worldly objects.

अधीत्य विधिवद् वेदान् पुत्रांश्चोत्पाद्य धर्मतः ।
इष्ट्वा च शक्तितो यज्ञैर्मनो मोक्षे निवेशयेत् ॥21॥

adhītya vidhivad vedān putrāṁśchotpādya dharmataḥ /
iṣṭvā cha śaktito yajñairmano mokṣe niveśayet //21 //

21. After studying the Vedas as prescribed, begetting sons under dharma, and performing yajñās to the best of his ability, he can then focus his mind on achieving final liberation.

Procedure of Saṁnyāsa

प्राजापत्यं निरुप्येष्टिं सर्ववेदसदक्षिणाम्[1] ।
आत्मन्यग्नीन् समारोप्य ब्राह्मणः प्रव्रजेद् गृहात् ॥22॥

prājāpatyaṁ nirupyeṣṭiṁ sarvavedasadakṣiṇām /
ātmanyagnīn samāropya brāhmaṇaḥ pravrajed gṛhāt //22 //

22. For realization of God, let a seeker of Brahman renounce his house and take Saṁnyāsa upon performing a yajña and abandoning all external signs like sacred thread, tuft or lock of hair. He should impose on himself the practice of five vital forces (prāṇās), i.e. prāṇ, apāna, udāna, samāna, vyāna in place of five fires of Yajña, i.e. Āhavanīya, Gārhapatya, Dakṣiṇāgni, Āvasthya and Sabhya. That is, he should perform prāṇāyāma instead of Yajñas.

यो दत्त्वा सर्वभूतेभ्यः प्रव्रजत्यभयं गृहात् ।
तस्य तेजोमया लोका भवन्ति ब्रह्मवादिनः ॥23॥

yo dattvā sarvabhūtebhyaḥ pravrajatyabhayaṁ gṛhāt /
tasya tejomayā lokā bhavanti brahmavādinaḥ //23 //

23. He, who leaves his home for taking Saṁnyāsa after rendering all living beings free from fear, that Brahmavādī (who

---

[1] सार्ववेदसदक्षिणाम्

disseminates the knowledge of God, i.e. Vedas) attains the state of eternal bliss called Mukti.

यस्मादण्वपि भूतानां द्विजान्नोत्पद्यते भयम् ।
तस्य देहाद् विमुक्तस्य भयं नास्ति कुतश्चन ॥24॥

yasmādaṇvapi bhūtānāṁ dvijānnotpadyate bhayam /
tasya dehād vimuktasya bhayaṁ nāsti kutaśchana //24//

24. For the scholar who causes no harm to any beings, there will be no danger from any direction after he is freed from his body.

अगारादभिनिष्क्रान्तः पवित्रोपचितो मुनिः ।
समुपोढेषु कामेषु निरपेक्षः परिव्रजेत् ॥25॥

agārādabhiniṣkrāntaḥ pavitropachito muniḥ /
samupoḍheṣu kāmeṣu nirapekṣaḥ parivrajet //25//

25. When a person has conquered all his desires and cares little for enjoyment, and when he has purified his mind and soul, becoming completely pacified, he can take saṁnyāsa directly from the Gṛhasthāśrama.

एक एव चरेन्नित्यं सिद्ध्यर्थमसहायवान् ।
सिद्धिमेकस्य[1] सम्पश्यन्न जहाति न हीयते ॥26॥

ēka ēva charennityaṁ siddhyarthamasahāyavān /
siddhimekasya sampaśyanna jahāti na hīyate //26//

26. A person attains mokṣa by himself–fully understanding this fact, without any desire for any companion to attain liberation, a saṁnyāsī should go alone. Thus he neither forsakes anyone nor is forsaken.

अनग्निरनिकेतः स्याद् ग्राममन्नार्थमाश्रयेत् ।
उपेक्षकोऽसङ्कुसुको[2] मुनिर्भावसमाहितः ॥ 27 ॥

anagniraniketaḥ syād grāmamannārthamāśrayet /
upekṣako'saṅkusuko munirbhāvasamāhitaḥ // 27 //

---

[1] सिद्धम्

[2] साङ्कुसुको

27. He shall neither possess fire (cook food or perform yajñas), nor a dwelling, he may go to a village for his food. He shall be indifferent to everything, pacified, meditating and concentrating his mind on Brahman.

नाभिनन्देत मरणं नाभिनन्देत जीवितम् ।
कालमेव प्रतीक्षेत निर्देशं भृतको यथा ॥28॥

nābhinandeta maraṇaṁ nābhinandeta jīvitam ।
kālameva pratīkṣeta nirdeśaṁ bhṛtako yathā ॥28॥

28. He should neither seek interest in death nor in life; instead, let him wait for his appointed time, like a servant waiting for his master's orders.

दृष्टिपूतं न्यसेत् पादं वस्त्रपूतं जलं पिबेत् ।
सत्यपूतां वदेद् वाचं मनःपूतं समाचरेत् ॥29॥

dṛṣṭipūtaṁ nyaset pādaṁ vastrapūtaṁ jalaṁ pibet ।
satyapūtāṁ vaded vāchaṁ manaḥpūtaṁ samācharet ॥29॥

29. Let him place his foot down, cleansed by his sight; let him drink water filtered through a cloth; let him speak words formed from truth; let him act with a pure mind.

अतिवादांस्तितिक्षेत नावमन्येत कं चन ।
न चैमं देहमाश्रित्य वैरं कुर्वीत केन चित् ॥30॥

ativādāṁstitikṣeta nāvamanyeta kaṁ chana ।
na chaimaṁ dehamāśritya vairaṁ kurvīta kena chit ॥30॥

30. Let him patiently endure harsh words, avoid insulting anyone, and not become an enemy for the sake of this perishable body.

क्रुद्ध्यन्तं न प्रतिक्रुध्येदाक्रुष्टः कुशलं वदेत् ।
सप्तद्वारावकीर्णां च न वाचमनृतां वदेत् ॥31॥

kruddhyantaṁ na pratikrudhyedākruṣṭaḥ kuśalaṁ vadet ।
saptadvārāvakīrṇāṁ cha na vāchamanṛtāṁ vadet ॥31॥

31. When faced with an angry man, he should respond without anger. Instead, he should offer blessings when he is cursed and avoid speaking falsehoods, which can be scattered through seven wholes (one mouth, two nostrils, two eyes, and

two ears).

अध्यात्मरतिरासीनो निरपेक्षो निरामिषः ।
आत्मनैव सहायेन सुखार्थी विचरेदिह ॥32॥

adhyātmaratirāsīno nirapekṣo nirāmiṣaḥ /
ātmanaiva sahāyena sukhārthī vicharediha //32 //

32. Finding joy within himself, seated in the prescribed yoga postures, self-reliant and completely avoiding meat, he shall live in this world with himself as his only companion, seeking the bliss of ultimate liberation.

कॢप्तकेशनखश्मश्रुः पात्री दण्डी कुसुम्भवान् ।
विचरेन्नियतो नित्यं सर्वभूतान्यपीडयन् ॥ 33 ॥

kḷptakeśanakhaśmaśruḥ pātrī daṇḍī kusumbhavān /
vicharenniyato nityaṁ sarvabhūtānyapīḍayan //33 //

33. With his hair, nails, and beard clipped, carrying an alms-bowl, a staff, and a water-pot, he should continually wander, exercising self-control and avoiding harm to any creature.

एककालं चरेद् भैक्षं न प्रसज्जेत विस्तरे ।
भैक्षे प्रसक्तो हि यतिर्विषयेष्वपि सज्जति ॥34॥

ēkakālaṁ chared bhaikṣaṁ na prasajjeta vistare /
bhaikṣe prasakto hi yatirviṣayeṣvapi sajjati //34 //

34. Let him beg once a day, without being eager to collect a large amount of alms. A renunciate who becomes addicted to gathering alms also becomes attached to sensory objects.

अलाभे न विषादी स्याल्लाभे चैव न हर्षयेत् ।
प्राणयात्रिकमात्रः स्यात्मात्रासङ्गाद् विनिर्गतः ॥35॥

alābhe na viṣādī syātlābhe chaiva na harṣayet /
prāṇayātrikamātraḥ syātmātrāsaṅgād vinirgataḥ //35 //

35. He should not feel regret when he receives nothing, nor should he celebrate when he gets something; he should only accept what is necessary to sustain life, [mātrāsaṅgāt vinirgataḥ] without caring about the quality of the charity received.

अभिपूजितलाभांस्तु जुगुप्सेतैव सर्वशः ।

अभिपूजितलाभैश्च यतिर्मुक्तोऽपि बध्यते ॥36॥

abhipūjitalābhāṁstu jugupsetaiva sarvaśaḥ /
abhipūjitalābhaiścha yatirmukto'pi badhyate //36 //

36. Let him reject all charity and other offerings received in a respectful manner. Even an ascetic on the verge of liberation can become bound by the chains of sensory objects when he accepts alms and other gifts respectfully.

अल्पान्नाभ्यवहारेण रहःस्थानासनेन च ।
ह्रियमाणानि विषयैरिन्द्रियाणि निवर्तयेत् ॥37॥

alpānnābhyavahāreṇa rahaḥsthānāsanena cha /
hriyamāṇāni viṣayairindriyāṇi nivartayet //37 //

537. By eating less and spending time alone, he should control his senses if they are drawn to sensory objects.

इन्द्रियाणां निरोधेन रागद्वेषक्षयेण च ।
अहिंसया च भूतानाममृतत्वाय कल्पते ॥38॥

indriyāṇāṁ nirodhena rāgadveṣakṣayeṇa cha /
ahiṁsayā cha bhūtānāmamṛtatvāya kalpate //38 //

38. By controlling his senses, eliminating love and hatred, and avoiding harm to living beings, one becomes worthy of immortality.

अवेक्षेत गतीर्नृणां कर्मदोषसमुद्भवाः ।
निरये चैव पतनं यातनाश्च यमक्षये ॥39॥

avekṣeta gatīrnṛṇāṁ karmadoṣasamudbhavāḥ /
niraye chaiva patanaṁ yātanāścha yamakṣaye //39 //

39. He should contemplate the plight of humanity, stemming from their misdeeds, their descent into lower species, and their painful experiences at the time of death;

विप्रयोगं प्रियैश्चैव संयोगं च तथाऽप्रियैः ।
जरया चाभिभवनं व्याधिभिश्चोपपीडनम् ॥40॥

viprayogaṁ priyaiśchaiva saṁyogaṁ cha tathā'priyaiḥ /
jarayā chābhibhavanaṁ vyādhibhiśchopapīḍanam //40 //

40. Regarding separation from loved ones, union with

disliked individuals, and being overwhelmed by aging and illness;

देहादुत्क्रमणं चास्मात् पुनर्गर्भे च सम्भवम् ।
योनिकोटिसहस्रेषु सृतीश्चास्यान्तरात्मनः ॥41॥

dehādutkramaṇaṁ chāsmāt punargarbhe cha sambhavam /
yonikoṭisahasreṣu sṛtīśchāsyāntarātmanaḥ //41//

41. On the departure of the individual soul from this body and its new birth in (another) womb, and its wanderings through thousand crores (ten thousand millions) of species;

अधर्मप्रभवं चैव दुःखयोगं शरीरिणाम् ।
धर्मार्थप्रभवं चैव सुखसंयोगमक्षयम् ॥42॥

adharmaprabhavaṁ chaiva duḥkhayogaṁ śarīriṇām /
dharmārthaprabhavaṁ chaiva sukhasaṁyogamakṣayam //42

42. Regarding the pain inflicted on embodied souls due to adharma and the attainment of eternal bliss resulting from actions aligned with dharma;

सूक्ष्मतां चान्ववेक्षेत योगेन परमात्मनः ।
देहेषु च समुत्पत्तिमुत्तमेष्वधमेषु[1] च ॥43॥

sūkṣamatāṁ chānvavekṣeta yogena paramātmanaḥ /
deheṣu cha samutpattimuttameṣvadhameṣu cha //43//

43. Through yoga, he recognizes the subtle nature of the supreme Soul, and its presence in all organisms, both the highest and the lowest.

दूषितोऽपि[2] चरेद् धर्मं यत्र तत्राश्रमे रतः ।
समः सर्वेषु भूतेषु न लिङ्गं धर्मकारणम् ॥44॥

dūṣito'pi chared dharmaṁ yatra tatrāśrame rataḥ /
samaḥ sarveṣu bhūteṣu na liṅgaṁ dharmakāraṇam //44//

44. Even if a saṁnyāsī is blemished by others, he should still adhere to dharma. Likewise, individuals from all āśramas (stages

---

1 देहेषु चैवोपपत्तिम्

2 भूषितोऽपि

of life) should also uphold dharma. It is important for everyone to treat all creatures and people equally, as external markers such as a stick (daṇḍa), clothing, garlands, and other appearances do not truly represent one's adherence to dharma.

फलं कतकवृक्षस्य यद्यप्यम्बुप्रसादकम् ।
न नामग्रहणादेव तस्य वारि प्रसीदति ॥45 ॥

phalaṁ katakavṛkṣasya yadyapyambuprasādakam /
na nāmagrahaṇādeva tasya vāri prasīdati //45 //

45. Though the seeds of a clearing-nut tree (Strychnos Potatorum-Botanical name) purify water (when mixed with it in powdered form), the mere mention of its name can never do so.

Benefits of Prāṇāyāma

प्राणायामा ब्राह्मणस्य त्रयोऽपि विधिवत् कृताः ।
व्याहृतिप्रणवैर्युक्ता विज्ञेयं परमं तपः ॥46 ॥

prāṇāyāmā brāhmaṇasya trayo'pi vidhivat kṛtāḥ /
vyāhṛtipraṇavairyuktā vijñeyaṁ paramaṁ tapaḥ //46 //

46. Let a saṁnyāsī (seeker of Brahman), therefore, practice prāṇāyāma accompanied by vyāhṛtis preceded by praṇava sound (syllable Om). At least three prāṇāyāmas done by the seeker will serve the purpose of the highest penance.

NB: There are seven vyāhṛtis, viz. Om bhuḥ, Om bhuvaḥ, Om svaḥ (these three can serve a purpose), Om mahaḥ, Om janaḥ, Om tapaḥ, Om satyam.

दह्यन्ते ध्मायमानानां धातूनां हि यथा मलाः ।
तथेन्द्रियाणां दह्यन्ते दोषाः प्राणस्य निग्रहात् ॥47 ॥

dahyante dhmāyamānānāṁ dhātūnāṁ hi yathā malāḥ /
tathendriyāṇāṁ dahyante doṣāḥ prāṇasya nigrahāt //47 //

47. Just as impurities of metals are blown out in a furnace, so does prāṇāyāma treat the body and mind of the impurities.

प्राणायामैर्दहेद् दोषान् धारणाभिश्च किल्बिषम् ।
प्रत्याहारेण संसर्गान् ध्यानेनानीश्वरान् गुणान् ॥48 ॥

prāṇāyāmairdahed doṣān dhāraṇābhiścha kilbiṣam /
pratyāhāreṇa saṁsargān dhyānenānīśvarān guṇān //48 //

48. So, impurities of mind and body caused by aggravated vāta should be treated by prāṇāyāma, guilt feeling should be treated by concentration of mind at one point (dhāraṇā), sensual attachments by pratyāhāra (withdrawal of mind from external stimuli), and all qualities that are not Godly and attributable to souls like joy, sorrow, and ignorance should be treated by Dhyāna.

उच्चावचेषु भूतेषु दुर्ज्ञेयामकृतात्मभिः ।
ध्यानयोगेन सम्पश्येद् गतिमस्यान्तरात्मनः ॥49 ॥

uchchāvacheṣu bhūteṣu durjñeyāmakṛtātmabhiḥ /
dhyānayogena sampaśyed gatimasyāntarātmanaḥ //49 //

49. By the practice of Dhyāna yoga (contemplation), let him then observe the presence of Omnipresent God in all small and big objects which are hard to understand by the ignorant and by those who are not yogis.

सम्यग्दर्शनसम्पन्नः कर्मभिर्न निबध्यते ।
दर्शनेन विहीनस्तु संसारं प्रतिपद्यते ॥50 ॥

samyagdarśanasampannaḥ karmabhirna nibadhyate /
darśanena vihīnastu saṁsāraṁ pratipadyate //50 //

50. Those who have true insight into the nature of the world are not bound by their wrongdoings, while those lacking that insight are ensnared by the temptations of the material world.

अहिंसयेन्द्रियासङ्गैर्वैदिकैश्चैव कर्मभिः ।
तपसश्चरणैश्चौग्रैः साधयन्तीह तत्पदम् ॥51 ॥

ahiṁsayendriyāsaṅgairvaidikaiśchaiva karmabhiḥ /
tapasaścharaṇaiśchaugraiḥ sādhayantīha tatpadam //51 //

51. By non-violence, by renunciation of sensory pleasures, by performing duties as prescribed in the Vedas, and by rigorous austerities, a Saṁnyāsī can achieve Mokṣa.

यदा भावेन भवति सर्वभावेषु निःस्पृहः ।
तदा सुखमवाप्नोति प्रेत्य चैह च शाश्वतम् ॥52 ॥

yadā bhāvena bhavati sarvabhāveṣu niḥspṛhaḥ /
tadā sukhamavāpnoti pretya chaiha cha śāśvatam //52 //

52. When a Saṁnyāsī by his temperament becomes indifferent to desires for all worldly objects, he attains eternal bliss here (as living liberation) and hereafter (liberation after death).

अनेन विधिना सर्वांस्त्यक्त्वा सङ्गान् शनैः शनैः ।
सर्वद्वन्द्वविनिर्मुक्तो ब्रह्मण्येवावतिष्ठते ॥53॥

anena vidhinā sarvāṁstyaktvā saṅgān śanaiḥ śanaiḥ /
sarvadvandvavinirmukto brahmaṇyevāvatiṣṭhate //53 //

53. Thus a Saṁnyāsī gets established in Brahman by gradually giving up all evils born of attachment to worldly objects and rising above the joy and sorrow. It is the duty of all Saṁnyāsī-s to enlighten men of all other Āśramas on true nature of all types of their duties, to dissuade them from all kinds of evil conduct, to dispel their doubts, and to persuade them to follow the path of truth and morality.

ध्यानिकं सर्वमेवैतद् यदेतदभिशब्दितम् ।
न ह्यनध्यात्मवित् कश्चित् क्रियाफलमुपाश्नुते ॥54॥

dhyānikaṁ sarvamevaitad yadetadabhiśabditam /
na hyanadhyātmavit kaśchit kriyāphalamupāśnute //54 //

54. All that has been declared above relies on meditation; those who are not proficient in the knowledge of Adhyātma, which pertains to the Soul, do not reap the full rewards of their actions.

इदं शरणमज्ञानामिदमेव विजानताम् ।
इदमन्विच्छतां स्वर्गमिदमानन्त्यमिच्छताम् ॥55॥

idaṁ śaraṇamajñānāmidameva vijānatām /
idamanvichchhatāṁ svargamidamānantyamichchhatām 55

55. Adhyātma is the refuge for the ignorant, as well as for those who understand the meaning of the Veda. It serves as protection for those who seek divinity and for those in pursuit of eternal bliss (mokṣa).

अनेन क्रमयोगेन परिव्रजति यो द्विजः ।
स विधूयैह पाप्मानं परं ब्रह्माधिगच्छति ॥56॥

anena kramayogena parivrajati yo dvijaḥ ।
sa vidhūyaiha pāpmānaṁ paraṁ brahmādhigachchhati ॥*56*

56. A scholar who becomes a saṁnyāsī, after performing the actions mentioned above, shakes off evil in this life and attains Brahman.

ब्रह्मचारी गृहस्थश्च वानप्रस्थो यतिस्तथा ।
एते गृहस्थप्रभवाश्चत्वारः पृथगाश्रमाः ॥57॥

brahmachārī gṛhasthaścha vānaprastho yatistathā ।
ēte gṛhasthaprabhavāśchatvāraḥ pṛthagāśramāḥ ॥*57*॥

57. The Brahmacharya, the Gṛhasthī, the Vānaprasthī, and the Saṁnyāsī, these (constitute) four separate Āśramas, which are sustained by the Gṛhasthāśrama.

सर्वेऽपि क्रमशस्त्वेते यथाशास्त्रं निषेविताः ।
यथोक्तकारिणं विप्रं नयन्ति परमां गतिम् ॥58॥

sarve'pi kramaśastvete yathāśāstraṁ niṣevitāḥ ।
yathoktakāriṇaṁ vipraṁ nayanti paramāṁ gatim ॥*58*॥

58. A scholar who fulfills the duties Fof all these Āśramas in the proper order as prescribed in the Śāstras achieves the highest state.

सर्वेषामपि चैतेषां वेदस्मृतिविधानतः[1] ।
गृहस्थ उच्यते श्रेष्ठः स त्रीनेतान् बिभर्ति हि ॥59॥

sarveṣāmapi chaiteṣāṁ vedasmṛtividhānataḥ ।
gṛhastha uchyate śreṣṭhaḥ sa trīnetān bibharti hi ॥*59*॥

59. According to the injunctions of the Veda and the Smṛtis, the Gṛhasthī is considered superior to all others because he supports the other three.

यथा नदीनदाः सर्वे सागरे यान्ति संस्थितिम् ।
तथैवाश्रमिणः सर्वे गृहस्थे यान्ति संस्थितिम् ॥60॥

---

[1] वेदश्रुतिविधानतः

yathā nadīnadāḥ sarve sāgare yānti saṁsthitim /
tathaivāśramiṇaḥ sarve gṛhasthe yānti saṁsthitim //60 //

60. Just as rivers, both large and small, reach the ocean, so too do individuals from all Āśramas find refuge with Gṛhasthīs.

चतुर्भिरपि चैवैतैर्नित्यमाश्रमिभिर्द्विजैः ।
दशलक्षणको धर्मः सेवितव्यः प्रयत्नतः ॥61 ॥

chaturbhirapi chaivaitairnityamāśramibhirdvijaiḥ /
daśalakṣaṇako dharmaḥ sevitavyaḥ prayatnataḥ //61 //

61. Therefore, all educated Brahmacharī-s (knowledge seeker students), Gṛhasthī-s (householders), Vānaprasthī-s (hermits/forest dwellers) and Saṁnyāsī-s (peripatetic monks) should observe ten-fold Dharma (ethical and moral code of conduct).

धृतिः क्षमा दमोऽस्तेयं शौचमिन्द्रियनिग्रहः ।
धीर्विद्या सत्यमक्रोधो दशकं धर्मलक्षणम् ॥62 ॥

dhṛtiḥ kṣamā damo'steyaṁ śauchamindriyanigrahaḥ /
dhīrvidyā satyamakrodho daśakaṁ dharmalakṣaṇam //62 //

62. 1. Patience, 2. forgiveness and forbearance, 3. self-control (to regulate mind towards dharma), 4. non-stealing (never to acquire things without permission, through fraud, betrayal or illegitimate means, 5. purity of body, mind and soul, 6. restraining sense organs from immoral and illegal actions, 7. sharpening of intelligence by avoiding intoxicants, bad company, idleness, lethargy and by use of healthy products, good company, yoga, virtuous acts, and celibacy, 8. acquisition of true knowledge right from earth to God and its proper application for public good, 9.truthfulness (to know a thing in its right perspective, and harmony of thought, word and deed), 10. abstention from anger, all the above form tenfold ethical and moral code of conduct.

दश लक्षणानि धर्मस्य ये विप्राः समधीयते ।
अधीत्य चानुवर्तन्ते ते यान्ति परमां गतिम् ॥63 ॥

daśa lakṣaṇāni dharmasya ye viprāḥ samadhīyate /
adhītya chānuvartante te yānti paramāṁ gatim //63 //

63. Scholars who understand the tenfold dharma and follow its principles enter the highest state.

एष वोऽभिहितो धर्मो ब्राह्मणस्य चतुर्विधः ।
पुण्योऽक्षयफलः प्रेत्य राज्ञां धर्मं निबोधत ॥64

ēṣa vo'bhihito dharmo brāhmaṇasya chaturvidhaḥ /
puṇyo'kṣayaphalaḥ pretya rājñāṁ dharmaṁ nibodhata //64

64. Here we have explained that it is the duty of a seeker of Brahman to undergo the training of Brahmacharya, Gṛhastha, Vānaprastha and Saṁnyāsa Āśramas. In this life, it yields high moral value and eternal bliss hereafter. Now listen to the duties of ruling profession.